Becoming American

PERSONAL ESSAYS
BY FIRST GENERATION
IMMIGRANT WOMEN

Becoming American

Edited and with an Introduction by
Meri Nana-Ama Danquah

New York

Designed by C. Linda Dingler

Library of Congress Cataloging-in-Publication Data

Becoming American : personal essays by first generation immigrant women /
    edited with an introduction by Meri Nana-Ama Danquah.—1st ed.
        p.   cm.
    1. Women immigrants—United States Biography.   2. United States—
    Emigration and immigration.   3. Acculturation—United States.
I. Danquah, Meri Nana-Ama.
E184.A1B288   2000
305.48'9691—dc21   99-37345
                                                                    CIP

ISBN 0-7868-6589-X

First Edition

10   9   8   7   6   5   4   3   2   1

Dedication

to

Gloria Loomis, my brilliant agent, for always urging me to defy all odds
and prove that I can, indeed, live by the word;

E. Ethelbert Miller, my mentor, for reminding me that I must also live,
with grace and integrity, beyond the boundaries of words;

Jackson Browne, my friend and hero, whose generosity of spirit and
commitment to craft leave me speechless;

and

Marc Cohn, the muse who carried the passion
of this project on his wings

EDITOR'S ACKNOWLEDGMENTS

Process is always as important as product. *Becoming American* exists only because of the love, encouragement, guidance, and support of many wonderful people.

I am deeply grateful to the Author's Guild Fund, the Carnegie Fund for Authors, and the PEN Emergency Writers Fund. Without their generous assistance the only thing I would have become was broke.

For matters pertaining to publication, I would like to thank: my editor at Hyperion, Leigh Haber, whose vision, courage, patience, and unwavering faith in both me and this project have meant everything; Katherine Fausset, at the Watkins Loomis Agency, who handles me and my work with such great care and constantly goes above and beyond the call of duty for me; all the writers who shared their personal stories of immigration with me, including those who, for reasons beyond our control, are not included in this collection; and Doug Adrianson for his honest, on-call editorial expertise.

To my fierce circle of sister-friends who keep me laughing, writing, and believing, I offer much love and many hugs: Anne Schneider Burrows, Sandra Stevens Pate, Wendy James, Danzy Senna, Rebecca Walker, Catherine McKinley, Eugenia Kim, Anne Beatts, Lisa Jollif-Andoh, Jonetta Barras, Akuyoe Graham, Yvette Nipar, Bee-be Smith, Julia Boyd, Erika Ellis, and Vanessa Williams Wiseman.

I will also be forever grateful to my fabulous fellows: those knights in tarnished armor—David Hatcher, Gregory Tate, Bruce Abrams, and Jamal Kadri—who shelter me through the storms and, also, celebrate the sunshine with me; Erik Burns, for being the big brother I never wanted but always needed; and Kenny Carroll, for putting up with my late-night loquaciousness and for being a reliable voice of reason. I love you guys.

I am deeply grateful as well to Rev. Michael Beckwith and the Agape International Center of Truth; all the folks at the Open Charter Magnet School, especially Dr. Grace Arnold, Connie Green, Sandra Shea, Cathy Furer, Kim Masumiya, Pat Cracchiola, Nathaniel Shultice, Dena Johns, Anne Granick, Denise Cole, and Dolores Patton; lots of positive vibrations to J. D. Heilprin, Sabina Weber, Lee Shirani and all the other MP3 mavericks at RioPort.com.

There are several friends, family members, and colleagues who have been a tremendous source of inspiration throughout: Camilia Schwimmer; my phenomenal immigration attorney, Warren Winston, Esq.; his assistant, Tonia Spriggs; Paul Guthrie; Eric Lynn; David Goldsmith; Richard Walden; Randy Hall and Dr. Freda Lewis-Hall; Yuri Vasquez; Susan Cheever; Scott Grossman; Shela Halper; Sven Birkerts; Stephen Harvey; Danny Peck; Gracie Browne; Akwasi Osei; Liam Rector; Priscilla Hodgkins; Ben Elsesser and Anedra Shockley-Elsesser; Ray Santos; Lisa Teasley; Belisa Vranich; Selina Payne; Mary Moffitt; Lynell George; Jeff Schatz; Nnamdi Mowetta; Steven Temple; Hope Frazier; Dianna Cohen; Jason Shinder; Raul Escuza; Robert Kipper, Esq.; Jonathan Fein, Esq.; Bob Shacochis; Anthony Foy; Mary Ann Hutchison and Ben Davis; Pamela Kawi; George Packer; my mother, Josephine Danquah; my father, Duke Brobby; my stepmother, Anne Brobby; my sisters, Paula Danquah-Brobby, Alexis Brobby, and Doriane Brobby; my brother, D.J. Brobby; and my uncle, Opoku Acheampong. Many thanks to all of you.

Finally, I would like to thank all of the children in my life who feed my spirit and fill each day with a world of possibility: Shane Browne; Ian Davis; Omar Wiseman; Aslan Moffitt-Rolston; Maya Hadash; Jackie Johnson; Noah Andoh; Ashley Payne; Maddy Goldsmith; Amiri Aje; Chance McDermott; Paloma Elsesser; and, of course, my amazing daughter, Korama, the one whose love guides my pen and gives birth to all of my dreams.

CONTENTS

As my feet touched solid ground
I felt a chill run down my spine
I could almost hear the sound
Of thousands pushing through the lines

Mothers and bewildered wives
That sailed across the raging sea
Others running for their lives
To the land of opportunity
Down on Ellis Island

"What is this strange paradise?"
They must have wondered
Through the cries and moans
After all they sacrificed
Their faith, their families, friends and homes

—Lyrics excerpted from the song "Ellis Island"
  by Marc Cohn

INTRODUCTION

MERI NANA-AMA DANQUAH

BECOMING AMERICAN IS ABOUT LANGUAGE. A language shaped more by longing than by landscape. A language rooted in both romance and estrangement. This book is about how we—not only as immigrants, but also as people—define ourselves. Perhaps more important, it is about how we either created or came upon these definitions.

It seems rather ironic that I should find myself writing an introduction to, let alone editing, a collection of essays for a book entitled *Becoming American.* Even though I have lived in America for most of my life, it has always been difficult for me to think of myself as an American. A native of Ghana, I came to America, with my family, at the age of six. Back then, I did not believe it was possible for people to "become" American; I felt that either a person was an American, or she was not. And, of course, the only way to be an American was to be born in America. There just wasn't any room for in-betweens. Even the naturalized citizens I knew still claimed their country of origin. When they spoke of "home," it was never America to which they were referring. It was always some other country that held their hearts. So I learned to view America as a place, not an identity—at least, not for me.

America, for me, was nothing more than a journey, an adventure, a world that spun seductively around my world, around my home, which was still the center of my universe, which was still governed by the influences of my native culture. When my family came to America and settled in Washington, D.C., they brought as much of Ghana with them as they could. Our apartment was filled with Kente and Adinkra cloths, with highlife music and wooden, hand-carved stools. Inside our apartment we spoke in our languages—*Ga* and *Twi*; we ate gari and fufu with groundnut soup, using our fingers instead of utensils; we wore batakaris and dashikis; we called each other by our "real" names, not those English names we answered to when we were out in public. We did nearly everything as if we were still living in Ghana. I had no reason to think of myself as anything other than a Ghanaian. In my mind, I was the same as any other Ghanaian girl my age. But, of course, I wasn't; and soon enough, people started pointing out the many ways in which I had changed. At first, they were subtle changes: a slang term, a gesture, maybe a new hairstyle.

Friends and family members would say, "You've become *so* American" or "You've become *too* American." Sometimes these sounded like words of praise and admiration; other times they sounded like accusations. Either way, I never knew how to respond. I never knew what the words, or the emotions behind them, were really implying. The process of becoming felt like a betrayal of what I was and, ultimately, of who I was. After all, in order to move toward something one must move away from something else. Even though I had already left Ghana, I didn't want Ghana to leave me. I didn't want to exist in the in-between. *What does it mean to become American?*

This was the question I found myself asking throughout my youth and well into my adulthood. It sparked an internal debate, a seemingly endless search for self that was fueled by pride and shame, determination and denial. It's a question that I found difficult to answer yet impossible to abandon. It's a question that at first generates more questions than answers: What is an American? Have I, in fact, become an American? Would I not be the person that I am now had I stayed in the country where I was born? In order to know what it means to become American, you must know what it means to have been something other than American. You must recognize the ways, large and small, in which you are no longer what you had once been. In order to know this, you must investigate your past. *What does it mean to become American?* It's a question that demands the writing of a story, a history, or the creation of a mythology.

❧

Stories are told through movement; they are exchanged in the making of things. They begin in the hands. They find their rhythms in the chopping, the hammering, the sewing, the bathing, the shuffling, the tidying. My grandmother used to tell me stories while she was braiding my hair or stirring a stew. She would tell me folktales about Kwaku Ananse, that mischievous half-spider, half-man. She would tell me about our family, about the relatives who were still living with and around us, the ancestors whose names and features I had inherited. There has always been a place for me in language.

As such, literature became the most immediate and effective way for me to ease my feelings of confusion and isolation. Throughout my youth, I had seen and read books about immigration. None of them contained any information that even remotely seemed to relate to me. There wasn't anybody on the *Mayflower* who looked like me. Or on Ellis Island. And if there were was, I would have never known it from the photographs or the text in the books I read. I had a strong yearning to be validated and it was hard for me to believe that there were no reflections of me, of my experiences, in any of those books. Where were the accounts of immigrant experiences through the eyes of a black African-born woman?

While browsing through a bookstore one day, I stumbled upon a copy of *Wife,* Bharati Mukherjee's novel about an Indian woman who emigrates to America with the new husband her parents have chosen for her. It was exactly the type of literature I had been searching for my entire reading life—a story that dealt with displacement. Though the novel was about Indian culture, the heart of the story—the dilemma of deciding how much of one's heritage and customs must be sacrificed to camouflage oneself as a member of mainstream society—spoke directly to me. In the years that followed, I read every piece of creative writing

I could get my hands on that addressed the personal aspects of immigration.

In the pages of the books I read were characters who were, as I was, dealing with the tediousness of having to constantly weight their desire to belong to one place against the possible consequences of betraying the other, all the while negotiating the undefined space in-between the two. I wanted to find as many interpretations of it as I could; I wanted to seek out all the possible answers to that single, haunting question. *What does it mean to become American?*

Fortunately, this hunger came at a time when the contemporary immigrant experience was inspiring a burgeoning literature. Ironically, it was also a time when America, a self-proclaimed nation of immigrants, had started to re-examine its policies, values and, in essence, itself by scrutinizing immigration—so much so that there was a growing hostility toward immigrants. I suppose this should not come at all as a surprise when one takes into consideration that literature has always provided society with a sense of self, place and history—especially in regards to immigration.

In his introduction to the anthology *Altogether Elsewhere*, Marc Robinson writes: "The constant threat of solitude in exile increases the value of language as a sustaining link to old and new worlds. Many exiles implicitly suggest that, for them, writing can no longer be private or inward-looking, no matter how much they would like it to be. From even the most reserved writer, some words written in exile can't help but sound like poignant, embarrassed pleas for attention—ways of reaching toward an indifferent group of people, potential readers who might anchor the writer with their interest. Other words are hopeful reachings—back to readers no longer known."

❧

This book is about the changing face of a nation, the personal geographies of some of its residents. It is a dialogue by and about women with newly hyphenated realities. Women who are no longer Korean or Chilean or Rwandese but Korean-American, Chilean-

American, Rwandese-American. These essays explore the complexities and contradictions of what is means to become American. They explore the hybrid cultures, foods and dialects we create along the way. As a whole, these essays are a true representation of the collective immigrant experience. Yet despite the fact that there are aspects of each journey through the assimilation process that are hauntingly similar, each immigrant experience is definitely individual and unique. Which is why, from essay to essay, there are wonderfully evident differences in grammar, spelling and style.

These sorts of differences are present even within a single essay. There are times when a writer opts to use the American spelling for some words, and times when she opts to use her birth country's spellings for other words. Every vowel, every consonant, comma and period is symbolic of the writer's presence here. In the introduction to *Darkness,* Bharati Mukherjee's collection of short stories, she writes: "The transformation as writer, and as resident of the new world, occurred with the act of immigration to the United States. . . . It's possible—with sharp ears and the right equipment—to hear America singing even in the seams of the dominant culture. In fact, it may be the best listening post for the next generation of Whitmans."

There are essays from women who immigrated to the United States when they were children, and essays from women who immigrated later in life. Some of the writers in this collection left their native lands by choice, others came by force, as a result of war or exile. While by their own definition each of the contributors to this collection is a first generation immigrant, someone who has come to this country from another country, not all of them are "technically" immigrants. For instance, because Judith Ortiz Cofer was born in Puerto Rico, a territory of the United States, she is not "technically" an immigrant. The same is true of Veronica Chambers; because she was born on a U.S. military base in Panama, she is also not "technically" an immigrant even though both of her parents are Panamanian. Rosanne Katon-Walden's story of her perfectly timed New York City birth is a classic example of how many would-be immigrants devise crafty ways to become American. As you will discover when you read these women's essays, the "technical" category into which they fall has more to do with politics than with cultural reality.

I am not sure that even now I know what it means to become American. Not in any absolute terms. There have been moments when I have felt completely American, completely at ease with my patchwork identity. And there have been moments when I haven't known how or what to feel. Ultimately, that is the beauty of this book, of these stories. They don't concern themselves with absolutes. They are as individual as their authors. Each one of these essays, in their own way, answers the question *What does it mean to become American?*; and each answer is a new experience of America, a new expression of not only what it means to become, but also of what it means to have been and, simply, to be.

All my friends are exiles.

Born in one place, we live in another
and with true sophistication,
rendezvous
in most surprising places—
where you would never expect to find us.

Between us we people the world.

With aplomb and a command of languages
we stride across continents
with the self-assurance of those who know
with absolute certainty
where they come from.

With the globe at our command,
we have everywhere to go,
but home.

—from *Testimonies of Exile*
   by Abena P. A. Busia

Doing Archaeology in My America

NINA BARRAGAN

DURING THE WINTER MONTHS OF 1944, travel arrangements were under way in Buenos Aires, Argentina. My mother, a small, pretty woman of twenty-six, was making the necessary preparations: passports and visas, inoculations, the farewells. Leaving her family and her country, she would travel with her two young children to an unfamiliar place with a strange language, the United States of America. There she would be reunited with her husband. She did not like having to leave everything she had always known and loved, but she wanted her husband.

In New York, those same months were summer, hot and humid. For more than nine months my father had been studying at the New School of Art on a Guggenheim Fellowship. As our anticipated arrival date approached, his excitement and agitation increased. He worried that there might be a hitch in our travel plans, throwing everything into confusion. Would we be met in Rio and escorted to a hotel, as he had arranged? Would there be someone from the consulate in Miami to assist us through immigration, as he had been promised? Emilia, my mother, did not speak English, nor had she ever traveled alone. The United States was a country at war, and my father knew that anything could happen in these difficult times. During his short stay in New York, he had already experienced mail censorship. Letters addressed to him from his Argentine family had been confiscated at the American border. He'd been summarily summoned and questioned by immigration inspec-

1

tors, by the FBI. Who was he spying for? The code names in the signature of his letter, Emilia, Pelado, Rocío Aitana, who were they for?
Pelado, "baldy" in Spanish, is my brother William's nickname. My
name, Rocío, is Spanish; it means "dew": el rocío. There is a shrine to
St. Rocío in Andalusia. I was also given the Arabic name of a Spanish
mountain, Aitana. My mother's heritage is Spanish, and in their youth,
my poetic parents nurtured their romance with the likes of García Lorca.
I suppose our esoteric names could present a suspicious package to
wartime America. Rocío, for sure, was destined to raise many a Midwestern eyebrow—I grew up in Iowa. As for the implication of spying,
that misunderstanding was eventually cleared up. My father managed
to convince the FBI that he was not a spy and that we were indeed his
family, and quite innocent. He was dismissed, only to resume his wor-
rying, as he waited nervously.

We entered the U.S. at Miami on August 28, 1944. I was almost
nineteen months old, my brother was five. From what I've been told,
it was a scorching day, and we were still dressed in our Argentine wool-
ens, including the hats and scarves that my maternal grandmother had
knit just before our departure from a cold Buenos Aires. The peeling
of layers must have begun in Brazil, continued in Trinidad, and by the
time we reached Miami, my mother was carrying a load of heavy garments in her arms. Things went smoothly at immigration, but while
we waited for our flight to New York, it seems I managed to create
more excitement for my already anxious, exhausted mother. My brother
was in charge of walking me around in the airport during our long wait,
and on one of our excursions, I spotted a large doll in a display case.
The die was cast. Apparently, I could not live without her; she was
nearly my size. I threw such a fit of screaming and wailing, refusing to
leave the display case, that my mother had no choice but to buy the
doll, breaking into one of her two fifty-dollar U.S. bills. This buttery-
skinned beauty in a blue gingham pinafore, become my first American
friend.

I still have my Argentine passport, issued in Buenos Aires. It's small—
the times were more conservative—only 4½ by 3½ inches, and genuine, maroon leather. The photograph is of a cute baby propped on a

chair, ribbon in wispy hair. I'm dressed in a white, hand-knit sweater-coat, complete with a collar scarf, a product of my loving grandmother's busy needles. In a certain, clear script, an Argentine bureaucrat has written that I'm blond, with a fair complexion and light eyes. A straight nose—base, narrow. The mouth—medium. The ears—medium. One might easily assume that given my malleable age and outward trappings, becoming an assimilated American could be as easy as apple pie. Yet fate would have that plate just slightly out of my reach, always. As I matured, I came to understand that the development of my identity in the process of "becoming American" involved the instinctive act of pushing that plate away, as much as pulling it toward me.

The little pages of my passport are filled with all the stamps and seals and visas of a cautious world. The first visa stamps are for one year, the renewals are for two, and then it discontinues, it ends. In 1953, just before my parents took us on a year's sojourn to Spain—another Guggenheim Fellowship for my artist father, this time to study the prints of Francisco Goya—my parents became naturalized American citizens, and my siblings and I were included on my mother's new American passport. It wasn't until I was twenty and just married that my older brother and I would present ourselves before a judge in Davenport, Iowa, go through the formality of declaring our allegiance to the United States of America, and thus receive our own U.S. passports.

When the war ended in 1945, my mother was pregnant again, and we moved from New York to Iowa City, Iowa, where my father had accepted a teaching position at the University of Iowa. He was to begin a printmaking program in the department of art. University housing was at a premium that first year after the war, but Virgil Hancher, president of the University of Iowa, very kindly offered us the guest quarters in the president's mansion. That act of American kindness and generosity helped convince my father that he wanted a future in this country, this democracy, and not in what had become of his homeland, the Argentina of Juan Perón.

For my mother, it was different. During those winter months in Buenos Aires, she had slowly prepared herself for the reality of her departure, her emigration. Immigration was another matter. Her understanding was that this would be a year's visit, and I believe she fully intended to return to Argentina. Nowhere on her map did it say anything about staying away from her country and her family forever. In fact she did, and the year became a lifetime. I remember my mother telling me that the saddest day of her life was the morning she woke up in our first, rented home in Iowa City and suddenly realized that she was here to stay, that she would not return. She was right. In over a half century of residence in the States, neither of my parents has ever returned to their homeland. My father simply would not go back, and my mother wouldn't go without him. Nor has my older brother returned. I have.

That first rented home was part of university housing, a big, white clapboard house on a hill. We children learned to sleigh and make snowmen, and in the summer, we had a pet duck in our fenced-in yard. We fed him tomatoes, and I was amazed that the following spring we had tomato plants growing in the yard. We played with our neighbors— their parents were schoolteachers, raised on Iowa farms—and from this family, we learned about America. We watched their mother bake bread and freeze vegetables from the garden. During his time off from teaching, their father worked on projects around the house. Once, he butchered some chickens he'd brought back from his family farm. As the bread rose on the kitchen counter, their mother helped ours study for her citizenship exam. She quizzed her about the structure of the federal government, the legislative branch, the judicial, the executive. How many congressmen and how many senators represent each state? How often are elections held? By then, two siblings had followed us, and eventually, two more would, for a total of six children. Within a couple of years my parents bought an old Victorian house on a wonderful, tree-lined street. We were no longer visitors, we were here to stay. Iowa City was our new home.

I wonder if most "New Americans" think their circumstances are unique. Now, in retrospect, I realize how unusual our situation was, although at the time, I didn't think about it. We did not come to a "community" of people from our homeland, as so many immigrants do. We did not come to a ghetto or an ethnic neighborhood of a large city. We came to a small, Midwestern university town. There were only a handful of Spanish-speaking people, very few from Argentina. We did not come to *family* that had preceded us. We came alone, and we would remain alone, always.

Two things made our situation unusual. The first was that I'm not sure my mother ever considered the United States the "land of opportunity." She was from Buenos Aires, the Paris of South America, and that had always been enough for her. When we moved to Iowa City in the mid-forties, Iowa was Iowa, with its corn and hogs, insurance salesmen, bankers, and the racks of "Better Dresses" in ladies' wear of Penney's department store. I believe there were days when my quiet mother felt completely estranged, wanting only to go back. By the time I could sympathize, I found her silent withdrawal bewildering, for by then, I was an Iowan. I knew about the hogs and Penney's, but I was also incredibly aware of the University of Iowa, right in the middle of this little town, only a few streets separating it from cornfields.

The other factor that contributed to our uniqueness was that as children, my siblings and I were given little of our parents' past, little was articulated. For the most part it was left behind; it seemed to be the only way my parents could do it. Once away from Argentina, my father was determined to "start over." He left behind a difficult country, struggling under political dictatorship and economic uncertainty, and he left behind a difficult family. For my mother, who was neither politically inclined nor eager to leave her own, loving family, I believe my father's attitude was a source of great pain. I knew that my mother's background was Spanish and my father's was eastern European Jewish, that their parents had been first-generation Argentineans. But certainly my father rarely mentioned family events, customs, or religious traditions from the old country. He often spoke about the hard times of the depression and his family's poverty. I always felt he'd had little joy in his childhood, although on a few occasions he mentioned his mother's delicious *teiglach* candy and the special copper pot used in its preparation. As I matured and became a young woman, my mother would occasionally tell me anecdotes about her childhood; about her aunts and uncles, her many cousins, how her father was so kind and her mother such a fine cook.

She always spoke happily of these things, but in a sort of hushed secrecy, for she knew that my father felt the "past is the past," and "when you leave, you leave." Because my parents met as young teenagers, my mother's story included quite a bit of my father's. Eventually I was able to fit enough pieces together to form a fairly complete picture of their lives in that other time, that other place. But I was an adult before I could do this.

Once established in Iowa and secure in his teaching position, my father sought the time and solitude to pursue his art, to forge new technical and aesthetic territories. Watching our father, we were raised to believe that productive solitude creates independence, which in turn helps shape self-integrity. Indeed, independence was our force. It nurtured the strengths of self-sufficiency and commitment to work that our personalities would come to demand. These strengths we carry today. But there were pitfalls. With such a strong emphasis on independence, the concept of "belonging" to an extended family, or "belonging" to a community, was virtually nonexistent.

Without a sense of "belonging," we were not taught or encouraged to develop a sense of responsibility for our extended family, not to mention communal responsibility. Just as our strengths are with us still, these shortcomings are as well. While friendships and social life were not encouraged, although marginally abided by our parents, all of us managed to develop close ties with companions at school. But basically, my family grew up alone, together. In over fifty years of American residence, my parents have had few friends, and this situation has become more pronounced with time. Initially there were some, like our first neighbors, the teachers. As the years progressed, my parents shunned close friendships, the result, I believe of several painful experiences. I recall my father telling me that in the beginning years at the University of Iowa he was given a raise. In his excitement, he told a couple of friends, colleagues teaching in the same department. They, in turn, complained to their department head about the "foreigner" who got a raise, when they didn't. Ultimately my parents were immigrants, carrying the common burden of "immigrant paranoia." We were taught it was best not to depend on others, even those *unknown* relatives in

Argentina. The existence of those Argentine relatives was so hazy that to this day, some of my younger brothers do not even know the names of their parents' siblings. They find any talk of them annoying—and now there is some talk, in my parents' softer, later years—the way name-dropping about strangers can be.

So we were to exist apart from society. And yet my father truly respected America. He loved the way Americans are not afraid to do things: to build and paint houses, to bake cakes, to garden, and that one doesn't have to be a professional contractor, a baker, or a gardener. He always encouraged us to use our hands, claiming that it would stand us in good stead, in more ways than one. When I was young, he told me I could have all the clothes I wanted, as long as I made them. He would buy me any fabric I wanted. I pretty well took him up on it, and to this day I sew. When my parents bought an old house on a Maine island for our summer place, my father took great pleasure in the physical work of improvements and restoration. He put us all to work, giving us the satisfaction of accomplishment.

I remember thinking that my family must have invented *machete*, the word, the blade. I had never seen one hanging above other people's Franklin stoves as one hung above ours, in Maine. In time, I realized it had been ordered from an Army surplus catalogue, along with a surplus parachute. While my mother helped me make a party dress from the bundle of white nylon, somehow even managing to incorporate the tenacious seams in the garment's design, my father and brothers put the machete to use on our Maine property. For my father, that was American freedom, ordering what he wanted from catalogues, no questions asked. He was impressed that American teenagers held jobs, even the children of judges, like the family that lived across the street from us. Yet he did not encourage his own children to get jobs; somehow that would be compromising. We were different.

Despite my father's love of country, my parents did not strive to assimilate. They fought it, remaining separate, my mother almost aloof. My father led and she followed, toeing the line, his word, among the children. I believe my father reasoned that artists were different and could not allow themselves to be absorbed by the prevalent culture. I believe he felt it was his responsibility to look after the family's collective creative temperament, the individual artistic personalities. In fact, all of my parents' children made the arts their lives' work.

My growing up became a process of rummaging through what I knew of my parents' history, searching for fragments and relics, doing archaeology in my America. I was eager to find out where and what I'd come from. Oddly, I was the only one of my siblings who had any interest in our parents' backgrounds. It was a topic that was as irrelevant to them as it was to our father. Or so he claimed. I've returned to Argentina several times in the last fifteen years, each time finding it an enormous source of pleasure. I've connected with my large extended family, and I've connected with my homeland, despite the distressing volatility and uncertainty that mars the beauty of its people and landscape. When I'm there, I feel at peace. During my first trip back, while visiting the city of Córdoba, my birthplace, I had to stop a lady on the street to ask for directions. After helping me, she asked which province I was from, sensing a difference in my language. I was proud to be mistaken for an Argentinean, considering that I'd been away for the better part of forty years.

My parents have thick Spanish accents. While my father's command of English has always been excellent, essential to his university teaching, my mother's English was adequate. When she didn't like what she was hearing, she pretended she didn't understand. As a child, I often repeated her words, so the person or people she was talking to could understand. I do it even more now. In her eighties, her control of language has slackened. She doesn't try. Often, she breaks into Spanish with the slightest provocation, not realizing the smiling person before her is completely bewildered, though charmed, by this still-pretty, white-haired little lady. I am bilingual, as is my older brother. We speak with our parents in both languages. For my other siblings, who were all born in Iowa, English is their main language, though they all understand Spanish.

So, from this, assimilation? Yes, but with difficulty and caution. I was always different, we were always "foreigners." Like all immigrants, I too experienced the occasional, predictable prejudice, I too have stories. In the third grade I was not invited to a classmate's birthday party because I was a "foreigner." In the fourth grade I was an afterthought guest at a party given for a classmate going to England for the year. At the last moment one of the mothers realized my family would also be spending the year abroad, so I was included. The other girl's gift was a large suitcase, mine was a pretty, tartan purse. There was a lot of bluster about how I *must* understand that size is not an indication of importance. It was embarrassing, I liked the purse. While I did not have many such experiences, actual events I can talk about, I did have my name, my beautiful albatross.

I've always felt that Rocío Aitana Lasansky was one of my biggest barriers to assimilation. My brothers' names—Guillermo (William), Leonardo (Leonard), Felipe (Philip), Tomás (Thomas)—all translated well. My sister, Maria Jimena, became Maria at school. At home, "La Nena," little girl—my parents' nickname for me—became "Nina" to my siblings. But at school, and everywhere else, I remained Rocío. Most Americans unknowingly mispronounce it, putting the accent on the first *o* instead of the *i*, and because it ends in *o*, I was often mistaken for a male. When I was a senior in high school, the U.S. Army actually tried to draft me. In grade school I didn't look different from the other kids, but my name said I was. Later, in my last years of high school, when I began writing poetry and fiction, I became attracted to the exotic. In my first year of college, I embraced my differences, my marks of distinction. I played them up. I wore my long hair braided and "up," when bouffant hair and pillbox hats were in. I wore soft, almost hippielike clothes, before there were hippies. I wore comfortable leather sandals, Dr. Scholl's, designed for orthopedic problems—though I have excellent feet—long before *the look* was in. I was developing my style.

Had I married someone from Iowa, and remained here, possibly the course of my assimilation would have been different. But at the age of twenty I married a foreigner, a Canadian, an artist. We traveled in Europe. We lived on the Spanish island of Ibiza in the Mediterranean for a year and a half; my husband painted, I wrote. For three years we lived in Regina, Saskatchewan, where my husband taught at the university. Then we moved to Ontario and purchased a hundred-acre farm, 125 miles northwest of Toronto.

Our first three children were born. I wrote my first collection of stories. We lived in Ontario for eleven years. We were in Canada during the first American presidential election after my twenty-first birthday, and I was desperate to vote, but I was too late to cast a ballot *in absentia.* Four years later I was smart enough to make the arrangements ahead of time, and I was thrilled to exercise my right. I loved our farm, our isolation, but I'd felt myself an expatriate for too long, and it was bothering me. Not long after, we made the decision to move back to the States. My husband taught at the University of Texas at San Antonio for a few years, and then we moved back to Iowa with our three children. Our fourth child was born in Iowa City, and I was home.

I re-assumed my assimilation process when I returned to the States. When we moved to Texas, I made the conscious decision to go by "Nina" instead of "Rocío." I was tired of hearing my name mispronounced. Only when I was in Spain and Argentina did I hear Rocío as it should be, and I loved it. I was tired of being known as "Mrs. Weinstein" to my husband's "Alan." My pen name, Nina Barragan—my nickname and my mother's maiden name—came into existence for a literary competition in Saskatchewan. The submission of a story required a pen name. My story was published, and the name looked good in print. It stuck.

I always enjoy traveling and I love our Canadian farm during the summer, but the States is home. I sincerely respect our democracy, though our society's faults—its unfathomable "black holes"—make me as anxious as the next American. I am very much first generation, an immigrant, but more, the child of immigrants. I believe in saving, conserving, recycling, *making do.* It makes me nervous if our credit card balance gets too large, and I don't like to owe money. I despair that my husband and I have failed to teach our four, wonderful, accomplished children how to save half of what they earn.

Today, when I cook for guests, I am flattered when I'm told my cooking is European, not American. I take it as a compliment. Does this mean I'm not an assimilated American? I don't think so. I can never imagine my nationality ever being anything but American. In all the years I lived in Canada, I was often asked two questions. The first: "But what was your *maiden* name?" This always followed an introduction, when the person learned my married name was Weinstein. Fully aware of English Canada's obsession with lineage, specifically with Anglo-Saxon heritage, I would smile and answer, "It wasn't any better; it was Lasansky." The second question: "When will you become a Canadian?"

"Never," I would respond, "because I'm an American, and it wasn't easy. You see, it didn't come naturally."

Turbulent Times

LILIANET BRINTRUP

BEAUTIFUL, SMART, ELEGANT, JUST LOVELY were some of the words I heard not long after I came to the USA for the first time in 1981 from Chile. These were the words I wanted to hear. But at twenty-five degrees below zero, they mixed with the cold weather my own fear and anxiety. There were more words. *Efficient, go for it, do it, just brilliant, intelligent, cool.* The words were unfamiliar to my heart, feelings, and mind. These new words were unexpected, with alien meaning, without transparencies. They were announcing my growing assimilation and acceptance into my foreign culture.

I had come to the U.S. to be a graduate student at the prestigious University of Michigan—Ann Arbor. I was to begin my Ph.D. in the Department of Romance Languages. I arrived in Detroit with my family—my husband and two children—a boy of five, Cosme Zvetan Andreas, and a girl of eighteen months, Colombina Mercedes. When I first arrived, it was the second of February and the winter was at its zenith, hard and implacable. People didn't smile. I supposed that they were in a hurry. I didn't see any sign of welcome, not even one small flag waving in the wind as a sign of welcome for foreign people. This lack of courtesy in a country of immigrants, many of whom had been exiled by brute force, really surprised me. I thought, "Well, it is just one P.M., people are having lunch or siesta, and the ones left here are showing their irritation and sadness." I wanted an explanation for this absence of courtesy.

Soon I became depressed and tired of waiting for somebody to explain to me what this oversight was all about. What I didn't know then was that in America, if you don't demand an explanation, no one will approach you to explain anything. But if you inquire directly about something, the accurate and precise explanations will be given to you immediately. In fact, one might even be overwhelmed with both the oral and written details of such responses.

The world that I had arrived in happened to be extremely structured, monolithic. Sometimes I thought it nice. Other times I saw this world as alienating because of its obsessions, its constant quest for knowledge and need for progress. I felt stuck. Not in mud, but in the pavement, walls, offices, elevators, and corridors. Only I was not entirely isolated. I was still able to hear the unpleasant noises of the city—the cars, the sirens of ambulances and fire trucks. Soon, in order to retain my already borderline health during my stint as a student, I developed a particularly necessary talent: I looked through the sealed windows to nature and its world outside—the birds, squirrels, and trees, the silent snow, the young and the mature people, the absence of children. And I learned that in places like this so-called university town, real life had very little space.

It seemed as if the people in this town were having a long, long, heartless sleep. So, in order for me to survive, I had to learn to "live" less, to have a minimal awareness of real life. This fragmentation would soon have a tremendous impact on me, my children, and my family as a whole. From the very first few months of my arrival, this disconnection between knowledge, people, and reality struck me vividly. Despite the seeming perfection of things, I sensed a big superficiality and arrogance in the academic world that I was to be a part of. When I established relations with all my wonderful and knowledgeable professors, they made me feel that if I were to sustain my presence in this academic world, the first principle that had to be learned was humility.

I had received the award of a fellowship, thus gaining the status of teaching assistant. Friends, professors, and Ph.D. classmates spoke about this wonderful fellowship that the American institutions gave to foreign students so that they would not be forced to work somewhere else. But, in truth, the only real support I received was the payment of my tuition and a very small salary. And the teaching assistantship was such a burden. It was an unbelievable amount of work, work, and more work. It was difficult to cope with everything, especially doing all of this with a family and no help at home. Things for me then were out of place. They were centered in the middle of constant stress. My mind was in incessant movement and I couldn't rest at all. Life became a turbulent race, leaving me ill-equipped to pay attention to my domestic world, much less to the other worlds around me.

I have never had as intense a sensation of chaos as I did in the midst of this supposed perfection to which I had immigrated. Even a duty like answering a phone call was a difficult and frustrating experience. Assimilation came most immediately to my son, who was five years old. My husband and I placed him in charge of answering all calls in English. He quickly learned how to get rid of calls from banks, offices, vendors, and other unwanted intruders. He was the tongue of the house, the role model of gestures and new ways of thinking. We looked to him as our permanent teacher. He brought in information about a variety of things. He taught us what to eat, how to buy it, when to eat it. He told us which people were our neighbors and educated us on the informality of dressing, the importance of sport, and the mentality of his teachers. I never felt more abandoned during the first year of our arrival than when my son was at school or when he went out to play with friends after school. Sometimes I would call him in because I had received a phone call that froze me, or sometimes simply because he was an American boy who seemed to gracefully understand and accept why we were in the USA. He, especially, always made me feel that I was in the right place. He had the capacity to erase all signs of my guilt. Many times, when I think of the ease with which he adapted, I believe that this country was built for children. He seemed to be so happy.

To be more effective and efficient academically, I received advice like this: "Don't cook and clean up your house every day. Buy food once a week and store it. Spend your spare time at the library or at your work." The most interesting advice I received was "Forget everything you have learned in the past and start again." How can someone just discard memory? The rupture of my academic tradition tore intensively at my soul. Yet I did not see any significance in discarding the memory of the process of my previous academic learning. Why this necessity of washing off my mind when the "new" information I was about to incorporate was only going to sustain the values of a society that seemed to value human relationships so little? Unlike my son, I was neither optimistic nor happy. I felt as if something had been taken away, like my skin and my verbal conception of the world. I was confused; I could see nothing more than contradictions. I even felt a little bit retarded in the midst of the intelligentsia. But I grew to realize that all this advice was coming from people who were actually a lot like me, and that the real problem was my lack of mastery of the English language. I became determined to communicate with and to hear the "Anglo-Saxon Americans."

I tried to find those Americans, but where were they? Where were the ones I came to see, to know—the Anglo-Saxon Americans? The only people that showed any interest in me were Latin-Americans, Greeks, Portugese, Iranians, Chinese, Germans, Egyptians, and Arabs. Over time, I found that even what I had interpreted as genuine interest on their part was, in fact, a curiosity born of self-interest. After all, we all needed to learn how to survive, and we all looked to others who were somewhat like us to see and learn how they were doing it. In time, my English improved. Nevertheless, my inability to find those Americans for whom I had been searching was not only a question of lacking mastery of their language.

My dear Americans didn't show up. They were all basically too busy working from nine to five or in overnight shifts, or else they were in breakfast, lunch, or supper meetings, or in special training, or dating, or in some sort of professional development or skills workshops, or in seminars, in phone conferences, gardening, in their cars between bowling, football, or soccer, in their cars commuting to and from somewhere, or in their cars for the fun of it. I had entered into an incredibly mobile society where people were on the move all the time. This ceaseless mobility often brought to mind the image of an ocean where each of us swims and swims in order to go somewhere, although we always curiously come back to the point of our departure. We always come back avoiding deterioration, the passage of time, death. Moving, working, playing. The perfect ménage à trois in this territory. Such an alliance admits no divorce. One is always somehow vaguely attached to something or someone, a part of, not apart from. A foreign person can't help but feel confused, isolated, and paralyzed trying to figure out which road to take in order to avoid being mistaken.

I watched myself standing in the middle of this turbulent way of life with complete astonishment, trying to hold my family together, trying to save them from falling into an empty abyss. Food was a problem from the beginning. My daughter ran up and down the stairs of the house shouting and crying for the soup she used to eat in Chile. It was a simple vegetable soup. I made all efforts to reproduce it, but she kept on shouting for it for months until she discovered white bread, yellow cheese, and bologna. At the supermarket, I never knew what exactly to buy for them, so I let them choose. Doughnuts, white bread, and bologna invaded my refrigerator. White bread, that sponge of a food, was my children's favorite. For me, the only food I wanted during those first long winter months was food with a lot of calories. It was too cold to think about salad and fruit. At the time, I never read the food labels, which always looked so attractive and clever to me.

During the weekdays, the children had cold lunches (a sandwich or fruit) at school. I also adopted this form of nourishment and took from our refrigerator—that artifact which was now regulating our lives—anything I could eat at my desk. Not eating together in the dining room of our house made me feel that I was doing something completely wrong, illegal even. I had all but forgotten the "happy hour" of lunchtime. I was sure that we were going to fall into this way of life, into something similar to a black hole of nothingness, where everything was taking place all at once. So, firmly, I refused any job obligations and did not study after three P.M.—the moment my son arrived home from school and when I picked my daughter up from nursery school—in order to be there with them. Religiously, I served them tea between four and five P.M. I prepared them some Chilean pastry. I washed, cleaned, and didn't give up my white tablecloth that proudly covered the table every day at mealtimes.

I was terribly sad, and more than once I thought about quitting everything and returning to Chile, where my children would be surrounded by family, friends, their sensible and generous nanas. As a mother, I was suddenly living the painful experience of being a working mother of young children in a modern society. The dissolution of socializing as a way of being and also of eating disturbed me. I didn't know exactly how to move on and out from my domestic life without tearing apart my heart, customs, and manners. The inside of my home was a constant battle which took most of my energy and occupied all of my time. I seriously considered the idea of bringing over a maid from Chile. The cook we had before coming to the USA seemed to me to be the perfect one to solve all of my domestic problems. She was wise in anticipating the possible problems I would have in America. "Señora, how will you go away if you don't know how to cook? You don't know how to fry an egg the way your husband likes it." "I shall learn. Don't worry. I shall learn," I used to respond to her.

Being in a big university in a big country where everything looked so big, and on occasion, out of proportion, it was easy for me to connect the size of fruits and vegetables with the size of the territory and the size of the buildings. The supermarkets I visited reproduced this ideology of being "super," being "super superior," and therefore having a "super supper." Consequently, I admired the huge strawberries, the gigantic carrots, the enormous cucumbers, the immeasurable pumpkins, and the monstrosity of the apples. I would find myself with "the largest pear in the world," in the biggest and the best city with the tallest buildings imaginable and the most immense prairies on earth where the greatest cows grazed, where the most amazing and extraordinary people came up with super projects and ideas like the creation of Superman and Superwoman. It wasn't easy to adjust to a society with such extremes. It leads to confusion—of the same sort that I had been feeling, suggesting that one is always on the way to accomplishing some "mission impossible." Reproducing our Chilean domestic life was an inferno for the children.

Before too long, I became as busy as everyone else around me, always moving. I traded my siesta time for laundry time, my healthy leisure time for the unbearable workout time. I began to observe the women around me. They were strong, fast, competitive, efficient, even dominant and controlling. My husband was busy as well, too busy trying to get research done, and then, later, trying to get tenure at the university, to pay attention or even notice the details of our daily life. He and I felt then that getting tenure would not only ensure that we could stay in the country, but also that we would be able to relax and enjoy the life that other successful immigrants seemed to enjoy. Big mistake. We had so many projects on our minds that sometimes we found ourselves saying sadly, "We should have come earlier. We are not young enough to cope with the demands of this place." Just coping with the material acquisitions of a house, car, microwave, refrigerator, freezer, carpeting, television, Nintendo, CD player, computer, nice furniture, and practical clothes seemed a task unreachable. How much more coping before we reached a certain economic status, one which would allow us to buy a house in a "good" neighborhood, enable us to send our children to a "good" school. It took us a while to even realize that the really good schools in this country were not necessarily private or religious schools in rich neighborhoods. Surely immigrants, in this regard, are no different from many dedicated Americans who work from sunup till sundown to attain the luxuries of this country. But not coming from such a democratic party "par excellence" makes it harder to understand it.

I started buying all sorts of things in abundance. This exuberant way of life made me feel that I was rich and powerful. But, really, my mental health was in danger. The order of my previous domestic life was replaced by another order that I was unable to fully comprehend. My children cried, laughed, and complained too often. My husband's adjustment process was rapid and abrupt. He was always a warrior, a person determined to win any battle, to fight any obstacle, to blow up any insect near his shoulder. He had to take charge of America. As much as I admired him, his ambitious attitude and his combative behavior tired me. We were losing, little by little, through his activities, the feeling of being interrelated. He was too much like any other violent and ambitious creature. I recognized, though not without difficulty, that it was the only way for us to survive here. Because of him, I always had a place to live, food to eat, clothes to wear, and many other luxurious objects. He had, in vain, designed a prospectus for our life in order to save us from chaos. That dreaded chaos, which surfaced as the breakdown of our domestic life, came without us even noticing it. The university was a magnificent system, but it was like a headless monster unknown to me. I was scared to fail the demands. I was scared I would not be able to face the monster. Fear and competition had wrapped us both up. All the while that we were determined to become winners, we had forgotten what we were losing.

Assimilation was *the* major and overbearing task. To speak, to think, to eat, and to dream in more than one language. I became insensible and silly. To immigrate to the USA is to come to a mobile culture, where everything is changing, and where the immigrants are nothing special because the dominant style of life will ultimately absorb them. At first, I felt that Americans never appreciated my coming. Looking back now, I see that I was wrong in this belief. Over the years, I have witnessed the tremendous efforts on the part of Americans to celebrate diversity, minorities, and cultural differences. The opportunities that this place promises to immigrants are rather fantastic, but we don't know exactly where those opportunities are located. We think that they are everywhere—in the countryside, in the small village, in the big cities, even in the space at the very bottom of that ocean I so long imagined as a metaphor for life here in America. One has to seek out those opportunities in the midst of a profound disconnection between people, institutions, corporations, regular offices. In a place like this, where everything seems chopped, cut, fragmented; a place where there is no sense of community; a place where one is forced to move from place to place without a transition of any sort, one can become disoriented. There is something that has been difficult for me to understand: how Americans refuse to understand that we as immigrants cannot be "super" or "superior" to anything. Becoming American is an experience that cannot be the same for every immigrant. The experience of selling tacos in Los Angeles and being a professor at MIT or a researcher at NIH produces very distinct human beings.

So where am I in all this? I have never picked grapes or apples and I have never worked at the factories. I came as a Chilean white European with two German names. Now I am Hispanic. But not a "super" Hispanic of the nation. This transformation interests me. Instead of becoming just an American, I became a little part of America and a little piece of Hispanic-Latino-Chicano. Curiously, only my Chilean background has given me the feeling of roots. Roots that I do not find in that country. My little American portion has to do precisely with knowledge. I have been exposed to readings and dialogues produced by critical American minds. Reading and listening, I was able, and am able still, to observe the seriousness of their thoughts, the deep level of information, the rigor of the data based on extended studies. This is the portion of America that I want to be a part of: the process of dismantling myths, stereotypes, and lies. Being critical is one of the most relevant aspects of becoming American for me. What America gave me was a space to write, along with my developing abilities to clean a house, to cook, to select smart food, to be my own maid, to be a worker, to be personae.

When I went abroad and someone asked me where I came from, I answered in two parts: I am from Chile, but I am living in California. What I really want to say when I say, "I am living in California," is perhaps this: I came to this mythical and controversial place through effort, through hard work, and now I have a social security number, a driver's license, credit cards, status as a Hispanic and as a Californian. I have enough courage to deal with the USA. I have grown in this way—fighting stereotypes, and fighting to be a kind of quiet, conscious, and nonpassive Hispanic immigrant, a human being.

Secret Latina at Large

VERONICA CHAMBERS

SHE'S A *PLATANOS*-FRYING, MALTA DUKESA–DRINKING, salsa-dancing *mamacita*—my dark-skinned Panamanian mother. She came to this country when she was twenty-one—her sense of culture intact, her Spanish flawless. Today, more than twenty years since she left her home country and became an American citizen, my mother still considers herself a Panamanian, checks "Hispanic" on the census form.

As a black woman in America, my Latina identity is murkier than my mother's. Without a Spanish last name or my mother's fluent Spanish at my disposal, I've often felt isolated from the Latin community. Latinos can be as racist as anybody else: there are pecking orders and hierarchies that favor blue-eyed blonde *rubios* over *negritas* like me. Sometimes, I feel that I put up with enough racism from white Americans, why should I turn to white Latinos for a second share? In much the same way that you can meet a person and not know if they are gay or straight, you could meet me and not know whether I was of Latin heritage. So I find myself making judgement calls—do I come out of the closet and when?

I was born in Panama to black Panamanian parents. My father's parents came from Costa Rica and Jamaica. My mother's family came from Martinique. I left Panama when I was two years old, we lived in England for three years, and I came to the U.S. when I was five. Having dark skin and growing up in Brooklyn in the '70's meant that I was black—period. I spent my childhood on Brooklyn streets that morphed, quickly, into worlds away. A stroll down Utica Avenue and the music or the smell of somebody's grandmother's cooking could transform a New York City corner into Santo Domingo, Kingston, Port-au-Prince. Long before I ever set out in search of the world, it found me. My friends, their families, and the histories they carried on their backs, kept me glued to the globe. I traced nations with my fingertips and knew that America was neither the beginning nor the end, just the crazy mixed-up right now that we all lived in. I also knew that we were only the latest wave of immigrants to make a home in our East Flatbush neighborhood. Every day after school, I rubbed my fingers across the Jewish mezuzah that ornamented our door frame. The super had painted over the mezuzahs, an ugly brown, but I never saw anyone ripping one off. I understood it to be out of respect, and I wondered how we would leave our mark.

Still, despite the international flavor of our neighborhood, I found it almost impossible to explain to my elementary school friends why my mother would speak Spanish at home. They asked me if I was Puerto Rican and I would tell them I was not. But Panama was a kind of nowhere to my young Brooklyn friends. They understood Puerto Ricans because there were so many of them and because of movies like *West Side Story* and groups like Menudo. Everybody knew where Jamaicans were from because of famous singers like Bob Marley. Panamanians had Ruben Blades and we loved him like royalty. But even if my friends knew who he was, because he sang in Spanish, they probably thought he was Puerto Rican too. So in my neighborhood, my brother and I were a sort of fish with feathers. We weren't so much Panamanians as much as we were assumed to be Jamaicans who spoke Spanish. An analogy that isn't without historical basis—Panama's black community was largely drawn to the country from all over the Caribbean as cheap labor for the Panama Canal.

My father didn't mind us considering ourselves black as opposed to Latino. He named my brother Malcolm X. If my mother hadn't put her foot down, I would've been called Angela Davis Chambers. It's not that my mother didn't admire Angela Davis, but you only have to hear how "Veronica Victoria" flows off of her Spanish lips to know that she was homesick for Panama and names that sang like *timbales* on carnival day. So between my mother and my father, there was a black/Latin divide. Because of my father, we discussed and read books about black history and civil rights. Because of my mother, we ate Panamanian food, listened to salsa music and heard Spanish around the house.

I learned Spanish at home like a dog learns English, and understood mostly commands: "*Callate la boca!*" ("Shut your mouth!) when I dared to interrupt grown-folk's talk. Or "*Baja la cabeza!*" ("Drop your head!") when my mother was braiding my hair and I kept looking up to see my favorite show on TV. My father was also Panamanian, but his mentality was simple. "You're in America," he ordered. "Speak English." It wasn't until my parents were divorced, when I was ten, that my mother tried to teach Malcolm and me to speak Spanish.

My mother was a terrible language teacher. She had no sense of how to explain the structure when we asked questions such as why we were supposed to say "*Toma café*"—literally, "He takes coffee"—instead of "He drinks coffee." Her answer to everything was "That's just the way it is." A few short weeks after our Spanish lessons began, my mother gave up and we were all relieved. I remained intent on learning my mother's language. Nosiness, mostly. What was she saying to her friends on the phone? But there was more to it than that. When my mother spoke Spanish, it was a fast current of words, a stream of language that was colorful, passionate fiery. I wanted to speak Spanish because I wanted to swim in the river of her words, her history, my history, too.

At Ditmas Junior High School, I had to petition the principal so I could take Spanish. All the other kids in the gifted and talented program were taking French. Apparently, to the powers that were, French was more cultural, more intellectual. The principal approved my request to take Spanish and for two years, I dove into the language, matching what little I knew from home with all that I learned at school. I never asked my mother for help with my Spanish homework; she never asked me about my lessons. But one day when I was in the ninth grade, I felt confident enough to start speaking Spanish with my mother and it's been that way ever since.

My brother, who was born in England, never learned Spanish and still doesn't speak it. When I was younger, my Spanish became a point of pride, a typical case of sibling rivalry. Now, I know that my Spanish was also an important bond that I shared with my mother. When I was little, she used to watch astrologer Walter Mercado and *telenovelas* on the Spanish language TV station. I would sit impatiently as she translated Mercado's horoscope for me or tried to explain what was going on in the latest installment of *La Tragedia de Lisette*. After I learned Spanish, I watched these programs with my mother—not needing translations, poking fun at the campiness of Spanish language TV. My mother and I would talk to each other in Spanish at our jobs or anywhere we needed some semblance of privacy.

When I spoke only English, I was the daughter, the little girl. As I began to learn Spanish, I became something more—an *hermanita*, a sister-friend, a Panamanian homegirl who could hang with the rest of them. I kissed *boricua* boys on my grandmother's porch and wondered when they whispered *prieta* whether that meant they loved me more or loved me less. When Puerto Rican girls talked about me in front of my face, looking at my dark skin and assuming that I couldn't understand, I would playfully throw out, "*Oye, sabes que yo entiendo?*" Being *Latinegra*—black and Latin, has become a sort of a hidden weapon, something that you can't see at first glance. I know that many people look at my dark skin and don't expect me to be fluent in anything but homegirl.

After college, I put Panama on the back burner for seven years, traveling instead to Spain, Morocco, London, Paris, even China. Then last year, at the age of twenty-seven, I wrote my first young adult novel, *Marisol and Magdalena*, about a black Panamanian girl growing up in Brooklyn who goes to live with her grandmother in Panama. In many ways, the novel was a way for me to live a dream that never came true. When I was a young girl, my *abuela* Flora came to live with us in New York. She was old, eighty-four, and sick, but we became fast friends. She told me stories about Panama, promising me that she and I would go together. My grandmother told me that she would make me a festive *pollera* dress and I could dance in the carnival. She died when I was eleven but writing *Marisol and Magdalena* I imagined what all of those things would be like. Then I decided that it was finally time. With or without my grandmother, with or without my mother, I would have to make my way home. The first thing I did was enlist my cousin, Digna. She was thrilled. "*Ay prima!*" she exclaimed, calling me as she always does, by the Spanish word for cousin. "To visit our *patria* (homeland) together. We'll have so much fun." We planned our trip for the last week in February and made arrangements to stay with my godparents, whom I had never met.

Like Mardi Gras in New Orleans and the big carnivals in Brazil, carnival in Panama is the year's biggest event. We had no problem finding cheap fares. I flew from New York to Miami, where most of the flights to Panama depart from. Arriving in the Miami airport was like stepping into a huge family reunion. The waiting room was filled with hundreds of black Panamanians, speaking in Spanish and calling out the familiar greeting, "*Wappin'?*" (It's short for "What's happening?") On the plane, I found myself seated next to a family friend from New York.

It's a narrow slither of a country. Panamanians like to say that is the only place in the world where you can swim in the Atlantic in the morning and backstroke across the Pacific in the afternoon. In Panama, the oceans are close—suburbs of each other. But for most of my life, the ocean has been a divide—separating me from my homeland. There were days, weeks, even years, when I could turn my back on the Atlantic, turn American and no one would know or care that there was another country that I called home. Other times, when I danced in dark Brooklyn basements to the rhythms of Celia Cruz and Tito Puente or sat at my aunt's kitchen table listening to the round rhythms of her Panamanian-accented English roll across the table like lucky dice, Panama seemed impossibly close.

When I was little and I told my friends that I was from Panama, they would invariably ask, "Were you born in the Canal?" And I would close my eyes for a second, and I would picture myself, a chocolate colored little girl, swaddled in pink, floating like the baby Moses down the Panama Canal. Then I would solemnly answer, "Yes, I was." I am not much of a swimmer. I am not even a water sign. But water is significant to me. There are days when I find myself longing to be near a river or a lake, to put my hand into water that stops with my touch then keeps on moving. Other days, in the midst of a crisis or a full-scale panic attack, I will sit in a bathtub full of warm water to clear my mind. As human beings, we are drawn to the water. But I think with me, there is another layer. If you could lift my soul, like a piece of parchment paper, and hold it to the light, you would see an *S*-like watermark in the shape of Panama. It is brown and green and blue along the edges. Even landlocked in New York City, there are days that my spirit awakens in the Atlantic and falls to sleep, dreaming in the Pacific. And on those days, I feel whole and secure. When the airplane touched down in Panama, bringing me home for the first time since I was two years old, I felt the same way.

My cousin Digna likes to say that women in Panama know how to be *mujeres de cache*. I grew up in a world of Panamanian women who used cocoa butter to make their skin smooth and coconut oil to keep their hair soft, women who never went out without nail polish and immaculately pressed clothes. Even poor Panamanian women wear gold with the lavish indulgence that some women wear perfume: dripping from their arms and their ears, fourteen-karat trinkets glistening between their breasts. The first thing my godmother Olga did was book appointments for me and my cousin to get our eyebrows plucked and our nails and feet done with Panamanian-style manicures and pedicures with names like *Medialuna* and *La Secretaria*. "It's carnival," she said. "And you girls have to look your best." We just laughed. It was already feeling like home.

I know that I belong to many tribes. Sometimes, I see a dreadlocked girl on the subway reading a book or carrying a canvas and a bag from Lee's Art Supplies and I identify her as part of my artsy boho black girl tribe. Or I'll be out with a multi-culti group of friends and we'll see another group as wildly diverse as our own and identify them as fellow members of the Rainbow Tribe. In Panama, I went from being a lone black girl with a curious Latin heritage to being part of the *Latinegro* tribe or the *Afro-Antillianos*, as we are officially called. On my first day in Panama, my godfather took me to a party for SAMAAP (Society of Afro-Antilliano People). I was thrilled to learn that there was actually a society for people like me; my only disappointment was that there was no secret handshake. Everyone was black, everyone spoke Spanish, and it could have been a fiesta on Flatbush Avenue because everyone danced the way they danced in Brooklyn, stopping only to chow down on the same smorgasbord of souse, rice with black-eyed peas, beef patties, empanadas and codfish fritters. I immediately started to call my cousin Digna, "Pipa" because the whole trip she kept guzzling *agua de pipa* which is coconut water drunk straight from a ripe coconut.

In the *Afro-Antilliano* museum, I took a quiet moment to explore my history. I was struck by the faces of the men who worked and died building the Panama canal. I thought of the feminist anthology that had changed my life in college, Editors Cherrie Moraga and Gloria Anzaldua's *This Bridge Called My Back* and the phrase took on new meaning. The famous Panama canal which so efficiently linked the East and the West was built on the backs of my ancestors. The locks of the Canal were made strong with the gristle from their bones. My ancestors' tears filled two oceans. I had been taught to be proud of my heritage, but there is a difference between head knowledge and heart knowledge. Standing in the Afro-Antilliano museum, I stood a little taller, knowing in my heart what my people had done. I looked at the pictures and I could feel the family connection in each of their eyes—they resembled my uncles, my grandfathers, the young men who were doing the *salsa con sabor* right outside the museum door. So many of the objects in the museum, like the beautiful *molas* (Matisse-like prints made by Panamanian Indians) reminded me of things that I had grown up with in my mother's home. It was remarkable how comfortable I felt in Panama. There was none of the culture shock that I'd expected. I had my mother and my aunts to thank for that. Although we came to the U.S. with so little material possessions, somehow my family had managed to carry whole bushels of Panamanian culture in their bones and in their hearts.

The actual carnival was the all-night bacchanal that you might expect: elaborate floats, brilliantly colored costumes, live musicians and dancing. The black Panamanian community had a formal dance which felt like a real debutante ball for a long-lost native daughter like myself. My godmother took my cousin and me to a photo studio where we had our pictures taken in the traditional costume of Panama, the *pollera*. Suffice it to say, it was a real trip. After an hour of makeup, hair, and a rented costume, I looked like a Latin version of Scarlett in *Gone With the Wind*. But when I gave the photo to my mother, she almost cried. She says she was so moved to see me in a *pollera* because it was "such a patriotic thing to do." I had become so Americanized over the years, but when I reached out to Panama, it reached right back to me. On the flight back home, I felt a quiet sense of completeness. To paraphrase the Jamaican tourist ads, I had come back to Panama, my old island home.

A friend left a voice mail message for me once, calling me a "secret Latina-at-large." The message made me ridiculously happy. I saved it and played it again and again. He had hit on a perfect description for me. Ever since I was a little girl, I have wanted to be like my mother—a Latina with a proud sense of self. In one of my most vivid memories, I am seven or eight and my parents are having a party. Salsa music is blaring and the refrain, "*Wappin'* Colon? *Hola*, Panama," is bouncing off the walls. My mother is dancing and laughing. She sees me standing off in a corner, so she pulls me into the circle of grown-ups and tries to teach me how to dance to the music. Her hips are electric. She puts her hands on my sides and she says, "Move these," and I start shaking my hip bones like my life depends on it. Now I'm a grown woman, and I have hips and booty to spare. I can salsa. My Spanglish is flawless, and my Spanish isn't shabby. You may not look at me and know that I am Panamanian, that I am an immigrant, that I am both black and Latin. But like my homeland, I am a narrow being flanked by two oceans of heritage. I'm a secret Latina-at-large and that is more than enough for me.

Rituals: A Prayer, a Candle, and a Notebook

JUDITH ORTIZ COFER

A Childhood Prayer

In the early days of my Spanish-language years
I was put under the care
of El Angel de la Guarda,
my Guardian Angel, the military sentinel
who required a nightly salute, a plea
on my knees for protection
against the dangers hidden in dreams,
and from night-prowling demons.

In the print framed over my bed,
he was portrayed as feathered and androgynous,
hovering above two barefoot children
whose features were set in pastel innocence—
crossing a dilapidated wood bridge
under which yawned a sulfurous abyss—
their only light being
the glow of the presence with wings
who was invisible to them.

I could take no comfort in this dark
nursery myth, as some nights
I lay awake listening to the murmur
of their voices sharing
their dreams of flight
in a well-lit kitchen, while I brooded
over the cruel indifference of adults
who abandoned children to the night,

and about that Comandante *in the sky*
who knew everything I did, or thought of doing,
whose minion could so calmly smile
while innocent children crossed over darkness,
alone, afraid, night after night.

TWICE A MONTH I TALK on the telephone with my mother in Puerto Rico. Today, after our usual exchange of news about people on the Island whom I barely remember and people in my life she has never met, I try to concentrate on writing in my notebook. But Spanish has entered my brain, unlocking memories, making me take one of my trips back to my childhood in New Jersey and our first years in this country. I get my notebook from my dresser and settle down on the couch next to my textbooks and papers which represent my real life now as an English professor in a southern university. At a safe distance from the chaotic world I grew up in—and if Tennessee Williams was right when he said that "time is the longest distance"—I now have enough space between my selves for my investigation to proceed. And that is why I write. I write to know myself, and it is a job that will occupy me for life.

Keeping track of my thoughts in a journal is a habit I acquired as a teenager experiencing the conflicts and loneliness of Puerto Rican immigrant life in the '60s. Now in my middle forties, writing my daily paragraph or two has become a routine, as indispensable as a daily prayer and weekly candles are for my mother. Most nights before bed, I take out my plain school notebook and write a few lines. Every morning at dawn, I write the poems or begin the stories that my recollections have filtered through my dreams. I do not, however, merely record the mundane activities of each day in my journal or in my writings, but rather I try to capture with clarity and succinctness what, if anything, the past twenty-four hours have taught me. Sometimes as I write, my fingers cease to be connected to my conscious mind and instead become instruments of revelations of my most painful memories and thoughts. On this night, perhaps because my mother's voice on the phone has caused a nostalgic wave to pass over me, leaving the treasures and debris of the past on my lap, I write about my father.

My father died with many things unspoken between us. Until his death in a car accident during my first year in graduate school, he directed my goals through his own unfulfilled dreams. He was an intellectual who did not go to college, a dreamer without hope, an artist without a medium. So I went to college. I became a teacher and later a writer. I had to finish what he had never even begun at the time of his death. My mother could not bear life in the States without him as her interpreter and companion, so she went home to her Island. She got what she always wanted, but not in the way she wanted. She wanted a return to *la Isla*; she got it, but without him. I stayed behind with my books, my memories.

To my father, knowledge was all the wealth and power he wanted. His only luxury was our education, my brother's and mine. He invested in us. He bought us books and paid our tuition at private Catholic schools when we could not afford to buy a house. Our times together were precious and rare since his job as a career Navy man kept him away from home during my waking hours and sometimes at sea for months. Our talks had to be carved out of the rare Sunday afternoon when he was home on leave—hours for which my mother competed also.

It was a solitary life we led, and I never quite understood why my parents chose to live in a social limbo. In piecing together from my notebooks what my mother talks about more freely now that she has returned to the Island, I began to understand that it was my father who chose to live in this country, and they had not really shared quite the same dream.

As a Puerto Rican family we were voluntary exiles, since we were free to go back to our homeland anytime. We could not even claim economic need because Father had a steady income through the Navy that kept us securely in our lower-middle-class status. The difficult part was that neither of my parents really assimilated into life in the U.S. The place my father chose to settle down was Paterson, New Jersey. Yet we did not stay for long in the rapidly growing Puerto Rican community; instead he rented us an apartment in a Jewish-owned building in a neighborhood of European immigrants where we were an oddity, once more strangers in a strange setting. Though I never experienced racism in its most brutal forms, our exclusion was as evident as a new silence as one enters a room.

I attended a school with the driven and overachieving offspring of Nazi camp survivors and Irish and Italian immigrants. It was among them that I learned how to concentrate on one thing at a time until I mastered it. The kids I knew centered their lives not around the normal flirting and cruising of mainstream teenage life, but on their complex family life and all the attending ceremonies. I felt my loneliness most keenly when a door opened and I heard the uproar of life shared with others under one roof, a family gathered around a television set, laughing at a joke they all understood, or arguing in one language. When we entered into our own quiet, orderly apartment we had to take off our English language and American ways at the door as well as our street shoes, for our mother would only speak Spanish and our father was determined that we would not provoke complaints from our neighbors.

My father was a good friend of the owner of our building, an immigrant Jew. The man was of Mediterranean heritage, and his dark features and curly black hair made him look more like a Puerto Rican than my father, who was a thin, fair-skinned man with an elegant bearing. I knew that my father stood out when he walked down our street, where the population was mainly composed of swarthy European men.

My mother hardly ever left our apartment, except twice a month when my father brought his black Oldsmobile out of the downtown garage where he kept it to the front of our building and we went shopping, first to the A & P and then to the Puerto Rican shops in the barrio where my mother bought the ingredients she needed for the dishes she liked to cook. The people in these bodegas shot Spanish at one another like machine-gun fire. So fast did they speak that I could barely understand what they were saying. And they stared at the three of us—overdressed by their standards, my mother in her brocaded black coat with the fur collar, my father in coat and tie or dress Navy blues, and me usually in the pleated skirts and plain white blouses my father liked to see me wear, with my neat cloth coat from Sears. My little brother's outfit was the masculine match for mine, dark trousers, button-up shirt. We were a family who dressed like the models in the store catalogues my father brought home to use as picture-dictionaries and my mother studied as manuals of American life. Yet we were suspect to the other customers. Little pockets of silence would form around us as my mother examined the yuccas, plantains, green bananas, and other *viandas* she would need for the week's meals.

I would watch the sharp bones of my father's cheeks and see his jaw clamp down hard. A look of haughty indifference would settle over his face as he "escorted" my mother up and down the aisles crammed with dusty bottles and cans bearing labels in Spanish. He kept his hands in his pockets and followed just behind her left elbow as if to protect her from dangers hidden in the stacks. She walked slowly, picking up cans and reading the labels, perhaps savoring the familiar smells of her culture, the sounds of sloppy Spanish as customers and clerks engaged in the verbal tag called *el gufeo* in barrio slang. It is a game of double entendre, of puns, semiserious insults, and responses that are *típicos*—the usual exchanges for Puerto Ricans in familiar settings. My father ignored the loud voices, the vulgar innuendos, and the uncontrolled laugher they incited. My mother obviously enjoyed it. Her offbeat humor and her need for laughter are to this day qualities I love about her. In the early days, she was timid in front of my father and the strangers in the barrio. Back on the Island, she is again quick with the word, the quirky metaphor—was she really the poet in the family? I tagged along in the bodega, as I did in the American stores, not really grasping until much later why we did not belong to either world: the quiet, clean world of my father, or the intense, confusing locales where my mother seemed most at ease.

In our apartment, especially during the hours that my father was not there, my mother followed certain rituals that got her through each day. At least twice a week, she walked the five blocks to the nearest Catholic church to attend mass. I accompanied her only on Sundays. We went to the Spanish-language mass celebrated by a priest from China who had been trained to serve as a missionary in Latin America and had somehow ended up in Paterson. He said mass in Latin and delivered passionate sermons in Chinese-accented Castilian Spanish that was just barely comprehensible to the Puerto Ricans whose dialect resembled his pure speech about as closely as American English does the dialect of the Scottish Highlands. It took faith and concentration to receive the word of God in Spanish from our determined pastor, but my mother relished each lisped word. Her Catholic training in Puerto Rico had been transferred intact to Paterson where her isolation made her develop the habits of the religious. She yearned for the others who believed what she believed coming together to celebrate custom. It was the comfort of the familiar that she sought in church ceremony and pious rituals. On the days when she did not attend mass, my mother lit candles in front of a popular depiction of the Virgin—the one where she is crushing the snake with a dainty bare foot.

My mother's religious practices included special prayers said on saints' days, candles every Saturday night, all night, left burning in the bathtub (a fire safety precaution), and rosaries in memory of dead relatives she kept track of through letters and dates marked on calendars; and of course, she supervised my religious education since the American nuns did not keep the busy liturgical calendar she followed. Every night while I was a small child my mother came into my room to say the prayer to my guardian angel with me. I still remember the words: *Angel de mi guarda/dulce compañia/no me desampares de noche ni de día.* Then she would kiss me, and I'd inhale the smell of Maja soap on the skin of her throat. It was a special soap that came in a box of three cakes, each wrapped in a fancy paper depicting a beautiful dark-haired woman in full Spanish costume of red and black satin and lace, an ornate comb and veil on her head, a black fan coyly held against her cheek. I saved the boxes and paper and kept them in my underclothes drawer to give my garments the sensuous aroma my mother imported for herself. Incense and Spanish castile soap, essence of my mother, scents of my childhood.

But though Catholic ritual filled the gaps in her life as an exile, they did not turn my mother into a dull, predictable person. She was rather an incurable romantic who was addicted to love stories. She read one Corín Tellado (the Spanish-language Danielle Steel of her time) romance novel a week. I was in charge of buying them, at a quarter each, from the only bookstore in Paterson that carried them, Schwartz's soda fountain and drugstore. As the trustee and executor of her literary needs, I had to learn early to memorize covers and titles so that I would not buy one she had already read. After she was through with a book she'd let me have it, and that is how I learned to read Spanish. The words that I still retain after all these years are mostly flowery adjectives and passionate verbs used to describe the appearance of the heroes (the girl always dark and lovely, the men always elegant and soft-spoken, unless they were the villains, then they were drawn more varied and interestingly). The actions of the protagonist were always performed within the same formula story, told in countless ways. My mother liked to discuss these *cuentos de amor* with me, and we sometimes dramatized the characters, reading aloud to each other as if we were acting in a soap opera. My father objected to my reading this *basura*, "trash." I once heard him threaten to forbid the books in the house.

"She is impressionable, *Querida*," he said in his perfectly enunciated Spanish. He avoided using slang in both languages and sounded like a foreigner when he spoke either. It was the peculiar slowness of his speech and his insistence on the clarity of each word that made him seem cautious in the way he spoke. "As it is, she is not spending enough time studying. Do not distract her with your silly *novelas*."

"My 'silly' *novelas* are the only reason I do not go crazy in this place, *Querido*. Shall I give them up, too? Should I read only the Bible and the prayer book until I become *loca*?" My mother's voice intensified like those of actresses in the Mexican movies she loved. Behind closed eyes, I visualized her rising from the table, standing before him, trembling in rage, in perfect contrast to his infuriatingly calm demeanor.

"*Controlate, por favor.*" Father usually warned softly. Our apartment was small. He knew that I could be listening, and only when they were arguing did I get a glimpse into the real conditions of our imposed solitude. When I asked directly why they had chosen to leave the Island, or why they had not returned, the answers were always predictable and vague. "We have a better life here." My father would state this with finality. "There is nothing there for us to go back for." I knew that his father was dead, and his mother was a perpetual wanderer with no permanent home, living with one of her sons or the other. But my mother received mail from her many relatives on the Island.

"No, *hombre*. You will not deprive me of my books. They are not harmful to our daughter, and they are my only company." Her words were meant to imply that she did not need to be so desperately lonely.

"You obviously do not remember your promise to me. Try to forget your idealized Island. It only exists in your dreams. I know that you feel lonely here, but there is no place for us back there. When I asked you to come to Paterson with me you said you would not look back. Do you remember?"

"I was eighteen years old. What did I know about *la maldita soledad* then? *Mi amor*, can it really be that bad for us in our own country?"

"Our life is here. Our family has a future here. There she would just be another girl waiting to get married. Our daughter would just end up a slave to some ignorant man. And our son would have to join the Army or Navy like I did to make a decent living. Then you would never see him either. Do you want that for them?"

"You are wrong to think that the future is hopeless in our own homeland. Just because your father was a tyrant and your mother a martyr . . ."

"Please be careful that you do not go so far that I cannot forgive your words. We had agreed not to mention my unfortunate family's past in this house."

"That is another promise you forced from me when I was too young to understand. Other people have tragedies and troubles in their families, and yet they lead normal lives."

"If you are referring to the population of the barrio—they do not lead 'normal' lives. So many of them are like cattle in a pen doing things in a group because they are afraid of venturing out. We are pioneers. We live our own lives and give our children the best opportunity for an education. So we do not socialize very much. I do not need it. You as my wife should not either."

And so it would go, around and around. Little hints for me to ponder: names of people I had never met and of places I had never visited would drop into their intense but subdued late-night arguments, which had become a passionate ritual summoning the painful past and casting a spell over our daily struggle, *la lucha*—and my dangerous, unfathomable future. I would gather their whispered words: discarded flowers to keep between the pages of my notebooks, clues to a mystery I hoped someday to solve. I write about tyrants and martyrs, and about lonely women who find solace in books. All the words I heard my parents trade like currency for each other's loyalties, like treaties to be negotiated so that their children might have choices, they are still with me. The memories emerge in my poems and stories like time-travelers popping up with a message for me. But I must first open the door with a ritual.

I finish grading my students' essays. What they don't know yet about life and literature can fill volumes. I can do something to remedy the gaps—if they are hungry at all for knowledge—I will add a drop to their half-empty or half-full buckets. But how can I fill mine? As I look deeper into myself, I discover that I left the place where my family's well is located. As a writer, I am always in the new territory of Myself

Alone. I am looking for new lands to discover every time I begin a sentence. I carry nothing but a dowser's wand and my need to make order, to find a few answers. So by recalling kitchen-table conversations in my notebook, re-inventing them as I go along, perhaps I am moving at a snail's pace toward understanding through my poems, stories, and essays.

Time to rest. I go to my bedroom and open the dresser drawer where I keep my notebook. I add several sentences. In the same drawer I also keep votive candles in different colors. I choose a green one. I can hear my mother saying, "*Verde-esperanza*," meaning that green meant hope; she always said it when she chose a green candle. My candle, bought at the drugstore, smells like a tropical rain forest, or so the label promises. I place it in front of the photograph I took of the statue of *La Virgen de Monserrate*, patroness of our pueblo. For a long while I watch the shadows dancing in solemn silence on the white wall. I am held by the complex flux of flame, shadow, reflection blending in a choreographed repetition of motion in precise intervals. I keep my eyes fixed on the flickering show until I fall into a deep sleep. I hope will be undisturbed by the dreams and nightmares that I keep locked away in my notebook for future reference. Sometimes, *most* times, I allow a prayer or a poem to drift like sweetly scented candle smoke into me.

AHA!

EDWIDGE DANTICAT

(Excerpted from a lecture presented at The Inter-American Development Bank's Cultural Center in Washington, D.C., on December 7, 1995.)

AHA!

I'D LIKE TO TELL YOU ABOUT AN ENCOUNTER I had a couple of months ago in a bookstore in Miami, Florida. I was doing a reading, and after the reading, a young man came up to me and asked me to sign a book for him. Before I could sign, he whispered, "Would you please write 'From one AHA to another'?" I stopped to ask him what he meant. What is AHA? "From one AHA to another" implied that I was one and he was one. What had I just become?

He said, "Well, AHA, spelled A-H-A, is an acronym for African-Haitian-American. That's what I am. That's what you are."

I had never heard that particular classification applied to either me or any of my friends before so of course I had tons of questions. He proceeded to tell me that this was a new way for young Haitians who had been in the United States for a while to define themselves, partly to combat all the negative labels they were bombarded with, among them "boat people" and "the AIDS people."

The term *AHA*, African-Haitian-American, had the following elements: African to acknowledge our ancestral roots deep in the African continent; Haitian, because of course most of us were either born in Haiti or were first generation born of Haitian parents; and American because we were from the Americas, living in the other "America," the United States of America.

1981

As I sat there in the bookstore, thinking about what this young man had said, I couldn't help but flash back to the time when I had just moved from Haiti to the United States in 1981. To catch you up with my life before that, I was born in Port-au-Prince, Haiti, in 1969. In a somewhat typical migration pattern, typical for many people I know, my father left Haiti when I was two years old. When I was four, he sent for my mother, and I was raised for the next eight years by an aunt and uncle.

I was twelve years old when I moved to the United States to be reunited with my parents. I came on a Friday night in the middle of March, not speaking a word of English. My father enrolled me in junior high school on Monday morning in a bilingual class. Now the spring of 1981, aside from being the time when Brooklyn, New York, and I discovered one another, was still a time of dictatorship in Haiti. Jean-Claude Duvalier (aka Baby Doc) was president. There was a swell of people coming by boat from Haiti to Florida to escape the dictatorship, the first large exodus of the 1980s. Every night on the six o'clock news, you could see dead, bloated bodies washing up on Miami beaches. This was often followed by some type of report on AIDS, still a fresh news topic then, too. Both items would keep all the members of my family anxious. The boat people, because coming from a poor Haitian family, any of those faces could have been one of our relatives. So we watched the television screen with great interest as the Coast Guard's white sheets were thrown over the dark, dead faces, already half buried in the Florida sand. And we watched with great interest those who had survived the boat journey to America and were able to walk away, only to be processed into detention centers in New York and Miami. We leaned in to observe their gait, their height, their body type, and we searched for traces of ourselves in them.

My parents belonged to a Pentecostal church in Brooklyn called Evangelical Crusade of Fishers of Men, which was very much involved in refugee work. So on Sunday afternoons after church, we would go and visit many of the refugees in confinement at the Brooklyn Navy Yard detention center. We would go to talk to them and pray with them, listen to their complaints, and, most important, get the names of relatives to contact on their behalf. After looking into their eyes and holding their hands, watching them cry and fully acknowledging once more how much they had sacrificed to come to the United States, I never understood why the children at school would shout their fate at us as a curse: "Get back on your banana boats, you dirty Haitians!"

As I said before, the spring of 1981 was also a time when AIDS hit the media in a major way. It was still a new disease, AIDS was, and there was a lot of speculation as to what the disease's origins were. All anyone seemed to know, all they seemed to be saying from the six o'clock news, was that there were only certain groups of people who got AIDS, among them homosexuals, hemophiliacs, heroin addicts, and Haitians. So the labels we were given in my Brooklyn neighborhood in the spring of 1981 were not very hip or self-assigned. They were like lashes from razored whips.

I am reminded of a particular day in the spring of 1981. After many taunts and fights with students who would continue to call us "boat people" and "AIDS people," a group of my fellow Haitian students decided to use a stereotype as our protection. We knew that among the many conceptions/misconceptions that the other students had about our culture was that we practiced a "dangerous" religion sensationalized in American films and denigrating political language as "voodoo." So the Haitian students all agreed to carry red handkerchiefs and spread rumors that the red handkerchiefs had spells and crippling powders in them. Soon whenever we were called names or taunted, up would go our handkerchiefs with a mumbling of some kind of abracadabra and our enemies would flee. Even those students who on other occasions had denied that they were Haitian participated in this wild scheme, reaffirming our solidarity.

Flash forward now some fourteen years, where my time spent in Haiti was at a deficit to the time spent in the United States. And in a bookstore unexpectedly someone is giving me this label that was part playful, part revolutionary in the way he presented it to me. And for some reason, it made me glad. I was glad about what this young man was calling me and was calling himself, because as he said, the moniker was "self-assigned" and self-assigned tags are always better than the ones other people holler as epithets against you.

Days after this encounter in the bookstore, I would think over and over about this meeting. Perhaps this AHA thing was a North Miami phenomenon. Maybe this was something this one particular person and his own group of friends called each other. I have never heard anyone use the term since. However this conversation left me with a sense of empowerment, given the many things that we have been called in the past.

DYASPORA

In Haiti, people like me are called dyaspora, meaning we are members of our country's Diaspora. We can also belong to something that is called the Tenth Department. Haiti has nine geographic departments, which are actual entities. The tenth department is not concrete land. It is not a specific place, but an idea to which Haitians can belong, no matter where we are in the world. We of the Haitian dyaspora maintain a very long umbilical cord with our homeland. People who live in the United States for twenty-five years still want to return to Haiti and run for government office.

I was once at the Haitian consulate in Manhattan with my mother when a man in his sixties walked in with his U.S. passport held high above his head. He marched up to the secretary at the front desk and denounced his United States citizenship so that he could run for parliament in Haiti. My mother, who has maintained her Haitian citizenship after more than twenty-five years of living in the United States, often says, "If I can't go to Haiti as often as I'd like, I might as well have my Haitian passport. At least I can look at it once in a while."

In spite of our own nostalgia, the term *dyaspora* can also be a painful epithet aimed at those of us who return to Haiti from abroad, acting as though we know all the answers to a country from which we had been absent during the most difficult times. Still, many of the well-intentioned dyaspora start businesses and build schools when they return to Haiti and, with their income capacity, are helping to bridge the huge gap between Haiti's majority poor and small elite.

MRS. CHÉ

In the building where I used to live in the spring of 1981, we all desperately tried to maintain the best of Haiti in our Brooklyn lives. The building had a very large population of Haitian families. On Sundays the families would exchange dinners and plates of sweets. Baby-sitting favors were taken for granted. If children were seen misbehaving on the street, any of the people in the building were allowed to scold them, and the minors would listen, knowing how much the adults trusted each other.

When I was teased at school, I would dream of that building and I would run home to it. It was a comforting leap into the most comforting elements of my life: social intimacy, community, kinship.

I remember there was an old woman who lived on the sixth floor of the building, Mrs. Chérubin; we called her Mrs. Ché. Mrs. Ché liked to say, "It is only my body that is here in America, but I am going to make the most of it." To Mrs. Ché, it was okay to look forward and back at the same time, to be melancholy about being away from home and joyful too, to have plantains with our Thanksgiving dinner, the proverbs of our language peek through the veil of our English sentences, to see the world with two eyes that do not always look in the same direction.

With Mrs. Ché, if something special was happening in the building, some party or special event that I couldn't attend, she would always say, "Edwidge, *map wè lonbraj ou la*," meaning "Even if you can't be with us, I will see your shadow there."

The other night, I spoke to an uncle in Haiti whose seventieth birthday was coming up. I told him I was sorry I couldn't come for the small celebration he was planning, he told me he would look for my shadow there.

These days my shadow is more often in Haiti and my body in the United States. (There are times too when I am in Haiti for a long time that people tell me they see my shadow or feel my spirit at events in Brooklyn.) These days, I feel less like an immigrant and more like a nomad. I try to see as many different places and experience as many cultures as I can. The more cultures I experience, the more Haitian I feel, because it is my birthright as well as my chosen foundation, what I compare and contrast everything to, my floating banana boat, for which there is perhaps no longer a singular harbor.

A friend once told me, by way of a cautionary tale, the story of a woman who ran away from Haiti in her late teens to go live in Puerto Rico. In Puerto Rico, she picked up enough Spanish to get by but never really mastered the language. While in Puerto Rico, she never had a chance to use either one of our two official languages, *Kreyòl* or French, so she forgot both of them. After a while, she didn't speak either Kreyòl, French, or Spanish well. She moved to the United States later on in life, where she never learned English very well either. So when she had daughters in America, she and her daughters developed a potpourri language and a series of gestures in order to communicate.

After hearing that story, rather than feel pity for that woman, I envied her.

"Wow!" I remember thinking. Imagine, she gets to invent a language of her own out of her fragments of memory.

I have always had what Baudelaire called the grand malaise, secretly relishing the role of permanent outsider, never expecting to belong. That's why I don't agonize over being told to get back on my banana boat only to be called a dyaspora when my boat sets anchor. I don't want to be a culture-clash victim. Nor do I need to be. We live in a more and more migratory world. I don't know that many people these days whose bodies and shadows are exclusively anchored in the same harbor. However, these days I, too, call myself an AHA now and then. Peer-assigned and equally a-geographical as poly-geographical, it seems as good a harbor as any for both me and my shadow to temporarily reside.

Coming Home

GABRIELLE DONNELLY

I CAME TO LOS ANGELES FOR A SIX-MONTH WORKING VACATION, a break from my real life as a London magazine journalist, and ended up staying for two years. After that, it was obviously time to go back to England. I was having immense fun racketing around in the sun, making new friends, and cycling by the ocean; still, I was thirty years old, not a kid any longer, and London, as I had always known, was where the sensible, grown-up world was. My family and my past were there; it certainly made professional sense for me to live there. More to the point, my elder brother had taken a job in Brussels and was offering to rent me his flat in West Hampstead. London has a crushing accommodation problem; it was an opportunity I would have been silly to refuse.

Very soon, I was back in the swing of London life. I rekindled old friendships and started some new ones; I interviewed interesting people for glossy magazines with whose editors I would have long, gossipy lunches in fashionable restaurants; I joined a community newspaper, went to play readings and gallery openings; I both gave and attended rambunctious dinner parties where people with strong opinions would shout and laugh and drink wine. I had become the complete young Londoner, the woman my teenaged self would scarcely have dared to dream of being.

Then, my brother decided to return from Brussels. Obviously, he needed his flat back, but, since he had decided anyway to move to a larger one, he very kindly offered me the first refusal of buying. Again, it was an offer that was both generous and timely. Most Londoners do own their property, and here was a golden opportunity for me to enter the market. The only problem was finding the mortgage. While other, more sensible, folk had been saving their money instead of floating off to California, my own bank account was slender at best. I was, besides, a woman, single, and self-employed. As bank after bank considered my case and, regretfully, declined, I started to panic. There were no other rentals to be had in any part of London I was prepared to live in, and I began to form the idea that, if I could not buy my brother's flat, I would simply return to Los Angeles, where a rented apartment was at least a possibility. It was not, after all, as if Los Angeles had been such a bad place; it was just that my life was in London. Always had been. Was always going to be. If only I could find a roof for my head there.

A friend telephoned in high excitement; she had heard of a bank in Hampstead, very close by, walking distance in fact, which specialized in cases precisely such as mine. Weary and discouraged by now, I nevertheless bundled up my paperwork one more time and trudged up the hill to the address she had given. This was the last time I would put myself through this, I promised myself, bending into the brisk spring breeze that ruffled the daffodils in the gardens and sent cotton-wool clouds scudding across the pale blue sky; if this bank refused me, then I really would go back to L.A. It was pay or play, I decided, London's last chance. A mortgage—or emigration.

I reached the bank, explained my situation, and produced the paperwork. The bank manager read it, frowned, and read it again.

"I think," he said, "that we can help you."

To my astonishment, I felt my heart hit the floor. And—to my everlasting relief, pride, and joy—I listened to my heart instead of my common sense.

"Thank you very much," I said. "I'll think about it. Good-bye."

I walked back down the hill and promptly began writing letters to alert Los Angeles friends of my impending arrival. In the many years that have followed, I have never, no, not even for a micro-mini-fraction of a second, regarded that decision as any but one of the best I have ever made.

I had to tell my mother on three separate occasions that I was leaving. The first time, she said, "Oh, don't go." The second time, she said, "*I'm* not going to beg you to stay." The third time, she said, "Going away? It's the first I've heard of it—where are you going?" When I actually left, she was heartbroken. My mother loved me a lot, and I certainly thought at the time that I loved her; but she was an impossibly difficult woman, angry and overindulged. In the important things that have happened to me since her death—loves and losses, my marriage, my two miscarriages, my failure to achieve motherhood—I have, sadly, been able to summon no emotion but relief that she was not there to make anything worse. Mine was not a happy family, and I have found it necessary over the years, for sanity's sake, to sever all ties with my father and three of my four brothers—harsh and painful decisions with whose ramifications I am still coming to terms. Presumably, if I had had a more loving background, then I would not have emigrated. But then again, maybe that was not such a disservice that was done to me.

Although I did well professionally in England, made friends, and led what an observer would consider a perfectly nice life, I never felt at home there. I did not realize this until I had had the experience of living somewhere else; I had assumed that my vague malaise, my frequent, uncomfortable sense of being different from other people, was simply part of the human condition, like paying taxes or having to go to the bathroom. But the fact was, that I was *not* at home. My family had come from Ireland, although it was long enough ago that we were not in touch with any relations over there. Even we didn't know quite which nationality we were, and were split among ourselves, between those who regarded us still as Irish, the race of our forebears, and those who insisted as firmly that a century of English living had rendered us Brits. Each side found the other faintly pretentious.

I was firmly in the Irish camp myself, although I knew from painful experience that when I presented myself as such to a real Irish person (one, to be just, whose ancestors, unlike mine, had not left that fair country when the potato crops failed), I was simply laughed at. Which left the English.

I didn't meet any English people until I went to university. Until then, my life had been my brothers, my cousins, my friends from the convent, and my parents' friends from the church—Catholics all, mostly of Irish origin, with a few Italians and French and the occasional Pole, although the Polish crowd was known to be clannish. Since I did not actually live in a cave—I did, after all, watch television, read the newspapers, and go shopping along the local High Street—I suppose I must have been aware on some level that the entire population of England was not composed of Catholic immigrants. Yes, of course I was aware of it, if only because, as children, we were continually urged to behave ourselves in public "to set a good example to the non-Catholics." Nevertheless, when I went to London University—and was for the first time thrust among real English people—I encountered the worst culture shock of my life.

While some of my dearest friends are English, I have to say that I do not, on the whole, get along well with English people. I find too many of them to be repressed emotionally, rigid socially, and actively—and often most offensively—hostile toward both my race and my religion. I find the famous English love of irony too frequently to be no more than a veneer for downright rudeness—and a coward's one at that, because it gives them the out, should anyone be so crass as to call them on it, of raising a disappointed eyebrow and murmuring, "What's the matter, old thing? Lost your sense of humor?" . . . A touch of bitterness here? Very possibly. I am a willing expatriate, remember, and that is not so very different from being an ex-wife. Happily, my new marriage—to continue the metaphor—could scarcely be more joyous or congenial.

I can breathe in Los Angeles. The sky is high, and the streets are wide, lined with tall palm trees, leading to the lofty mountains or the expanse of the ocean. Americans, by definition, are survivors, descendants separated by one generation or by ten of those who had imagined a better life, had the courage to pursue the vision, and the strength to realize it. They are large people, with grandiose plans and, just like the song says, high apple pie in the sky hopes; they believe in treating themselves well, spending more money on themselves, ordering more food in their restaurants, and taking more luggage on their vacations than any European would dream of. They expect good service in their shops and efficient plumbing and labor-saving devices in their homes. Americans believe in celebrating their ancestors, wherever they came from, romanticizing them with a gleeful abandon that simply would not be countenanced in understated England. Americans—unlike the English—both admire and respect strong women.

I am a strong woman myself. I am opinionated, I am unconventional, I am (and I am too old and too battle-scarred to be coy about this) more intelligent than most. I make jokes that people laugh at, and when someone else makes one, I am usually able to come back with a retort that is at least as clever. In England, I found that these were qualities that made most of the men around me—and many of the women, too—distinctly nervous. I was labeled as "eccentric," a terrible and pa-tronizing word that suggests that there is somehow a "center," a one right and correct way of being, and that I, poor dear, am simply not part of it. In America—land of the tough pioneers, of Fannie Brice, of Jo from *Little Women,* of the feisty, gun-totin' granny from television westerns—there is a place for me. I am sure that not everyone likes me: I am a good and honorable person, but I am undeniably a strong taste, and, even in America, there are those with whom I have dealings who look at me with open fear. Still, there are enough who get the point of me. Most gratifyingly, my husband thinks I am perfectly marvelous.

My husband, Owen Gerald Bjornstad, could only be American—six feet tall and three hundred pounds (he's trying to diet down to two-fifty) of mostly muscle, with hands like hams and forearms like thighs, a ruddy beard, a rafter-ringing laugh, and a personality to match his size. When we travel through villages in Europe, children quite literally stop to stare at him. "He's *very* American, isn't he?" was the comment of more than one London friend on first meeting him. To which I would respond, "Well, what did you expect?" which was dishonest of me, because I knew exactly what they had expected. They had expected someone more recognizable to them, more similar or at least more familiar, a tweedy New Englander, perhaps, or another European immigrant—maybe even an Irishman. Owen, with whom I am happier and more comfortable than I have ever been with another human being, is an in-your-face reminder of how far I have left both England and Ireland behind. As I have embraced America, so I married an American.

He is not only American, but Californian, Angeleno born and bred, and fiercely proud of it, which, loving Los Angeles as I do, is one of the qualities I love in him. Many people, when they think of our city, picture impossibly shaped starlets, semi-cooked philosophies, and a morality as shaky as the terrain. That's not Los Angeles; that's Hollywood, and, yes, in the show business circles of this town, that stereotype does hold chillingly true. However, there are whole sections of people also living in Los Angeles who have nothing to do with the entertainment industry, whose lives are as solid, as straightforwardly decent, as those of any Midwesterner, with the only difference being that they happen to be part of one of the world's most sophisticated cities. Owen's family are farm folk from North Dakota, upright Scandinavian Lutherans, who came to the West to find work. He has always lived within a few miles of the house where he was raised and where his mother still lives; many of his best friends are men and women he has known since they were all in Mrs. Morgenthaler's class in elementary school. The way we met was almost comically small-townish: through my neighbor, Kym, who happens to be the oldest friend of the wife of Owen's oldest friend, and who had moved into the top half of my rented house in Venice because the landlady is the mother of the best friend of her eldest brother. Kym and I—and now, of course, Owen—live there still.

I envy the solidity in Owen's life, and when I hear him laughing with his friends or family and exchanging reminiscences of this or that schoolmate, or movie theater, or pizza parlor long gone, I feel a pang of yearning that is almost painful—not for London, nor for any particular person there, but for the comfort of shared memories, the sweet familiarity of it all. Sometimes, they all seem to me to be very young, they who have not packed up and moved across the world. At other times, they seem more mature than me. Unlike myself, they are able to live the life they were born to. And them—how do they see me? Not, I think, particularly as a foreigner. I am quite sure that when Owen first announced that he had fallen in love, he received his share of teasing for its being with a British novelist (as he rather grandly describes me) rather than a Culver City girl; but Americans are well accustomed to the idea of immigrants, and these days, I am neither British nor novelist to them, simply Gabrielle, a good cook and a poor timekeeper, someone who is hot-tempered, kindhearted, absentminded, hospitable, and, most important of all, reliably in love with Owen. They openly like me, which, after my sad history, gives me great joy. In a speech at our wedding, Owen's brother BJ remarked that I was "real people." A very American compliment, and one of the most welcome I have ever received.

I am perhaps unusual for an emigrant in that I bring so little of my old country to my new. I certainly do not run with the Brit-pack, and if occasionally I cook a British meal or rent a British video, it is to show curious friends how things are done in another country—my contribution, if you will, to the cultural melting pot—rather than to indulge any nostalgia or nationalism of my own. I cannot even fully remember by now how it felt to regard England as home. To me it is simply a place, far away and increasingly foreign, where I happened to live for the first decade of my adult life. What a contrast to my own ancestors who brought such love of their native land all those years ago across the Irish Sea. But then, my ancestors were driven to emigration for survival's sake; I had the privilege of leaving through choice.

I don't think—and neither, he says, does Owen—that my nationality is particularly a factor in our marriage. Any man who marries a woman marries an alien creature; and while in our particular case there is still the odd hurdle of idiom to be crossed (I now know, for instance, not to be offended that, when offered a cup of coffee he will say, "Yeah, sure, I'll take it," instead of "Yes, please, I'd love it"), it is nothing to the morass of miscommunications that must be negotiated daily between any card-carrying male and his mate. For us, a bigger gap than the national is that between Owen's practical Lutheranism and my own complicated, emotional, often morbid ("Oh, God," he has been heard to groan. "Are we talking about death *again*?") Irish faith. A bigger difference still is that his family life was happy, while mine was not. That is the dangerous ground between us, the place where preconceptions are challenged and hurts can be inflicted. It is a cultural fissure that is far deeper, and far more perilous to cross, than that of who says tom-ay-to and who says tom-ah-to.

I myself say tom-ay-to these days, as I say pross-cess instead of proe-cess and skedule instead of shedule. Otherwise, for some reason, my accent remains unchanged, which is surely one of God's little jokes, considering the number of British people in Los Angeles who, for reasons of snobbery or nationalism, strive to keep their accent but lose it. Sometimes, I hear myself talking and think, with a mental start, "My God, I'm foreign!" Because it is the American cadences that are natural to me these days. It is how my husband speaks, and my in-laws, and the vast majority of my daily contacts. It is the cadence that I hear inside my most rudimentary thoughts, while the noises that actually issue from my mouth are strange even to myself. Oddly enough, though, the longer I am in America, the less often my accent is commented on. I look—as indeed I am—so thoroughly at home here, my bearing, my clothes, my frame of reference, even the expressions on my face having become so completely assimilated into my new culture, that my unusual vowel sounds are often overlooked. More and more in late years, people who do notice the difference in my speech are taking me for an Irish-woman, which pleases me greatly. So much for the "English" Donnelly family.

Which is not to suggest that I have completely lost touch with Britain. I still write for British magazines and talk by telephone to one or another editor in London most weekday mornings. I have many, and dear, friendships still alive there, with cousins, with fellow journalists, with former flatmates, and increasingly, with their now teenaged off-spring, and it is a rare few months that go by here which do not involve a British visitor, for a night, or a week, or, occasionally, a year or more. Los Angeles is an attractive city on many levels; and my circle tends to the peripatetic.

I visit London every couple of years, for a book publication, a wedding, or a birthday party, and when I do, I base myself with my friends the Barbers, who—English to the core—are these days the closest things this London Mick has to an immediate family. Richard is an old journalist buddy who for a couple of decades has been the merry, kindly teasing big brother I failed to find among my own kin. His wife, Patti, is a lecturer at London University; they live with their three children, a couple of cats, and the English family's obligatory dog, in a rambling, high-ceilinged house in Islington, overflowing with books, theater programs, tennis racquets, pottery jugs, framed prints from London art galleries, fixture listings for Arsenal Football Club. Owen both loves them personally and is fascinated by their life. He can spend hours sitting contentedly in the corner of their long kitchen, watching the comings and goings, although when I ask him precisely what it is about them that sets them apart from an American family, he is hard put to identify it. The pots of tea, maybe, or the school uniforms, or the milkman who delivers in the mornings; the gray light, the variety of newspapers, the talk of the Labour Party versus the Conservative, Arsenal versus Manchester United, of train rides to Nottingham, or tube journeys to Turnpike Lane.

I used to find these visits to London painful and distressing. I was a stranger and yet not a stranger; I missed California, and, walking the gray streets that had been familiar from my earliest years, I would find myself almost wondering if Los Angeles were all a fantasy, a childish made-up Utopia, romanticizing an innate inability of my own to get along with anyone, anywhere, ever. It is far easier now that I go there with Owen. I have an American with me, a comrade with whom I can laugh, and point things out, and say, "Yes, that's strange, isn't it? It might be better, it might be worse; but it's not how we do things at home." He is a reminder that England is not my only option, that there is, indeed, for me a place on this planet which I can comfortably call home.

On a visit some years ago, before I met Owen, I was dropped off by friends on a Sunday morning at a small train station in Kent. I was to spend the day and night with my one remaining brother and his family, and according to the railway timetable I had consulted, I could travel directly to the center of London, change trains once, and arrive at my brother's house in the suburbs within two hours. What the timetable had not thought to mention was that Sunday is the day when the railway tracks are worked on and the trains rerouted, and that, far from being direct or swift, my trip would involve numerous changes of trains, much waiting time, and several extra hours of duration. I am not often able to spend time with my brother; I had luggage and little in the way of reading material; it was cold. I went out of the station and into the taxi company next door to ask how much the journey would cost by cab.

"You want to go *where?*" said the sales clerk. He whistled a bit, consulted his book, and at last looked up, shaking his head with sorrowful finality. "That'd cost you fifty quid," he said.

When an Englishman says quid instead of pounds, it means a serious sum of money is involved. Fifty quid is about eighty dollars. An English person, and particularly an Englishwoman, and most particularly, for some arcane English reason, an Englishwoman of the educated professional classes, would think it a shame to spend such money on a few hours of her own comfort when people were starving. She would have taken the train, or rather, the series of trains, and have done so, moreover, with admirable good humor. She would have dragged her luggage expertly across bridges and through tunnels, and sat patiently in windswept stations, lunching cheerfully on an overpriced dry sandwich and weak tea. If the delays had built up, she might have exchanged with a fellow traveler an occasional eye-roll of half-humorous frustration, but she would not have dreamed of voicing any irritation to any British Rail employees she had encountered. She would have known that none of the delays were their fault, that the railway tracks must be worked on sometime, and besides, these poor people were already having to work on a Sunday. She would have arrived at her brother's house late and cold, but philosophical, and would have immediately set about enjoying to their very fullest the few hours that remained to them.

Me, I took the cab. The driver was shaking his head throughout the journey.

Very soon after that, I took a plane home.

Embracing the Alien

BY LYNN FREED

I FELT ABOUT BECOMING AN AMERICAN as I would have felt about becoming a Hindu—very silly. For five years I had been answering Americans' questions: apartheid, the revolution, my family and how they got there in the first place, sharks, shark nets, blacks, whites, Jews, apartheid, the blood bath, the Blue Train, surfing, winter in July, the revolution, Christian Barnard, did I go back to visit?, anti-Semitism, Cry, the Beloved Country, *Gary Player, and wasn't I glad I'd got out?*

And now this . . .

You must demonstrate, said the immigration official, that you can write an English sentence.

I laughed lightly at this, as if it were a joke we shared. But he stared soberly at me through small pale yellow eyes, the same colour as his hair. He pointed to a blank on the form and then sneezed. Write, The Constitution can be amended, he ordered, reaching into a pocket for a handkerchief.

I wrote, wondering whether I'd catch this man's cold.

Who's the first Chief Justice of the United States? he asked.

I shook my head. Sorry, I said. I haven't a clue.

It's in the booklet. What is the First Amendment?

This much I remembered. I recited it word for word, noticing the frightening shape of his head revealed by his crewcut. I wondered whether he would rather be in Vietnam, and if one could fail at becoming an American.

55

Please stand, he said, and raise your right hand. Swear after me—

The heater hissed and spat. Outside, the sun shone brightly although the temperature had dropped below zero. In England the sun had seemed to be a shadow, a ghost. But in America I'd learned not to trust it at all. There it was, blazing down directly on people muffled up in furs and boots.

Answer yes or no to the following questions. Are you now or have you ever been a member of the Communist Party?

No.

Are you now or have you ever been—

Clive was at home. The blizzard and then the drop in temperature had brought the city to a standstill. He couldn't dig the car out, nor were the trains running. I had thought, perhaps, they'd cancel my citizenship test, but Clive had insisted I take a cab down to find out. Who cared about the cost? He loved the whole idea of my becoming an American. He himself had taken pains to change his accent, flattening out his a*'s and putting in the* r*'s. He'd adjusted his voice, too, using the sort of monotonic cadence of television newscasters.*

Do you abjure homosexuality? Do you swear not to overthrow the state? Will you bear arms for your country?

Yes, yes, yes, I said, watching a small drop of snivel swell at the rim of his nostril.

Do you abjure polygamy?

I smiled, determined now, for some reason, to win him over. With regret, I said.

His pupils shrank to pinpoints. He pulled out the handkerchief again and wiped furiously at the nose. This is not a joke, he said. I remind you that you are under oath. Measures can be taken. Your application can be closed now if you wish.

I flushed. I'm sorry, I said.

Then, I will ask you again: Do you abjure polygamy?

I do, I said.[1]

⚜

---

[1] *The Bungalow*: A Novel, by Lynn Freed. Poseidon Press, 1993; Story Line Press, Fall 1999.

The closest I have ever come to understanding my life in America has been in writing about it. The same thing is true of South Africa, where I grew up. It took me fifteen years in America to be able to write about South Africa with anything more than nostalgia. Until then, I had been too homesick to make much sense of the place on the page—the characters were prototypes, the situations predictable, the fiction flat.

But then I began my third novel, *Home Ground*, the story of a girl who, like me, had grown up there. Whose family, like mine, were Jewish. Whose parents were actors, as mine were. And who spent much of her childhood, as I had, dreaming of escape into the "real world."

Such dreams were common among South African children, then as now. Apart from the remoteness of the country itself, its colonial history had always pointed north, usually to England. As a new university graduate with a scholarship to study overseas, I, too, would probably have gone to England (and probably been just as homesick there). But I did not; I was off to America to consider marrying a South African who was living there. It seemed like a delightfully mad thing to do—so far, so foreign, and to marry a man I hardly knew.

To the quasi-colonial in the '60s, America was never a serious choice as a place to live. With British hauteur toward all things American, South Africans considered America too young, too unbaked, a country that did not take itself seriously. America was a cartoon life, a comic life—people hitting each other over the head with frying pans and roaring with laughter. As for a serious education there, well, for this there was no historical validity. Oxford and Cambridge were the goal of the serious student. Attending graduate school in New York, as I was, seemed frivolous, illegitimate. English Literature in America? Ridiculous!

Still, there I was. And there we were on the corner of 112th and Broadway, living in Columbia graduate student housing. The building itself was quite standard, the apartments well-furnished, and air-conditioned. At twenty-one, I was delighted with the idea of what I had done. And with the pots and pans and sheets and towels of this strange new life. It felt like playing at real life—making meals, making beds, making love.

And yet, within weeks of moving in, I slipped into what I now recognise as a form of shock. I dressed, I attended classes, I made new friends. But nothing I did seemed connected to anything that had gone before, or to what might follow. In the urban cacophany in which I lived, my spirit seemed sunk in silence—deep and wide and terrifying.

New York alone had not done this. Nor had the homesickness from which I was suffering so acutely. The problem was of more existential proportions. It went something like this: If nobody knows me, who am I? If nothing is familiar, where am I? And, if I don't want to be here, why am I?

Twenty years later, long out of the crisis and living in California, I wrote in my journal: "I do not belong here, and I have had to turn not belonging into triumph." The triumph, such as it was, was modest. I had a Ph.D. I was teaching. I had written three novels and published two. And I was working on a fourth, a sequel to *Home Ground* called *The Bungalow*.

It was only in the writing of this new novel that I began at last to understand those first years in America. The novel takes place in 1975. Ruth Frank, my protagonist, now an adult and living in America, returns to South Africa to visit her aging parents. Wound into the novel, in flashback, are scenes from Ruth's life in America, starting at the beginning, in the late '60s in New York.

That first summer in New York City, I found that my clothes were all wrong. The flimsy shorts and strappy sundresses that had served quite well at home couldn't be worn there without subjecting me to the wild antics and suggestions of men. Or to the ravings of some mad person at large on the streets. But when I tried on a wraparound skirt and a blouse that covered my arms to the elbows, I seemed to vanish in the department-store mirror. On the way home, searching for my reflection in plate-glass windows, I decided I'd be better off indoors.

Anyway, there was little to go out for. The sun was of no use in such a place. Worse than useless, it was a torment. Without a breeze, without a beach, and hot at the wrong time of the year, there was no festival in the season. Every patch and stretch of grass was circumscribed. Each tree placed and fenced. And everywhere there was the stench of traffic and rubbish and dogs.

Sometimes, Clive brought home mangoes, and, once, a bag of lichees from the Chinese store. These gifts I accepted gratefully. But the mangoes had been picked too soon. They were sour and green. The lichees were old and watery. I threw them down the chute. And broke down completely when my sheets were missing one night from the dryer. It wasn't as if I didn't understand theft. I had grown up with it. But when I thought of my mother choosing them for colour and thread count, with wool blankets to match, the crime took on a significance beyond what I could explain to Clive.

Time, that first summer, was different too. There were no ceremonies to mark things off. I had lunch standing in front of the refrigerator, tea in a mug at any time of the day. In our two rooms, with the traffic roaring fourteen stories down, and the air conditioner buzzing, I found myself warping hour into day, day into week, waiting for Clive to come home.

George Bernard Shaw once referred to England and America as two countries separated by the same language. As I wrote on in *The Bungalow*, I remembered how much more severe the paradox of that barrier had seemed during those first years in America, dividing my life here from there, present from past. Language itself is only one aspect of the extended vernacular of a culture. There is also the timing, the rhythm, the sights and smells and sounds of daily life. Putting on a winter coat, facing into the icy wind off the Hudson, crossing the road to avoid the madwoman screaming obscenities at the corner of 113th, stopping at Chock Full o'Nuts for some coffee and a doughnut and then standing at a high table to eat and drink because no seats were provided by the place—well, I felt every bit as foreign as the Cambodian graduate students who lived in the apartment next door.

In South Africa, I had grown up in the middle of a sizable city, in a large Anglo-Jewish, quasi-Bohemian, quasi-Victorian household of family and servants. There was also an enormous extended family, including grandparents, aunts, uncles, and twenty-seven first cousins. My sisters and I were sent to an Anglican girls' school, where there were very few Jewish girls. And then, in the afternoons, we went to Hebrew school with other Jewish children. At night, when most parents were home from work, ours went off to rehearsal or to a performance. Every Friday night, we gathered for dinner at one or the other side of the family— twenty, thirty, forty of us sometimes. Our lives were noisy with family, with theatre parties, with performances, and with our own private dramas.

In America, by contrast, there was only my husband and I—no standards but what we might set ourselves, no familiar rituals, no duties, no audience for our lives. Although we had come from quite different sorts of families, with different educations, different social sets, different manners, different everything, we were more alike here than we would have been at home.

Feeling alien among American Jews had made Clive and me less alien to each other. "High Holy Day" was a term we both found hilarious. We also laughed at the price of the tickets, at temples that looked like churches, at organs, and choirs, and responsive reading in English. And, even though I myself had never read Hebrew well enough to follow the services intelligently at home, I liked to think—as I stood silently among American Jews, missing home on purpose—that what mattered to me was to have things properly done.

In his brilliant story "One Out of Many," V.S. Naipaul tells the story of a servant in Bombay who comes to Washington with his master. In Washington, he discovers the immigrant's truth: Stay away long enough and you belong nowhere anymore. In the profoundly sad finale, he says, "I was once part of the flow, never thinking of myself as a presence. Then I looked in the mirror and decided to be free."

This, in a sense, is what had happened to me. I had looked into the mirror and taken myself out of the flow. I had decided to be free, and now there was no going back—not in the same way, not ever. Nor did I really want to go back, although I continued to long for what I had once been part of.

I should say here that, at the age of eighteen, three years before I came to New York as a graduate student, I spent a year in America as an American Field Service exchange student. AFS placed me with a

Jewish family in Far Rockaway, New York, where I was completely miserable for six weeks. (I was then moved to a family in Greenwich, Connecticut, where I stayed out the year.)

It was this first experience of America in Far Rockaway, however, that, years later, gave me my voice as a writer. Once I had returned, married, settled in, I began to tell my American friends about Far Rockaway, about me in Far Rockaway, and about the family I had been placed with there, their trips to the bowling alley, and to Grossinger's, and to the wholesale houses. Over time, the stories became polished and refined to a gloss. The whole experience became a mine of entertainment among my friends.

People who tell stories are always being enjoined to write them. "You should write that!" someone will say, not understanding how different the written story is from a story told to a live audience. For years, I had been told that I should write the story of Far Rockaway. But, when I considered doing so, it seemed to fall flat on the page. I had told the story too often. It already had a shape, which seemed to rely on a live audience.

At that point, I had written two novels—the first published, the second never published. The voice I had used for these first two novels, and for the shorter fiction I had written, was the rather earnest feminist voice of a '70s woman flirting with defiance. I had written about American women in an American cast of characters, and had gone about as far as I could go with the subject and the voice.

But then, one day, considering the fact that I, a Jew, had been placed by Gentiles in a family of American Jews on the assumption that we would all get along like cousins, I wrote the opening paragraph of "Foreign Student," a short story:

I was once told by a displaced Rumanian, fellow Jew, in a variation on the old adage, that each country gets the Jews that it deserves. What was I to make, in the light of this, of my first day in Far Rockaway, New York, with the family Grossman? I knew already that all Jews were not the same. But what, I wondered, did America do to deserve this?

This sort of bad behaviour has always appealed to me. It loosens my tongue, sharpens my teeth. Gleefully, I moved through the story. It took on quite a different shape from the one that I had told to others, and from the one that I had lived through myself. I bit into the subject as a dog takes hold of a doll, shook it and shook it until I had shaken the life out of it. (Some years later, the story was included in an anthology of Jewish women writers, published by the venerable Jewish Publication Society. No one else would touch it.)

Irony requires perspective—distance not only in space but also in time. Living in America now had given me this distance. It also gave me the benefit of the doubt as a professional expatriate. America is kind to expatriates, particularly to those who have what passes for a British accent. Confronting daily the anomaly of my presence in a country that was both my home and could never be home to me, I found it easy to contemplate the conundrum of alientation and belonging.

What was salutary for me in writing "Foreign Student" was discovering the joy of that particular brand of irony. And also of daring myself down into the truth. In a sense, the whole experience set me free to write *Home Ground.*

After *Home Ground* was published and reviewed, I took on the life of a writer. I wrote articles on South Africa, always from the perspective of someone who had left. I wrote about revisiting the house in which I had grown up, about revisiting the country both before and after Mandela was set free. I wrote a short story about a young Zulu woman leaving home to go and seek work in the city. The subject of leaving home seemed to have no bottom to it. I wrote a story about a young English woman who leaves home to go out to South Africa to make her way there.

Why then did I not simply return to South Africa, one may reasonably ask? Why leave the place and the people that I loved only in order to be able to return for a few weeks a year? Even though I pretended to ask myself this question, it did not really interest me. Or, rather, the answer seemed to lie in an impulse that was as familiar to me as the rhythms of my breathing. It involved not only the foolishness of reclaiming a future in a country mired in political mayhem, but, even more than this, of giving up on the chances of a future in the real world. Of giving up choice.

I was not alone in this. Among my expatriate South African friends, the phenomenon of longing for home while staying steadfastly away from it was old hat. Bring expatriate South Africans together, serve them a strong curry, *biltong, boerewors, melktert,* and *koeksusters,* and, sooner or later, you will have a maudlin crowd, a crowd mourning lost paradise. Or a crowd laughing at the funniness of life in America.

In America, I discovered a new kind of privacy.

Coming back to the apartment after my first day out, I stopped dead in the living room. The place was in chaos. Clothes lay strewn across the floor, just where I had dropped them. Drawers that I'd left open hadn't been closed. The bed was unmade.

I stood still for some moments, waiting for the fright to subside. Then I began to pick up the clothes and put them away. I pulled the bedclothes off and made the bed completely, put on the bedspread. I went through to the kitchen. There were dishes in the sink, food out on the counters. I cleaned it up and went back to the living room with a mug of tea to consider the possibilities of my new life.

If I opened the drawer to Clive's desk, looked through his letters, and then put them back again, who would see? No one. I could also climb onto a chair and bring down his box of memorabilia from the shelf in the closet, spread them out on the bed, and examine them closely. What's more, if I talked on the phone, no one could overhear. I could fall asleep without warning anyone not to wake me up. I could take off my clothes. I could walk around naked if I wanted to, day and night. I was free.

. . . I liked the ads on television. Every night, between bouts of news, smiling white women vacuumed their houses, washed their clothes, their cars, their faces; they polished their furniture and their floors, fed their dogs and their children. At home, it had been different. The ads had come over the radio; there was no face to the voice. At home, there was no joy to cleaning. Every morning, the servants dusted the house, they Hoovered, they cleaned the bathrooms, made the beds from scratch. Monday was wash day. Friday, the silver was polished. Once a month, the books were painted for

bookworm, the hairbrushes soaked in ammonia and then laid out in the sun. Every now and then, my mother had run her finger along a windowsill or over a lampshade. Then she'd ring the bell for the servant so that she could tell him to do it again, and properly this time.

I consulted the Hoover manual and found out that there was more than just the floor to consider. There were places underneath the furniture, and underneath the cushions on the furniture, picture mouldings, invisible flakes of skin that filtered down into the mattress. Nothing, however, was said about windowsills as such, where the dust was not dusty, but stuck to the paint like glue. Nor could I find a solution for the pots and pans that gathered oily grime. Nor for the seam of thick, black slime that kept returning, week after week, between the toilet and the floor.

When I mentioned this to my new friend, Anna, she just laughed. Why bother, she asked? The sky won't fall in if you don't vacuum, or clean the toilet. Who cares? Who's going to see?

Apart from the odd South African expat, my main connection between the two worlds in which I now lived were the letters my mother wrote me every day, the letters I wrote back to my parents. I told them what they wanted to hear—real-world things—the opera, the plays, the star performers I had seen, the essays I was writing, exams I had taken, honors, degrees, publications. Performing for the audience of my parents was an old routine. And it made sense of my life in America through all those early years of longing to go back.

There is an odd phenomenon in place among certain South Africans. It is the discouragement, loud and clear, that comes in the face of any suggestion of return. The reasoning behind this is fairly simple: If one person can leave and thrive, then the chances of others being able to do so are higher. By the same token, if an expatriate returns, immense failure is implied, not only for oneself, but for all those looking to ensure their futures in the real world.

What is being played out here involves a colonial brand of ambition that speaks to the phrase so often twinned with "real world"—"making it." Making it in the real world is not something to be given up lightly, certainly not to return to a country as politically fraught as the South Africa of the '70s and '80s.

And so, what I could not tell my parents in the letters I wrote—what I hardly understood myself yet—was the scope and range of the loneliness in my new life. The cost of the bargain in which we had all tacitly taken part.

Everyone . . . had accepted without question that I was going to America to get some more degrees, a clever girl like me. I had almost come to believe it myself. The fact that my parents couldn't afford an overseas education for me, that I would have to use up my scholarship money for the plane ticket alone, was still an unspoken secret among us. The whole plan seemed to fit well with Clive's green card, with the way he kept apart from other Jewish men ready to take a wife. Just as I stood apart from the sort of Jewish women who majored in psych and socio at the local university and announced their engagements just before graduation. . . .

[Nothing] could upset my mother's delight in being lifted so miraculously into the real world. In having a daughter married and living overseas. Letters to read out to the family on a Friday night. Parcels to send. Biltong to smuggle. Anchovette. Golden syrup. Mrs. Ball's chutney. All the paraphernalia of separation and nostalgia. . . .

There is an odd lag between playing the life and writing about it. By the time I was writing *The Bungalow*, the longing to return had died down. I was reconciled. More than reconciled, I had begun to understand that it was no accident that I had chosen to stay on in America. In America, I could play myself, free of the sort of colonial categorising that I would have had to overcome in England (a South African, a Jewish South African). In addition, I now had an American child, American friends. I was an expatriate, living in America. And that is where I would remain.

For eleven years I had been coming and going like so many others who had left to live overseas. Peered out of the plane window at the sun roaring

up over the African plains, and felt my heart heave with joy. Filled my
weeks at home with dinners and lunches and teas and shopping. And then
wept when it was time to leave again.

Sitting around the swimming pools of women who had stayed behind,
observing their nannies and drivers and hairdos and varnished nails, I had
liked to think myself above hairdressers and manicures. With a husband
who washed the dishes, with foreign degrees and foreign stories to tell—I
had felt, among these women, delightfully unconventional. They, too, had
seemed to think so. They had told me how much younger I seemed than
they. How thrilling my life was in comparison to theirs. And even if they'd
believed this only for the assurance that they too could seem younger and be
thrilled by living in the real world—so what? If I gave them hope, they, in
turn, made me feel very fortunate to have left.

So too did my parents. I loved my parents the way some mothers love
their children—without ambition, and full of lies. With other people I was
different. Fretful, critical, proud. If there were a meaning to these differences, I hadn't yet tried to find it. All I knew was that only by leaving had
I been able to give them the happiness of my coming back. Seeing them
behind the airport barrier, their arms around each other for once, I felt, as
I had felt since first I left, that I was the only person who could make sense
for them of their old age.

When I took my daughter back to South Africa for visits, she amused
everyone with her accent, with her American ways. She could not, for
instance, understand the phenomenon of servants. Nor had she ever had
much to do with old people. In America, there was her father and I, our
friends, their children. In South Africa, there were cousins and second
cousins, and second cousins once removed. There were aunts and uncles
and great uncles and grandparents, all to be visited. It was a whole society that knew where she fitted in, from whom she had come.

As it turns out, she has come to feel half South African herself. She
loves the place. After she finished college, she lived there for a few years,
and then she came back to San Francisco, only to go off again and live
in London. I see her coming and going, I receive her e-mails and her

phone calls, and I smile. One can pass this on, this ambivalence of place. One can play the audience oneself.

I have never understood the concept of assimilation, not for myself anyway. How would I disappear into America? And why would I want to? As a writer, I need the specifics, I need the differences. I also need the distance at which I keep myself from my subject, from my life, past and present. I have always needed this. If I have learned the language of life in America, if I have made friends here and found in them a generous audience for the performance of my life, then this is what I have become, what I have always been, in fact: a performer of myself.

Just after finishing *The Bungalow*, I went back to South Africa, accompanied by two American friends. In my twenty-five years in America, this was the first time I had taken anyone other than my daughter home with me. When we reached Durban, I took my friends to see the house in which I had grown up, where my father had grown up before me—a colonial, pillared splendour, commanding a ridge high above the city. As we stood on the upstairs verandah, looking out over the city and the bay, the Indian Ocean beyond, one friend turned to me and said, "How could you bear to leave this place?"

I stared at her. No one had ever asked me this before. And yet, of course, it was a question I had been asking myself all my life. Being asked it now, though, and by a dear and intimate friend, brought the whole issue back *de novo*, all the deep and suspect sadness of my self-imposed exile.

And then suddenly, standing there on the old verandah, I saw my bifurcated life for what it was: as a failure of daring. I had not dared to remain. More than this, I had been a show-off in my leaving. And I was still showing off—leaving there, leaving here—keeping the truth for the writing itself, hiding it away like a criminal. For what is writing, after all, but a bid for the truth? And what is truth if not the life at the very heart of failure?

The Remembering

AKUYOE GRAHAM

This essay is dedicated to Dr. Rev. Michael Beckwith.

I REMEMBER WANTING TO BE MY MOTHER'S DAUGHTER because she knew how to dress, had a face as bright as the sun and a soul wrapped in skin so pretty it made me want to cry. I remember thinking that the man who was going to be my father was a sad, solemn creature. And that maybe, just maybe, if I was lucky, I'd remember that I'd wanted him to be my father to teach him how to smile. I remember riding half asleep on my grandmother Afio's back, tucked snugly in the folds of her rose-scented cloth only to later eject myself up and out like a rocket into my mother's waiting embrace. I remember knowing at age three that something was about to go down, something that I wasn't going to like. Even then I think I realized that this something was going to change the entire course of my life. And so it came to pass. My mother left Ghana—to do what it would take other women twenty years or so to even think about doing—to find herself. I remember how, in giddy anticipation of my mother's flight of fancy, I stopped smiling the entire year before. And I remember how regardless of my various protestations, she left Ghana anyway.

What I didn't remember was that I'd forget. I'd forget that I would have to remember.

Stripped of all memory I came to America in the early '70s at the age of eleven. After a tumultuous seven years in England I was happy to flee what had been, for me, years of swallowing my breath and biting my tongue. I had been warned about America by my British friends. They told me not to drink or eat anything given to me at an American party because it would be laced with some evil drug that would kill me. But their advice came too late. I'd already been seduced by the big cars and luxurious homes I'd seen in American movies and could see no wrong in anything coming from that country. "America. Oh sweet America." I practiced saying the name over and over again. "I'm going to America. One day I'll be an American. Wow! America, oh sweet America." I was a willing conquest lusting after their affections and loot. Besides, I was on a personal mission to find the Jackson Five and make a home for all those lonely brothers whom I was convinced needed nobody else but me.

Always the visionary, my naive young mother had been to the States on holiday the previous summer and now she too was in love with brassy, bold America. Or perhaps it was the childhood sweetheart with whom she had reunited. Either way, we got into what looked like a do-it-yourself chartered plane and by the grace of Almighty God landed safely at John F. Kennedy Airport in New York. That was the most frightening night I have ever experienced. Two young women on their way to the good life. . . .

We came to New York and stayed with friends in Spanish Harlem. Loud, sexy, and hot. This was not the America I'd been dreaming about. Where was all the whiteness? Except for the Jackson Five, I hadn't expected any "coloured" people in this land of milk and money. My British friends needn't have worried that I'd be duped at an American party. I'd already been taken on a huge ride. You see, I grew up on Hollywood. I grew up watching television shows like *Bewitched* and *Primrose Lane*, and was sure that everyone in America lived like the people on those programs. The fact that I didn't see any black people on the shows didn't mean a thing to me; in my eleven-year-old mind, all the coloured people lived on the next block which was never shown. Spanish Harlem was that block. And it was unacceptable to my white-bread sensibilities. Where on earth was I? I repeat: This was not the America that I'd been dreaming about. Where was Bud and Hank and Bobby? Why were these streets so dirty? There weren't supposed to be any dirty streets in America.

Well, after many attempts, I finally met the Buds, Hanks, and Bobbys of my television fantasies and they didn't look as pleased to see me as I was to see them. In fact they were downright hostile. They greeted me with the word "nigger" and taunted me with the rhyme "If you're white you're all right, if you're brown stick around, if you're black stay back." I'd never been called a "nigger" before. Unsurprisingly, it didn't feel good. The Brits, regardless of how they really felt about you, would never do that to your face. In America, especially in Spanish Harlem, it was up close and personal: overflowing trash cans and creaky tenements filled with the nauseating stench of hatred and human prejudice. Where were the lavender hills with spruce tops, the manicured lawns and smiling faces? Where was the freedom I'd been waiting for? My first few months were hell, but I didn't like where I'd just come from either, so there was no turning back.

In my attempt to become as colourless as possible in England, I had taken a hot comb and singed the life out of my beautiful curly hair. I had renamed myself Katherine, after Queen Katherine of Aragon. Since Londoners couldn't see the blue blood coursing through my African veins, I became a Spanish royal, my native tongue banished forever from my lips. And like my hero Eliza Doolittle, I learned the queen's English proper. On the phone I could pass for a member of Parliament. In America this make-over was hideous. My days of sipping "high" tea and eating crumpets were definitely over. Who would I have to become now?

It seemed as if I was an embarrassment for black Americans and a painful reminder of the ancestors who had sold them away into slavery. I became an easy target for their pent-up rage and anger. "Yo, yo, boo-wana, where's yo' spear? Do y'all live in trees?" White Americans found me a "curiosity." Intellectually too proficient to be a "savage," and yet, because of my dark skin, I had to be "inferior." And so to them, I became an "exotic." Like a rare animal. Something to be looked at, petted, fawned over, and even lusted after, but never to be loved. Because the television shows I had been weaned on never dealt realistically with race, I didn't know the level at which I would have to deal with it too.

At eleven, I had no words for what I'd had to become in order to survive England. "Uncle Tom," "assimilationist," "oreo," "square," "golliwog,"—but I was smart enough to know that something was, if not wrong, then, not quite right. Once I was in New York and face-to-face with all the beautiful shades of ebony and caramel, I couldn't help but notice my own discomfort. I felt shame. I felt fear and disgust. The other black and brown children around me felt my secret disapproval of them and they hated me for it. After all those years of watching Tarzan, did I really believe that we were savages? Did I really believe that it would take a white man, one not even educated but raised by monkeys and chimps, to elevate our minds and teach us right from wrong? Did I really buy into that tired old story? Apparently I did.

No wonder the dark brown "sistahs" tormented me with their verbal assaults. If I could have, I would've turned my nose right up at them. Fortunately for me—and, perhaps, them—my sculpted nose sits ever so proudly in the middle of my face. Classically African, broad in the middle, tapering down to a saucy soft-tipped curve. This nose could never snub anyone. Even so, they heard my voice with its perfect enunciation of every letter in every word and they went for the verbal kill. They never laid a hand on me but delighted in waiting for me after school with their prolific ammunition. "Yo, yo, boowana, where's yo' spear?" "Do y' all live in trees?" "What kind of African is you?" Eventually when they realized that in spite of being from "The Motherland," I was truly lost—wandering in the geography of a new world which did not seem to have a safe place for me and my heritage—they left me alone. Consequently the "sistahs" did me a great service. Their constant badgering began to dislodge the years of shame I'd secretly harbored. Slowly, I began to take baby steps back to the little African girl that I had long since discarded. Now my journey toward remembering could really begin.

❦

America has been like a big mirror held up to my face. High definition, a magnification of every thought and sigh. Somewhere in between my extremes I've had to find a sense of myself and the place where I can connect, where I can bridge my diverse realities. My mother often reminds me that America was my destiny. She said she had to bring me here. I thank God that she did. I shudder to think who I might now be had I remained in England. Charlotte Katherine Graham. Fashioned after Queen Katherine of Aragon. Luckily, I had to put all affectations aside once we hit the rebellious shores of these United States. Tough, no-nonsense New York was the perfect environment for the African "white" child that I used to be. New York slapped me in the face and demanded that I learn to respect myself. No one cared how high my little pinky was raised when I was drinking my tea. New York kept repeating the question, "What kind of African is you?" until I could finally answer, "I am the African who knows the strength of each tight curl upon her head."

One year after my arrival in NYC, I was welcomed into the High School of Performing Arts and began training to become an actor. I practiced the roles of Curley's wife from John Steinbeck's *Of Mice and Men*, Blanche Dubois from Tennessee Williams' *A Streetcar Named Desire*, and Laura from *The Glass Menagerie*, also by Tennessee Williams. I identified heavily with these female characters. I knew, for instance, that underneath her grit and grime, Curley's wife felt like a heap of no-good trash. Invisible, tormented. These were feelings I knew well. Beneath my tall spine, beyond the walls of my womb, lay buried the fragile voice of a young woman waiting to take center stage. And that young woman, in her adulthood, eventually gathered up enough courage to leave New York and travel to Hollywood.

My original motive for wanting to be an actor was "to move people, to touch their hearts and stir their imaginations, perhaps to inspire." I remember saying those words when I first auditioned for the High School of Performing Arts, and again when I went to study with the internationally renowned Uta Hagen and Herbert Berghof, and still again I uttered those words while training with the legendary Sanford Meisner. Throughout all those years, I had never been afraid to say those words, to know them and mean them. Now, the thought of saying those words in Hollywood and trying to live up to them frightened me. I knew well the images and portrayals of Africans through Hollywood eyes. Images carved out of ignorance, created to ridicule and wound. What marvelous words could I speak "trippingly on the tongue?" And on whose soundstage? Who in America would hear me and allow me close enough to touch their heart? Whose imagination could this kalua princess stir? Would I be able to "play" in Peoria?

In taking an overview of the situation in Los Angeles, I realized that here, too, just as in England, I would have to remake myself in the image of my detractors if I wanted to be accepted into the mainstream. It seemed that the price of admission would once again have to be the betrayal of myself. But this time something inside of me roared "NO." I just could not take one more step in that direction. I just could not do it. The Frankensteinian changes begin first with the hair, and then the nose or perhaps the breasts, with a chemical skin peel thrown in for good measure. I'd become too accustomed to change and disguises. A master dialectician with a bag full of different behavior and speech patterns. Acting was nothing new for me. The only character I'd never explored was me. "NO," the voice roared. Then it whispered firmly, "I am an ancient warrior come at last." I could see, without any question or doubt, that this was the appointed hour. This spirit, my spirit, was going to awaken.

I come from a long line of storytellers, from my great-grandmother, Adorkor, to her daughter, Afio, down to my mother, Lamiokor. I remember sitting in the family house courtyard and listening to great tales of fishermen and farmers, tales which espoused the virtues of honesty and humility. One of my favorite tales, told to me often by my mother, was about a lowly stonecutter who toiled day and night in the fire-hot light of the sun and the eagerly awaited cool of the moon. One day, while at work, this stonecutter accidently dropped his ax into the river and it immediately sank. The poor man could not swim and so he sat desolate by the riverbank, his entire livelihood completely submerged. With no other means to take care of his family, he cried shamelessly, his tears dropping steadily and rhythmically into the water like rain pellets. Shortly, a beautiful mermaid appeared from the water to console him. She told him that one of his teardrops had worried its reach all the way down to the bottom, where she and her sisters were sunning themselves, and had stung her straight in the heart. The mermaid asked the stonecutter why he was disturbing the balance of heaven and earth with his sorrow and grief and the stonecutter shared his tale of woe. The mermaid then delved into the water and brought out a strong, sturdy ax made of silver and malachite and asked the stonecutter if it was his. The stonecutter answered that he wished it were, but unfortunately, his was not such a fine instrument. Then the mermaid brought out a golden ax decorated with rubies and diamonds and the stonecutter again said no, that his was a simple ax made only of wood. The mermaid then brought out his ax and gave it to him, which pleased the man to no end. Moved by the stonecutter's honesty, the mermaid gave him the other two axes with all of her blessings. The stonecutter was overjoyed, and from then on, his fortune and good works increased a thousandfold.

Countless other villagers and stonecutter wanna-bes rushed to the river, throwing their simple wooden axes into the water, hoping to imitate the first man's mistake and, in so doing, duplicate his miraculous good fortune. What they couldn't imitate was his integrity and sense of truth. The mermaids were not fooled by any of the rogues. Annoyed, they disappeared them from the river's edge.

I so loved this simple tale that I had my mother recount it to me many, many times. For me, the stonecutter's purity of heart and loyalty to himself was exemplary. I took him in as a member of my own family, a link in the chain of my own personal history. Bit by bit, with the fabric of one story and the soul of another, I began to weave a history of myself and my heritage which I could own and be proud of. I began to remember. I began to create my own stories and I quickly discovered in me a spiritual odyssey which goes far deeper than even my ancestry. I began to understand that to reconstruct myself into an alien form solely for the search and acquisition of temporary treasures would be a gross denial of my own unique, unreplicable story.

So Los Angeles has become my spiritual mecca. In the land of pink tofu and jasmine rice, I found an intimate relationship with God. I am able to define my own tastes back, and up, to the people and places that I find beautiful. I now walk miles on the beach in the noonday sun unafraid of my very own blackness. I live here on my own terms, not waiting or hoping for anyone to give or/allow me anything except what already rightfully belongs to me. I have created jobs and opportunities for myself. I am an original storyteller, traveling to near and distant places, sharing my stories with diverse audiences. Hollywood doesn't scare me anymore.

As I open myself to the vastness within me, the world too opens up to me. I find myself welcomed into those places, those circles that once seemed to spin so far away and be so impenetrable. In America, I have found my voice. Ghana would have made me only African, and I am that and so much more. Now, I remember who and what I have been, who and what I can be. Now, I can move beyond that to become whatever it is I choose to be. In America. I can become. I have. I remember now. I am.

The Country of Childhood

LUCY GREALY

I WAS FORCED INTO BECOMING AN AMERICAN CITIZEN in my early thirties. My publisher wanted to submit work of mine for a prize, but only afterward did anyone read the fine print; only U.S. citizens were eligible. I called the prize committee to confirm; my thirty-year-old green card status meant nothing. I had to be a bona fide citizen. I'd lived in this country for all but four years of my life, but I did *not* want to become a citizen. Why? The best answer might be to say that though technically I am an immigrant from another country, a truer thing to say might be that I immigrated from a myth. Let me try to explain.

My family left Ireland for America when my twin sister and I were only four, after my father, a journalist, was offered a job in New York. Though I have lucid and muscular memories of Ireland, they are still a child's memories: pictures of un-narrated events punctuated with stark details and odd choices of focus—the penguin's beak poking through the bars in the Dublin Zoo, the moss on the stone wall outside our house, the soft triangular ears of the spotted dog which belonged to some blurry neighbor.

Ireland, however, was the locus of my family's first migration; some seven years before arriving in Dublin, they'd lived in England, my mother's homeland. Though my father was Irish, and my sister, Sarah, and I were Irish, everyone else in the family was actually English. Such gradations of geography did not matter to the Americans, however, once we arrived there in 1969, after our second migration. The Americans interchanged the two countries out of ignorance; Sarah and I did so out of instinct; both places were important parts of the family map, and we were just as likely to respond with either when asked where we were from.

Sarah and I occupied last place in the family lineage. Sean was so much older, thirteen years, that he was both technically and metaphorically a stranger by the time I could string my days together eloquently enough to live them in linear time, when I was perhaps around seven. This is precisely when he left home for good, to go live in California, three thousand miles away. I only saw him once more, when I was eleven or so, before he died in a road accident.

Nicholas was only three years younger than Sean, but more inclined to stay at home, and he took over the role of older brother after Sean left. Suellen was comparatively young, only three years younger than Nick, but six years older than Sarah and I. It was quite obvious to all concerned that Sarah and I were mere infants without rights, while Susie and Nick were adults. They perpetuated this idea, claiming adult privileges of bedtimes and food choices and tempers and any-show-they-wanted on the television. Sarah and I perpetuated this hierarchy also, because anything they said we automatically assumed to be more important than anything we said, or could even possibly imagine saying.

And they had a lot to say. My older siblings did not like America, and they particularly hated Americans; part of their arguments were viable, but a large part of their contentions, I recognized only later, were tempered by the anger endemic to all teenagers and, in particular, teenagers who have been forcibly relocated. "America is an *awful* place," they told us repeatedly, in a wide variety of contexts. They said bad things about the States with an inventive zeal that bordered on fondness. After all, their distaste was tempered by a poorly disguised nostalgia. As they spewed on and on in scandalized tones about how *bourgeois*, how *tacky* and *vulgar* Americans were (despite the fact these last two terms were invented by the bourgeoisie), my older siblings had a clear picture of what they were comparing the States with.

Sarah and I, however, were on the other side of this European door, and the only thing we could see through this door was the hated thing itself. We had no solid memory of the country that came before, only images which belonged as much to the country of childhood as to any literal map.

"American television is so *vapid*," Nicholas announced after walking by and seeing me sitting on the floor in front of the television. There was a reasonably good chance I was enjoying whatever it was I was watching—television enthralled me as a child—and all I could do was wonder what personal defect made me enjoy it so. How profound, how intricate, how enlightening Irish and English television must be. The fact that I couldn't understand at all the appeal of *Upstairs, Downstairs* on public television was only one more mark against me, I reasoned.

My Irish accent was ironed out of me by the time I was nine or so, though it occasionally makes sporadic appearances depending on whom I'm speaking to. But growing up I toed the family line and believed fully that I was not an American. Every year on St. Patrick's Day I scoffed at all those silly Americans wearing green and claiming to be Irish. "Real Irish people don't give a damn about St. Patrick's Day." And I was right; to focus on it so is an American trend. Years later, I met a woman who said, "I'm Italian," and I was shocked. "But you speak English so well," I said, and was laughed at. Of course she did; she was born in New York, as were her parents. National identity, to many Americans, includes the claiming of another country as one's own.

It was summer the day I had to make the choice to become a legal American. Only my father had ever actually become a citizen (Susie and Nick returned, as adults, to live in London) and only my sister Sarah understood my reluctance. My publisher, however, did not. Finally, partly because a Republican was in office and changing immigration laws (it was not inconceivable I would lose certain rights; terrible stories were circulating) and partly because I wanted the option to return to live in Europe and then return to live in America if I wished (something you can't do legally on a green card), I called the Immigration and Naturalization Service's 800 number. I was at a writers' colony at the time and had to cramp into a sweltering phone booth. The automated service listed dozens upon dozens of options (I hung up after the voice told me "press 29") including the option ("press 14," I think it was) to report an illegal alien. It dawned on me that this might be quite a process.

While growing up, foreign goods sometimes appeared in the kitchen; Irish sausages and Cadbury chocolate, Weetabix for breakfast or bright cardboard tubes of Smarties after dinner if we were good. It's not that I didn't love these foods (even I could recognize the superiority of Cadbury over Hershey). But they were talismans from mythic "olden days" when the general state of family affairs had been better than it was here in America. Things were not going well on this side of the big pond; garrulous money problems, a generally bruised outlook tendered by illness and unemployment, a deepening sadness that became the background rhythm of daily life. I felt I'd missed out on the earlier, better times of the family (I accepted a priori that they had been better) simply by being born too late. America was the land of our discontent, I was told repeatedly, and the luminous appeal of nostalgia, a nostalgia for something I knew only in the abstract, began to haunt me.

Nostalgia. Who has not fallen for its wiles? Advertising companies use it blatantly: sepia pictures of old men on bicycles, delivering bread; whiskey distillers inviting us to "share the tradition"; catalogue companies perfectly mimicking the styles and slang of a long-dead generation. Politicians coax it out of us too: "old fashioned values" and "a return to strength" as acceptable campaign promises. But note that the modus operandi of these examples is a nostalgia for an unclear, or even nonexistent, past. To long for the past is a very human thing, but what does it say about us when we long for a past we never actually participated in? And when we do long for the specific, it seems that any event is up for grabs; it's not uncommon for people to become nostalgic for what were objectively difficult, even miserable, times of their lives.

In Gabriel García Márquez's *One Hundred Years of Solitude*, there is a learned bookstore owner known simply as "the wise Catalonian." He's an important figure toward the end of the book because he becomes the sole protector of real-world wisdom in a town that is falling inexorably into a world of loss and forgetfulness. The wise Catalonian is the last holder of insight and erudition, despite the fact he spends most of his time in the doomed town of Macondo wistfully wishing he were back in his hometown on the Mediterranean. And yet, when he finally does return to his original home, he finds himself missing Macondo.

> *One winter night while the soup was boiling in the fireplace, he missed the heat of the trees, the whistle of the train during the lethargy of siesta time, just as in Macondo he had missed the winter soup in the fireplace, the cries of the coffee vendor, and the fleeting larks of spring-time. Upset by the two nostalgias facing each other like two mirrors, he lost his marvelous sense of unreality and he ended up recommending to all of them that they leave Macondo, that they forget everything he had taught them about the world and the human heart, that they shit on Horace, and that wherever they might be they always remember that the past was a lie, that memory has no return, that every spring gone by could never be recovered, and that the wildest and most tenacious love was an ephemeral truth in the end.*

One of the many things I watched on television as a child in the bright, endless, almost viscous space of the weekends were old movies made in England, mostly black-and-white mysteries and romances. Meanwhile, in color, I could watch documentaries on public television, *Monty Python's Flying Circus*, any other number of "grown-up" shows I didn't always get. But what I was watching for was not the content of the shows and movies themselves, but the details, the background: the always wet streets, the phone boxes, the door handles, the teapots, the road signs, the stone walls and hedges; the million details of daily life that are the true separators between cultures. All these details accumulated and came to represent a parallel world which very quickly became abstract. It's not exactly that I doubted such a landscape existed; it's that I automatically confused what was on television with what couldn't possibly be real, simply because it *was* on television.

I left America for several years in my twenties; I lived in Berlin, London, and Scotland, while visiting other countries as well. (How I was able to return to this country in my early thirties after three years abroad is a story I can't confess to in print.) One Sunday in Paris, before my return to the States, I read an astute observation by an ex-pat in *The International Herald Tribune*: America is like death: everything we ever learn about life is discovered in the process of trying to escape it. It was true; I only really learned to *see* America once I left it. And the fact that I even call it *America* was, I learned, itself a symptom. There is no such country as America, my European friends corrected me; America is a continent, not a country, and only Americans themselves and people in third-world countries call it America, instead of its real name: the United States.

What did I learn about America while living away from it? First, that no matter how much I wished to see myself as a non-American while growing up, I was acutely American. I possessed the very sense of entitlement I'd accused others of, an entitlement that came across subtly in the fact that I spoke only English, and embarrassingly in that when I first arrived in Europe I genuinely believed others would be interested in me simply and only because I was from America.

On a smaller level, the level of details, I found myself missing American things. I became fanatical about finding Reese's peanut butter cups, and I avidly watched American programs like *Roseanne* and *ER* on TV. Once faced with the small details of European life that I'd held suspended in the halcyon amber of nostalgia my whole childhood, my two nostalgias, as they did for the wise Catalonian, mirrored each other. And it's not that I came to see that what I had pined for all my childhood (that life was better in Europe, that people were smarter, kinder) was untrue (because I do believe Europeans are better educated than Americans, and that education does create an arguably "better" society on a number of levels), but that I recognized something much more personal in the endless repetition of images: There is always something to want, a place we would all rather be than where we are. Though I may have a very complex relationship to America, I can no longer dislike it simply because it is the place that I am.

The most inevitable and frustrating part of becoming a citizen of the United States of America is waiting in lines. Simply to enter into the

INS building in downtown New York takes several hours, and all that happens once you get in is that you get to wait on more lines. But, I was acutely aware, I was white (blond haired and blue eyed to boot) and I spoke fluent English. It was immediately understood that I would have no trouble getting my papers, and that it was only the tediousness of the process that was any obstacle. That this should be so angered me, and made the self-motivated skepticism behind my decision to become a citizen (which I freely admitted) that much stronger.

Before taking your "test" as part of the naturalization process (which includes knowing what Congress does and being able to write in legible English "I promise to be a good citizen") prospective citizens have to wait in an obscenely boring and decrepit waiting room. The only decoration in this windowless room is a group of drawings made by a second-grade class that had obviously visited the INS on some field trip: wobbly Statue of Libertys and out-of-proportion American flags, plus several drawings that were outlines of hands, with each finger named Liberty, Justice, Freedom, Equality (the thumb, oddly, had no name), and then the hand as a whole identified as the United States, then the whole thing colored in red, white, and blue crayon. How fitting, I thought with my inherited cynical air, that here in this room it is the childish, simplistic view of America which prevails.

When the papers finally came through informing me of when and where to show up for the final ceremony, I treated it as a joke. What a lark, I thought, all for a silly prize I didn't even get. Almost a whole year had passed since that first phone call to the INS, and the prize had been awarded, meanwhile, to someone else. Also meanwhile, my brother, who'd been living abroad a few years, tried to return to America and was turned away; he'd simply been gone for too long. It would behoove me, I saw, to stick with it and have dual citizenship (though the U.S. does not recognize dual citizenship, Ireland does, and I travel with both passports).

My letter informed me I had to wear formal attire, which was odd, seeing as the ceremony was at nine o'clock in the morning. I put on a black cocktail dress (it was too hot to wear anything long), invited my boyfriend (himself a Canadian), rode the subway with all the commuters in my odd garb, and showed up exactly on time.

The building had a huge lobby, and they were not quite ready for us in the auditorium, so my fellow soon-to-be citizens and I waited en masse. There were about two hundred of us altogether, plus at least two hundred family members there to cheer us on. The costumes and the colors were resplendently intricate and liquid; the flow of fabrics and details from all over the globe were not just dazzling but moving. Along with the many "American-clad" people such as myself, national costumes from Africa, Asia, and eastern Europe made not just their wearers but all of us that much more gorgeous.

When we were shepherded into the auditorium and sat down in rows, I began to hear the sound of weeping around me. There were many, many reasons we all filled those rows that morning, and there were just as many emotional landscapes. I had been taking it for granted that everyone else saw this whole thing, as I did, as a charade, as a major inconvenience. Somehow, beforehand, I had thought we would all understand this was just a silly, bureaucratic, even propaganda-laced ceremony—but no, I saw now how meaningful this was to so many. I felt vaguely ashamed of myself for having so underestimated the feelings of these other people, most of them nonwhite and most probably poorer than I was.

At the end of the ceremony, which included pledging allegiance to the flag (which I'd refused to do in high school), taking the oath of allegiance, hearing a speech or two, and ritualistically handing in our green cards, a woman I recognized from the INS offices stepped forward to sing the national anthem. The weeping grew louder around me as the woman sang this song so beautifully (this song I'd always laughed at before), and though it's almost embarassing to say because it is so predictable, I actually loved America in that moment, if only because I saw how much these other people truly loved it, and I could only guess at what they had been through to arrive at this love.

Still, when I am in America, I rarely feel completely American. When I am in Europe, I don't know what to feel. This is probably a good thing; uncertainty can be a privilege when one doesn't have to live in it all the time. Where I am now is more important to me than it used to be. Meanwhile, where I am from, whether that is Ireland or America or upstate New York or simply a place called the country of childhood, is harder to name now, an image that shifts all the time, wobbly and out of proportion, like any child's idea of what a country is.

A Road Still Becoming

SUHEIR HAMMAD

UTFO's "Roxanne Roxanne." I had heard other rap songs before, but this was the one which introduced me intimately to Hip-Hop. I was no more than ten years old and on my way home from school. Three fine Puerto Rican teenage boys were walking toward me down Fourth Avenue in Brooklyn's Sunset Park. One was carrying a flattened cardboard box under his arm, another, a boom box, and the last one was just smiling at the little girls who were admiring them. They were going to our now-empty schoolyard, the cardboard to be laid out on the concrete, so the boys could break-dance on top of it. The music from that huge radio could be heard from at least a block and a half away. But it wasn't until they were right in front of me that I heard the chorus to the song: "Roxanne, Roxanne, I want to be your man . . ." Word.

I rushed home, excited by the energy of the sound, and the smile the flyest boy had blessed me with. My mother was cooking fish. I loved the way she made fish—not breaded to death and served with tartar sauce, like in school. Mama would hook the whiting (forever to be called "ghetto fish" by my sisters and our friends who also grew up on it) up with some sumac and cumin, and the juice of a lemon. I put my books away, changed clothes, washed my hands, and came to help. I repeated the new chorus I'd learned under my breath as I placed olives and peppers on the table. Baba was home for lunch that day, a rare thing, so we had to set a proper table.

Smoking his cigarette while waiting for the food, Baba asked us what we had learned in school that day. My two sisters were two and four years younger than I, the first son was in kindergarten, and then there was the baby boy, who was spared the inquisition. We lined up in front of Baba as Mama took the fish out of the oil. As one of my sisters was reciting her ABCs, my pops heard me still humming to myself. "What are you saying?" he asked. And like an idiot, I rhymed the words for him. Pandemonium, as my brothers' favorite wrestling broadcaster would have said.

"What are you saying? This is what you learn in school? This is why we came to this country? So you can come home with filth in your mouth? No more. No more friends, no more music. Allah, what is this? What are we going to do with this? This music, this black music, rap, whatever it is, not in this house. We are not black, or Spanish. I'll break your teeth if I hear you repeat this trash again. Not in this house."

All this said at a decibel that made it clear Baba was more than a little upset.

❧

My parents are of the first generation of Palestinians born and raised outside of their ancestral home. Both sets of my grands were evacuated, or forced, from their towns in 1948. Their homes were taken over by Jews who left Europe's horror to embrace my grandparent's land as their own. How many people were murdered during what the Palestinians call The Catastrophe, the creation of the state of Israel, no one knows for sure. Entire villages were killed off, the most famous one being Deir Yessin, where nearly three hundred people were massacred overnight. But the people I come from, those who survived and were violently uprooted from their land, were taken to emergency refugee camps set up by the United Nations.

My dad was born on the way out of Palestine and into Jordan, in the West Bank. A transit baby. Mom's family had already moved out of the camps when she was born, three years after the expulsion. Both were raised in Amman, my mother on the outskirts of the camps, my father in the heart of them. And both were raised in the shadow of the land just lost. My paternal grandfather carried the key to his house in Lydd with him until he died in 1985. The key hung like a rosary on the wall of his refugee home, a reminder and false hope, after his vow never to return until he was free to live in his own land. Never was.

I, too, have grown up under that shadow. When I was five years old, my parents left what they knew in Jordan and came to Brooklyn, looking for their American Dream. It was 1979. The Iranian hostage crisis was brewing, and oil was a precious thing at gas stations all over America. The country was on the verge of a Republican presidency, and the Sugar Hill Gang was recently famous and on top of the music charts for what was later called the first mainstream Hip-Hop jam, "Rapper's Delight."

My parents believed many beautiful things of America before they immigrated. *Amreeca* was the place where no one bothered you. Where your religion and race did not matter as long as you worked hard. It was the one true democracy in the world. The police here did not harass people or get away with murder, the way did in Jordan or Lebanon. Money was to be made by anyone strong enough to work and smart enough to save.

This trip to a new land, the land of golden streets, was to be my father's first real chance at life. The camps had offered him no educational direction and no trade to learn. As the last-born child of his mother and the ninth out of his father's fifteen children, Baba had been raised in the unique position of being considered the baby and a middle child. As a man, he was expected to fully support his own growing family. Both of my parents graduated high school, my mother working as a teacher's aide briefly afterward, my father attending one year of college. But Baba left the university, as was in vogue during his youth, to join the popular resistance to Israeli rule. And like so many of his comrades, his dreams of a liberated homeland were eventually deflated and carried around as failure.

One of my paternal uncles had already been living in the States for a decade and had set up a business. My father was to come work for him and pay off the money my uncle spent on bringing me, my two younger sisters, my pregnant mother, and himself over to Amreeca. My brother was born a few months after we arrived, and with him came the first snow I remember.

Cold. My first memories of America are white, frozen over, magical, and cold. And I guess no matter what I have experienced here as a citizen, I more often than not come back to this same memory. I have a mean-ass cousin, who pushed me into that first snow, sticking snowballs into my ears and down my shirt. I got sick, but I didn't die. I became an American, accustomed to the cold.

~❧~

I grew up, along with my brothers and sister, in a cramped two-bedroom apartment in Sunset Park, Brooklyn. At the time a predominately Puerto Rican neighborhood, Sunset was loud with salsa music and botanicas. The park the neighborhood is named after is a scraggly-looking city lot with some grass and scattered trees which goes on for five blocks in one direction and three avenues in another. I remember seeing my first crack vials in that park. The 1980s drug epidemic affected my neighborhood deeply. Crack especially, since it is so potent and cheap. It seemed as if it was overnight, but in over a year, I witnessed neighbors who'd been healthy, hard-working people become gaunt, haunted by the monkey on their back. Girls I had been at grammar school with, shiny, beautiful girls, became involved with and had babies with drug dealers, the same boys who'd been at school with us. The drug dealers became the ghetto superstars of our day. Many of them were shot, jailed, or killed.

My father busted his ass working off his debt and trying to feed his growing family. He worked in grocery stores all over the borough, always in poor neighborhoods. And poor neighborhoods most often translated into black neighborhoods. It's a phenomenon still alive today. You won't find many Arab, Asian, or Latino-owned business in white neighborhoods. And it seems rare to find black-owned businesses any-where.

My father found himself in areas of Brooklyn, like East New York, Coney Island, Flatbush, which seemed to come right out of bad '70s gangster movies. Many of the stores he worked in were surrounded by broken-down, burned-out buildings. And more than once desperation, poverty, and substance abuse held my pops up at gunpoint. Robbed him of his pay. Pressed a revolver into his back and made him open up the cash register. For me, it was like Baba really was in a movie. He once came home with a bullet wound in his foot and blood dried on his forehead, evidence of where another bullet had grazed. As he care-fully took his shoes off, he told us of how three masked men broke into the supermarket he was working in, with shotguns blazing. Drama. And the music to all of this? The first stages of Hip-Hop. No wonder he didn't appreciate my UTFO sound bite.

⁂

"We are not these people. We are Arab. We are not American or Spanish or black. *Ihna* Arab."

These sentences were a kind of mantra both of my parents used when they wanted to get across to us that we were not to dress, eat, do, talk, study, or simply be like anyone else. I always found it interesting whom my parents thought Americans were. When they said, "American, black, or Spanish," they were clearly differentiating between the "real Ameri-cans," and the others, the Africans, the Latinos, and, eventually, the Arabs. America was, and is, to my parents, still the frozen, white, and magical fantasy, with no room for us.

Being Palestinian in America has been a trip. Like my parents, I found no room available for this particular identity in mainstream America. The America of apple pies and Fourth of July picnics. Whether this America, the one of toothsome corn-bred beauty queens and football-playing patriotic blond boys even exists, I don't know. The America I witnessed, was shaped by, and am myself shaping, is carved out of concrete and soul. This is the Other America, and it is made up of the spaces we have created in order to survive. And the soundtrack to this notion of a nation for me is Hip-Hop.

The Black Nationalist–inspired lyrics of Public Enemy coming out of my headphones accompanied the television coverage I viewed of the popular Palestinian uprising of the late 1980s, the *Intifada*. This visual and aural climate created around me a new notion of identity. Chuck D's thick voice mouthing the condition of oppressed peoples in neighborhoods similar to my own, the images of young Palestinian kids throwing rocks at Israeli soldiers helped me to understand my place in the world, my place in America, and my place in my self. I was of more than one place. The shadow, which had followed my father out of his camp, merged with the shadow America had created for those citizens who didn't exactly fit.

These people, the ones who didn't fit, were not of one color, one religion, or one race. These people came from everywhere, and some of them came from here, before the United States was even an imperialist twinkle in the eye of some European. The ancestors of my friends all have different stories. Some were captured on their own land, sold, and shipped here as commodities. Others came on planes to find the financial opportunity promised them after America's Navy took control of their island. One of my friends' grandfather came here fleeing the Nazis, his hand tattooed with the numbers which replaced his name to make it easier for the keepers at the gas chambers to record.

My own people were affected by the Jewish Holocaust in a different way. Using the horrifying effects of Europe's "anti-Semitism" as a justification, Zionists and their supporters were able to fulfill their goal of creating a Jewish state in Palestine. I place the quotations there because history has found identity to be fluid. My grandparents, Semites by ancestral, cultural, linguistic, and geographical definition, found themselves on the receiving end of a racism intent on erasing them, or at best, relocating them for the convenience of European Jewry, who became the epitome of the word Semite. The West approved of and funded the state of Israel, and in that way, tried to forget about my people, about the people who were living off of, and for, that land.

Knowing the U.S. government has given aid to Israel for so long, and so unconditionally, has always created a tension within me. Especially recently, having just turned twenty-five years old in 1998, the fiftieth year of the Palestinian Diaspora. I find myself asking who would I be if things had transpired differently. I am an American now. My passport says as much, as does my Brooklyn tongue. But on my first trip to Palestine, I was treated as a straight-up terrorist at the airport. I had to remind the security people I was an American, not a threat to them. But I was the one needing to be reminded. I will always be of more than one place. And that can be threatening to some.

And that's what it often comes down to. Reminding people. Reminding myself where I come from. I will never be as American as apple pie. And thank Allah, 'cause I ain't never liked cooked fruit. I'll have some of my mom's ghetto-fried whiting with the Arab spices over fillet o fish, any day. But if being from a place is about where, and what, you have lived, I am from here, more than I am anywhere else. This is what I know. What I have lived. Being a citizen ain't only about paying taxes, although sometimes it feels like it.

So, with all of our histories, with all of the different paths taken to be here, we find ourselves together. Hip-hop is more than music, it is a culture and a mirror of the times for many of America's youth. Created in the Bronx, by DJs throwing block parties in burned-out lots and rhyming over beats, the music is now heard all over the world. In true oral tradition, MCs remind. Many, if not most, lyrics are somewhat autobiographical, and in that way, young urban people, who are not the recipients of the best educational programs nationally, use vernacular and rhythm to define themselves. My friends and I used rhymes to define and defend ourselves. We are the generation the media had called X, not after Malcolm, or a sense of righteousness, but to define us as unknown.

Some people threw graffiti up on the walls of their neighborhoods. What the police and most residents (including my parents who kicked my butt the time I pointed out my tag "Fresa Fresh" on the hallway banister) saw as vandalism, these artists saw as proof of their existence, for all to see. The use of the bright spray paints on city transport or depressing project walls has also been a try at bringing nature into areas where trees are sparse. A good piece is like a dance caught in the air, all movement, color, and open space. And the memorial walls, now famous, of neighborhood kids who died too young are a testament to the violence so many people have not survived. Faced with dehumanizing building design, kids beautified their hoods with the materials available. Survival.

B-Boying, the break-dancing those fine Puerto Rican boys were off to when they changed my life, has connections to African dance that are clearly visible to anyone who will care to look. Watch B-Boys dance alongside Capoiera players of Brazil and you will see amazing flexibility and similar movements. In Brazil, during the last century, enslaved Africans were not allowed to exercise their martial arts skills, but ingeniously, they did so as though they were dancing, right under the noses of plantation owners, who got off on watching captive people move. The fact that kids from Brooklyn and the Bronx brought the same movements to concrete and cardboard, one hundred years later and across the world, says as much about the conditions of poor neighborhoods in America as it does about the incredible retention capabilities of people. Survival.

Caribbean immigrants were the most popular DJs in the Bronx during the late '70s. Some of the best were young Jamaican men who had come to New York with their working-class parents to find a better life than the one in the Yard. These DJs were familiar with different sounds, Jamaica being well known for DJ clashes and different sound systems. By sampling beats from different music, the DJs brought the world to the streets of New York City. Punk, Ska, Rock, were all early influences on Hip-Hop, as much as Jazz and Bebop. Like my mother's best gumbo (*makluba*), choice ingredients have gone into the pot. Survival.

Immigrants add as much to this culture as we gain from it. We have to remind ourselves that many of the things which are now popularly considered American were once marginalized as "the ways of colored folk." Jazz, Rock-and-Roll, Southern food. And now, what the media calls Rap. Survival.

And the MC. The front person, the face of Hip-Hop. The voice heard, the words memorized instead of homework. While all the elements are fundamental, each person has one that truly moves them. For me, it's the lyricist. The person who not only puts pen to paper, their heart on their sleeve, but also rhymes the words over a beat, to make you nod your head and think at the same time. It's about music, keeping an internal rhythm, and never missing it. My parents always told me the most perfect poetry was God's word. Between the Quran's teachings and Rakim's rhymes, I found myself in love with words, and wanting to record not only my story but the stories of those around me, so history would know we existed. Survival.

❧

There is a huge part of me that thinks breaking down my lifestyle into parts is stupid. As though the experiences my sisters and I went through could each be boxed and checked off a list. The world doesn't work that way. Neither does being an American. The lens I look out of has been shaped by more than one movement, and many moments of tension, contradictions. All the "-isms" have played a part, including socialism, feminism, nationalism, and a racism not based on economic superiority but on limited contact with white Americans. My parents' religious beliefs and their cultural traditions have affected the way I walk in the world. Shit, just being a woman affects the way I walk down the street.

But I have to remind myself, I am more than a woman. I am more than a kid who grew up poor in Brooklyn. I am more than a type of hair or a way of wearing clothes. I am dynamic, as we all are. As America is. As this thing called Hip-Hop is. And I walk with a certain step. A particular one. Not the exaggerated hoodlum with the one-pant-leg-up-and-one-down walk Hollywood has decided is hip. Nor the head-held-high-and-shoulders-back walk I would wish for myself. Not yet. I walk with my ancestors in my bones. They are heavy. I walk with history on my shoulders. It is heavy. I walk with a beat in my head, usually a beat with a rhyme laced on top of it. Not too heavy, but deep. I am walking into the millennium. And America is walking alongside of me, many of her youth with the same step. No longer walking behind, not interested in leading the way, but together. Down a road still becoming. Nothing is static, and we change with every breath. I may never be apple pie, but more and more, America is becoming like me, like us.

Code Switching

GINU KAMANI

I NEVER MEANT TO LIVE AN EXEMPLARY LIFE. I never imagined that my own experiences could, like tea leaves at the bottom of a cup, gather into forms so compelling that their symbolic order could dissolve the time capsule of my being, allowing me to look at my life experiences without being contained by them, using the vessel of my being as a lightning rod, or a prism through which a passing light beam inexplicably unsheaths a rainbow.

I am bemused by the degree of self-referentiality that has come to mark my life, self-awareness that has crept in through the back door of cross-cultural confusion stemming from migration, heightening my senses and intuition to such an extent that I accidentally evolved a level of sagacity that even now feels alien to me, even now occasionally irritates and burdens me with its ubiquitous presence and strength of feeling.

What is this self-consciousness that has befallen me in the move from India to the United States? Starting at the age of fourteen, I began shedding the skin of being a group member of Bombay's urban, upper-middle-class, merchant-caste, top-dog culture, where nothing about my "identity" or my "culture" or my "background" need ever have come under scrutiny; and began accepting, even collaborating in the repositioning of myself in the semblance of a Midwestern suburban, hardworking, economically viable citizen, who could presumably put aside

race, class, caste, name, gender, and language issues to passionately embrace and then fearlessly overthrow underdog status with the mother-
of-invention adaptability necessary to overcome social, psychological,
and cultural hurdles—emerging finally as a free individual, a successful
American, comfortably ensconced in personal goals and ideals, dedicated to the pursuit of happiness, blessed with inalienable rights and
just a few rag-tag social responsibilities.

In reality, in more than twenty years in the United States I have
routinely fallen through the cracks of gender, class, and race, of culture,
nationality, and sexuality, all predicated largely on binary oppositions
that continue to feel unsatisfactory and almost infantile long after I have
come to understand them intellectually. My responses to being posi-
tioned and re-positioned, of turning my yearning one way and then
another, tripping all over myself, experimenting demurely or equally
without restraint, risking money, shelter, status, affection, pushing the
envelope on all sides, and finally grappling with the immense fund of
self-knowledge that now dogs me down every alleyway of action and
reaction—all have transformed me into a thinker and writer situated
on the intersection of various destabilizing fault lines. And it is this
shaky ground exactly, like the rich soil that can only manifest itself
through volcanic eruption, that provides the best clay for molding the
mythological American ideal, but also, simultaneously twinned, the Indian ideal. Just when I think I have a handle on the "new world," I find
myself unceremoniously dumped on the doorstep of my birth culture,
but this time with a fullness of permission to excavate the overt and
covert forces of history, culture, and psyche that have shaped my very
breath, bones, and sinew. The only avenue for understanding who I am
is by understanding what I am not in one cultural context, and then
turning around and investigating the same in the other. Becoming
"American" is for me inextricably tied up with becoming fully aware of
what it is to be "Indian"; being born again as a self-aware Indian is what
I equate with becoming American.

Moving actively between cultures has the effect of leaving one in a
constant state of becoming. My younger self in India was already accustomed to switching codes—language, gender, class, modernity. I

grew up in Bombay speaking four languages by the age of four. Gujerati is my mother tongue, but already by the age of four I am certain English (that is, Indian English) must have surpassed it in importance. I have gleeful memories of being able to exclude my dour grandmother from my world simply by speaking English. I also spoke Marathi, the language of the state that Bombay is situated in and the mother tongue of the majority of household help in my youth, and Hindi, the national language, which we accessed mainly through the movies and school lessons. In fifth grade, French was included in the curriculum as a "foreign language."

In my childhood, Bombay was easily the cosmopolitan center of India, as well as being its financial capital. When the British fortified the harbor several hundred years ago, they purposely invited groups from all over India to relocate, and unlike the relative cultural isolation of their native places, the new migrants of Bombay lived cheek by multiethnic jowl on limited land in a situation akin to Manhattan. In the heady decades after Independence, Bombay grew into a bustling industrial center built around an international port, and the migrants continued pouring in from all over.

In this loosely amalgamated urban network, my identity as a Gujerati girl never wavered. There was no need for it. Even though we stood up and sang the national anthem at the conclusion of movie screenings, and attended flag raising on Independence Day, no one openly claimed themselves as "Indian" back then, since we all belonged to our own specific groups.

After moving to this country, I discovered that the label "Gujerati" conjured up no images amongst suburbanites. I was suddenly emancipated from my childhood culture, and projected into being Indian, and I had to work on new strategies to enable this shift, to conjure up answers to the kinds of questions posed within a nationalist framework by white suburban Americans who imagined Indian as a uniform country where everyone did everything the same way. To flatten India into a uniform country is like leveling Europe into one federation. To ask an urban kid who'd lived in Bombay on the twenty-fourth floor of a high-rise about tigers in the jungle was as good as asking Sicilians about reindeer in Lapland. Over time, I marked the recurring patterns of inquiry: the Kama Sutra and Khajuraho, wild animals and thick jungle, ubiquitous poverty, Kali, arranged marriages, the forehead "dot," saris, and hash. As a teenager, my answers on all the above subjects were rather pitiful. There was a cartoon-like portrayal of India that everyone I met seemed to subscribe to, and somehow no one seemed able to imagine how the space of my urban, cosmopolitan, English-language-based, upper-middle-class life could have spared me intimate knowledge of these subjects. I was expected to "explain" myself, and I couldn't. To me, the natural ambiguities of the Indian world—urban and rural and in-between, rich and poor and in-between, modern and traditional, space-age rockets and widespread illiteracy, eighteen major languages and a highly contested national language, manual and animal labor, a pantheon of gods and goddesses of fierce and colorful demeanor—all made "sense," all had their place, and their logic, and their own per-mission to carve out a piece of the "chaos." But I couldn't explain any of it, couldn't wipe off the skeptical looks even when describing my own life, and in this atmosphere of casual dismissal until proven artic-ulate, I began to generalize in a monolithic fashion about India. This was my first training in the identity of being "Indian" and, simultane-ously, the practice of being "American," by explaining and categorizing and forcing sense out of Otherness. The prime motivator may well have been my own bewilderment about, factually, being from India, but never having been self-reflexive on that account, and certainly never having been exposed to the kind of framing of India that Western media routinely engage in. The other problem was that rather than evade the questions, or falsify my answers to the needs of the questioners, my new American training had me receiving them head-on, and attempting to respond honestly, as though my answers mattered.

This "assault by question" as I often experienced it, only later came to make sense to me as the preferred form of white middle-class en-gagement: hearty communication, verbal intercourse, IV injections of intimacy through dialogue. In a country of immigrants like the U.S. highly verbal interactions and assessments make eminent sense. In the community-based, hierarchically ordered cultures of India, verbal communication is often unimportant compared to the constantly unfolding nonverbal codes governed by gender, role, age, and status.

I grew up surrounded by big, dark, animated eyes capable of conveying the greatest subtlety. Recently I was reminded again of the exquisite power of Indian eyes during a Satyajit Ray retrospective. As I watched his films, I realized what one of my biggest confusions must have been as a young immigrant to the U.S.—my American peers appeared cold even when trying to be friendly. I depended so much on eyes to magnify both silent and verbal transmissions, that communication from my American peers often left me in a dissatisfied limbo. I had to adjust to a different sort of communication, all talk and less than expressive glances.

I remember my first day in American high school. I had to wait outside my counselor's office until he was free to see me. It seemed like an eternity of waiting in the hallway, watching the American kids passing by. I was overcome with tension. I felt like I'd been dumped in an Arctic zone. I didn't understand exactly what vibrations I was picking up, but I had a sinking feeling that friendship as I had known it up to that point had come to an end. What became abundantly clear in a matter of weeks was that I would never duplicate the effortless intimacy of companionship with an Indian girl.

I grew up with females—raised by female relatives and servants, fighting and conspiring with two sisters and many cousin "sisters," attending an all-girls school where I was always attached to one female best friend with whom I strolled arm in arm through the lunch breaks and at whose house I slept over on weekends. In American high school, my female peers wore an air of semi hostility toward each other, constantly competing for boys. The fourteen- and fifteen-year-olds had already turned hard, already scared by intimacy but well rehearsed in the mimicry of desire. They fussed constantly over the attractiveness of their bodies, unaware of how the fear of rejection led them to blank out their faces. Their eyes revealed little about their cliquish, lemming like motivations, utterly insecure for all their claims on individuality and freedom. I could not imagine that they had experienced the delicious intimacy of friendship I had once known. I did not trust them with honoring my being.

Indian lore is full of the magical power of the eyes—justified in my view, as Indian eyes are truly incomparable. The cultural emphasis on implicit rather than explicit communication, on keeping emotions in check, on placing others before self, and observing duty-bound restrictions on words and action, transforms ocular communication into a high art. In the Vedas, the visual gaze is considered as potent as the transmission of semen between bodies. Westerners are often entranced by the eyes of Indian gurus and holy men, whose gaze casts an enticing spell. Many have felt hypnotized, submitting to a power they cannot fathom.

In America I was approached with words, and expected to communicate fully with words. Unconsciously, I did not trust words in the way I could an open face studded with shining eyes. In Indian culture, a large component of talking is equated with shame. Talking is heavily circumscribed, as it must be, in a culture marked by hierarchies, roles, self-censorship, and the constant anticipation of the needs of others. To speak openly and plainly, which is the American cultural mandate, to "come clean" on information, ignorance, feelings, speculations, judgments, fears, and desires is still largely taboo in India, and considered bizarre, with personal information generally used deviously against the fools who reveal it. The American method of approaching everyone verbally as an equal, regardless of age, gender, status, or degree of interest might as well have been a Martian mandate, judging by my discomfort.

In high school, the people who showed the greatest interest in me were my teachers, drawn to my unusual combination of being a foreigner, a straight-A student with high self-esteem, and having complete disregard for my dumbed-down, smoking, drinking, fashion-obsessed schoolmates. In addition, I was the only student from India in the class of '80, and many of the liberal teachers had near or distant connections to India that they delighted in sharing with me. These adults were friendly, enthusiastic, and extremely open, but even as I thrilled under their attention, I was inhibited. I couldn't hold my own across the hierarchical lines of teacher-student, adult-teenager, native-foreigner. Where I meant to communicate enthusiastically, I often dredged up confused silence. Friendship in that situation was a bit too far-fetched, given the memories of sour, distant, authoritative teachers who had filed predictably through my life back in India. I recall one math teacher in Bombay, who begged a ride for herself and her daughters in the chauffeur-driven car that collected me each evening from school. Agreeing once meant agreeing forever, and we rode together for more than a year while she ignored me completely, her teacher's mask never slipping beyond a terse "thank-you" as she slammed the door shut.

Interestingly, the power of words had been sown in me long before my move to the U.S. Starting around the age of eleven, I received extensive training in talking about my feelings, listening to my family members share their feelings about me, and learning how to integrate that information into my life in a healthy way. I resisted all this new openness quite thoroughly, as I found it as appalling as being brainwashed, and was convinced this was just another trap set by my mother to humiliate me. My mother came to the U.S. when we were young and studied Transactional Analysis, a system devoted to bettering interpersonal communication. She wanted to showcase her family as beneficiaries of her newly learned openness, and urged us to learn how to engage in a systematic, humanistic, but still thoroughly alien, way of resolving conflicts and empowering ourselves. With the zeal of the recent convert, week after week, she insisted that we learn to communicate by these new rules, until the habit began to form. However, there is a world of difference between speaking openly with one's family members and doing the same with the general public. The public/private dichotomy in Indian culture is very strong, with loyalty and secrecy around family life expected above everything.

When I finally did get around to unclenching my verbal fist in the U.S., the wellspring of articulation shifted into gear naturally as part of a friendship with a boy. His family moved in across the street and we discovered we were taking the same classes. He had a sunshine smile, and his openness hooked me. We could talk for hours. He was an immigrant outsider like myself, but raised in Europe. We had both been accustomed to long-lasting, same-sex friendships, and missed our old friends desperately. We commiserated about the severance wrought by migration and shared photos and letters of our long-lost companions.

Several months later when sexual feeling entered into the relationship, it came as a shock to both of us, but being friends first, we handled our physical intimacy cautiously, graciously, with respect. With intimacy back in my life, I felt human again. This time the intimacy had been cemented in the verbal, and suddenly this American custom of talking and articulating didn't seem so outlandish anymore.

My next relationship with a best friend was also sexual, also with a man. Given my Indian upbringing, this was all very new. But given my Indian upbringing, this was also all very familiar. I had a new angle on an old experience, or a well-mapped route for a new experience. I knew how to get close. I sought out intimacy and loved it. It had never crossed my mind that I could create this situation with males, an unfortunate hangover from my gender-segregated childhood.

"There is no greater aphrodisiac for me than having a man open himself up to my probing, revealing himself with subtlety, honesty and wit," says the narrator of one of my stories. Approaching men with strong expectations of self-revelation and intimacy, honesty, and equality, then actually being rewarded with responses commensurate with my audacious probing, freed me in a profound way from the gender suspicions, prejudices, and distance I had been raised with. I was lucky to stumble across men eager to take risks with intimacy, swift to up the ante of self-disclosure, generous with opening up their dreams and fears to (respectful) scrutiny. In many cases, no girl before me had ever evinced such interest. Past intimacy had been brokered though sexual contact, not a mutual exchange of spirit. This close access busted down the walls of mystification that both Indian and American cultures regurgitate in their own way, turning men against women and women against men in a love-hate charade that succeeds in obscuring all of our basic humanity. Demystifying one taboo area quickly led to demystifying others. Analyzing transactions, especially sexual and bodily transactions across cultures, forms a large part of my work as a writer and educator. One of the last avenues of communication to fall under scrutiny are often those with our relatives.

In my college years, as my parents grew comfortable with their adult children, we were told in detail of how my father had undergone intense sensitivity training and psychoanalytic therapy in the '60s in India, pushing the boundaries of his self-awareness through strategies completely alien to the culture. He took that route literally to save his life. In taking apart who he was in certain family and cultural transactions, he re-created himself anew. Later, in my mid-twenties, finally certain of my path as a writer, I realized I was fundamentally doing the same.

The realization was eerie, a collapsing of time and space and body. In ten years in the U.S., my sense of self had been squeezed, and expanded, and reshaped, and squeezed and expanded again. Returning to India for three years opened up the process all over again. As I approached thirty, I finally felt comfortable with the pushing and shoving and out-of-body experiences that bridled the wildly disparate Indian and American sides of myself, the parent-to-child links of psychic connection, the male and female blurring into a gender-neutral zone—all the oppositional points of my experience coalescing onto one track, where like a stunt woman commanding two horses with a firm leg planted on each, I could look inside and outside the galloping process of self-revelation without panic, denial, schizophrenia, or guilt.

As I write this essay, a few years shy of forty, I am on my way to "Becoming Mexican," to settling into a future tryst with Oaxaca as my third home culture, and inevitably the process will include being born again as Indian, and again as American. I'm getting accustomed to this odd process of midwifing my own births, trusting the intuitively prescribed actions and reactions that still burst the bag of my boundaries to push aloft deep, rumbling belly laughs that cushion and lubricate the challenge, the promise, and the irrevocable bounty of becoming, and continuing to become.

My New World Journey

NOLA KAMBANDA

THE ANTICIPATION OF COMING TO THIS GREAT COUNTRY and all of its physical, social, and economic capacity was overwhelming. It made me feel like a toddler in a toy store, unable to decide which adventure to tackle first. Coming to California from Burundi—a place that I had grown to call home, a place that was so very different in every aspect from the United States—I was in complete awe. The first thing that hit me was the speed with which everything was going. It seemed too fast-paced. The movement of the people was rushed, and no one was looking anywhere else except where they were going; the cars moved too fast; there were too many lights, too many buttons to press, too many escalators. I was suddenly asking myself if these people ever stopped to talk to one another. The longing to be back home suddenly came upon me. The need for some kind of familiarity was so strong and yet I had just stepped off the plane.

In many ways, I have lived my life as an immigrant of one sort or another. I was born in Burundi to native Rwandese parents who had each left the country in the early '60s as a political refugee to escape the ethnic cleansing which was going on. Despite the fact that they met, married, created a home, and had all seven of their children in Burundi, my parents never considered themselves to be anything other than Rwandese. There was no such thing as assimilation, as becoming a citizen of Burundi. As such, they raised their children to identify themselves as Rwandese. So I grew up with the understanding that where you were born has little, if any, bearing on who you are, let alone what you will become. You will always be followed by the shadow of heritage and of ancestry.

All refugees grow up with this understanding. You grow up knowing that you do not automatically belong, that you have to always prove yourself, earn your place in the society which has so graciously allowed you the freedom of life. In my household, it was just assumed that we would do well in school. There was no room for failure, for being anything other than the best. I, like all my siblings, excelled in my academics. I left Bujumbura, the capital city, to complete my secondary education at an all-girls boarding school in Kiganda, a small countryside town.

I had always wanted to be in a boarding school. My friends and the various acquaintances I met who had attended and/or graduated from boarding school told me about the lifelong bonds that were developed by the girls, about how it was an experience that had forever changed their sense of who they were as women. Though relatively unexciting, my first year at school in Kiganda was pleasant enough. My second year, however, was another story. A story that my parents, having left the violence of their homeland behind, had hoped I would never be able to tell.

Not so unlike the rival gang warfare that I have grown accustomed to hearing about in Los Angeles, the territory of Central Africa where I am from is marred by tribal warfare. The two main tribes in both Burundi and Rwanda are the Hutus and the Tutsis. The hatred and rivalry between the tribes has existed from the beginning of this century's colonial occupation of these two countries. Even though most of the world has recently appealed to both the Tutsi and the Hutu tribes to put an end to the genocide, it will most likely continue into the next millenium. It is hard to change when you know no other way of life.

I suppose that this was the case with the young Hutu student at the boarding school who was plotting to have me, a Tutsi, killed. Actually, she and a small group of her Hutu friends were planning to extinguish all the Tutsi students. I just happened to be at the top of the list—

literally. Mine was the first name on a list of over thirty names that the administration discovered. After the girls were found out and threatened with expulsion, they quickly abandoned their murderous plans. But for me, it was a serious reminder that I was a refugee and that meant I was never safe, always susceptible. I was never truly home. When I told my parents what had happened, their reaction only cemented this. "This is what you have to live with, Nola," they said. "This is who you are."

So there I was, at the Los Angeles International Airport, just one short taxi ride away from meeting the family with whom I'd be living. My aunt and cousin from Swaziland, where I had been living for most of the previous year, accompanied me on this, my first trip to America. More specifically, to what would be my new home—at least while I was attending school. While I was standing there outside the airport watching cars and buses of all sizes and shapes drive by, I thought about how I had reached this point in my life. I realized the sacrifice that not only my parents but also my siblings were making to send me out here. I was the first one of all seven of my parents' children to move so far away from Burundi. I should have felt privileged. I should have been excited and on top of the world about coming to America—the country I had been made to believe was the richest and most technologically advanced of them all.

But a sense of guilt was washing over me, one which became more pronounced as I kept thinking of the economic burden it would place on my father. An economic burden which I felt was too large for him to bear in order to accommodate just one child. This guilt and the realization that stemmed from it brought on a tremendous sense of responsibility for me. Even more so than in Burundi, failure was unacceptable. I could not fail here in America. I was going to have to be the best. I was going to have to do extremely well in school so that I could go on to get a decent job so that I would be able to contribute financially to my family's well-being.

The family that I was going to be living with in Los Angeles were strangers. They were well acquainted with my uncle and aunt who came to vacation in the States each year. But I had never met them before. I wondered how awkward it would be to live with people I had never met before. When I walked into their house they greeted me very warmly. The sound of their voices calling me by name was not strange but, rather, familiar. It eased the pain of separation that I had been feeling from the moment our plane landed at the airport. I felt welcomed and at ease. I felt at home in their home.

Even still, I found myself growing ever-conscious of the way I spoke. This was the beginning of what would be my lengthy battle to translate myself in a language not my own, to communicate in English—not just any English, but *American* English. It seemed like I would never be able to speak as fast and as well as these people. I would never be able to say or remember their names, names I was not used to, as easily as they seemed to be able to say and remember mine. I wondered if they were, in meeting me, as aware of our differences as I was in meeting them. How did I seem to them? Did I sound too soft? Too slow? Too self-conscious? I must not have, because my new family—a Jewish-American social activist, a Jamaican-American actress-cum-writer and their prepubescent daughter—were very caring and hospitable. They never made me feel like I didn't fit in just right. I felt, in their eyes and in their home, like myself, like an individual, not a representative of Burundi, Rwanda, or Africa at large.

This was not the case with other people that I met. I couldn't believe the questions that were posed to me. Questions about my country and about Africa—although in many instances there was no real distinction because so many people think that Africa is just one big country, not a continent with many, many countries in it. People would ask me if I spoke "African," if I could speak a little "African" for them to hear. One day while I was visiting the elementary school that the family's daughter was attending, one student asked me—with genuine sincerity—if we rode on elephants in Africa as a means of transportation. That blew me away.

When I went to apply for my Social Security card, the clerk looked at my passport, pointed to the printed name of my country, and asked, "Where is that?" Upon being told by me that I had recently arrived from Burundi, by way of Swaziland, a young man asked, "How did you get here from there?" The thought that I could have flown in a commercial airplane from there to here did not seem to ever cross his curious mind. At times, I received these questions with humor. At times, I received them with confusion and took great offense. Why didn't these people know anything about Africa and its people, its geography? Why was there such a deep pit of ignorance? Where was the knowledge and wisdom and greatness I imagined everyone in America would have?

Surprisingly, most Americans I met in Los Angeles had no concept of African modernity. They still thought of Africans as people who lived in a jungle, people who had no access to airplanes, cars, televisions, telephones, CD players, or any of the other household appliances and urban facilities that I grew up enjoying in Burundi. The fact that these Americans were not aware of African modernity was not as surprising as my discovery of the fact that they also knew little about American history. In Burundi, geography, history, and anthropology were a critical part of our educational curriculum. And not just our geography, our history, and the study of our culture. We learned about the entire world. By the time I finished secondary school, I knew all the significant details of all the countries in all the continents. I knew the capitals of all the states in America. I knew who the presidents of the country were. Living in the glamour of Los Angeles and not knowing what a Tutsi or a Hutu is, not knowing where Burundi or Rwanda is, can somehow be rationalized. Not knowing who Andrew Jackson was or where the capital of California is, cannot. This is how my romanticized idea of America died and the recognition of my journey into *a* new world—not *the* New World—began to take form.

The world I eventually came to embrace in America, in Los Angeles, and in the home where I was living was both comfortable and complicated. Even though my new family made it as painless as possible for me to merge into their way of life, there were many things I had to learn. The differences in our cultures and lifestyles continued to display themselves as the days went by. Everything was rushed, was too this or too that, was always being pushed to the extreme. There just seemed to be a ton of information to recall. Where had all the simple things gone?

I had used a telephone plenty of times before and I had always thought of it as a pretty basic unit. You pick up the phone, you dial who you're calling, they answer and you talk. If someone is calling you, the phone rings, you answer it and you talk. No interruptions, no complexities. Until I learned that there was such a thing as call waiting. And then three-way calling. And call forwarding. And single telephone units with multiple lines. What was all this? Was it all really necessary?

I wondered about the level of sophistication toward which everything seemed to be aspiring. It was a sophistication intended to facilitate, to make life simpler. But how is it possible to be simple and sophisticated at the same time? Take, for instance, the washing machine. I had neither seen nor used one before. You put your dirty clothes and some soap into a machine, close the lid, press a button and within minutes, your clothes were done—clean and ready to be placed in yet another machine to be dried!?! Back at home, in Burundi, we would put our dirty clothes in a basin, soak them a bit, hand wash them with soap, and then hang them up to line dry. I will admit that the American way is definitely more convenient. But it lacks a certain ritual of intimacy. There is a care that I like to put into the cleaning of my clothes, those things that cover and protect my body, so I still invariably find myself hand washing.

Only recently did I realize that the majority of all these cultural contrasts stemmed from the same root, the concept of time. Americans have a way of wanting to accomplish as much as possible in as little time as possible. Even something as sacred as eating. Fast food. It was amazing how many fast-food restaurants there were in Los Angeles, even in just our small neighborhood. Everyone ate at fast-food restaurants. I noticed how many ate while driving or being driven. I had not seen anything like this in my country. We ate three meals a day—breakfast, lunch, and dinner; and this was rarely done outside of either your own home or someone else's home. Eating out was a very formal affair. People didn't go to eat out by themselves. It was what you did in large numbers, something the whole family did together. Regardless of whether it was done in the home or out, dining required time. Food was never fast.

⁂

It didn't take long for me to catch on, for me to grab ahold of America. Especially after I started doing what I had come here to do—go to school. Once I started going to school and working a part-time job, I knew the meaning of busy. I knew why people ate and talked on the phone while driving from one place to another. Before long, I started doing it myself. I'd never gone to school and worked at the same time. I don't think I'd ever known anyone in my life, certainly not in Burundi, who was working and going to school at the same time. School was your job. You were obligated to study and do well until you were finished because only then would you be qualified for employment. That was our incentive. Nobody wanted to hold a job for which you didn't need qualifications. Those petty positions were for the uneducated, for those who couldn't finish secondary school or university. Education was something that was taken seriously in Burundi. If you failed a class, you were not only castigated and harshly punished for it, you would also have to repeat that entire year of school before being allowed to move on to the next grade level. Out of fear for authority and all elders in society, we gave our professors the ultimate respect.

When I began attending Los Angeles City College, I was completely thrown off by the casual relationships between professors and students. The students appeared confident of their circumstances, unafraid of any consequences. The school was overflowing with options and choices. You could decide what classes you wanted to take, how many, and when you wanted to take them. You could miss a class and still make up for it. You could miss class and never make up for it and still graduate.

Working and going to school was grueling, but I managed to do it because that was why I had come to America to begin with. I had to prove myself. There would be no reason to return to Burundi without a degree. Any of the students back home would have killed to be in my shoes. So why not use them to carry me someplace, somewhere of significance? After I completed my studies at the community college, I transferred to California State University—Los Angeles. I declared electrical engineering as my major. It did not go by unnoticed—by me or anyone else—that I happened to be the only black person, not to mention black woman, sitting in most of my classes. My strong accent made every verbal answer I gave a staring session for the rest of my classmates as they tried to figure out my words. The same is true of my present coworkers.

After receiving my degree, I was immediately offered the opportunity to begin my career. I took a position at Boeing Reusable Space Systems, where I am, again, one of a small few. It seems that I have always stood out. In Burundi. In America. My parents were right when they urged me to become used to the fact that I would always be the "other." Everywhere I go I come back to their words. "This is what you have to live with, Nola. This is who you are."

No doubt, I am not American. I am a Rwandese Tutsi refugee who is becoming more and more understanding and appreciative of America each day I am here. This appreciativeness and understanding creates an awareness that makes me unique in every circle I could possibly travel in. It keeps me on my toes. If I was still in Burundi, I would also be busy, but not in the same way that I am in America. I would probably be married with a couple of children. I would be busy with the kids, busy tending to the housework, busy taking care of my extended family and local community, busy helping my husband with his career and his dreams. I would be busy being a typical Rwandese housewife.

Sometimes I do think about going back home. I think about the rewards of having an extended family and a local community that depends and insists upon my involvement. I think about finding a mate, that person I have not yet been able to find in the United States, the one who will be able to accept and relate to all aspects of my background and my culture. I think about the food, about the cassava leaves and the fried green bananas. I miss what I used to have, and what I used to want, who I thought I would become. Then again, I don't.

Sometimes I am not sure whether home is behind me or in front of me. I am not so sure this longing is really recognizable. I might just be attaching it to those things that are familiar to me. Home might very well be a place that I have not yet discovered, that I have not yet created. Or it might not be a place at all. After all, Rwanda, that place that I have called home all my life, is a place I have only visited for one month.

I don't know its rivers, its mountains, intimately. All I know of Rwanda is its people, my family. So home might be family, and nothing more. It might be the people who make me feel. The people who define and occupy and receive my emotions. The people who reciprocate, who give me the most sought after, most valuable and intangible gifts—acceptance, trust, laughter, comfort, love. In that case, Burundi is home. And so is Swaziland. And so is America.

Beyond Boundaries

HELEN KIM

MORE THAN TWENTY-SEVEN YEARS have passed since our family crossed half of the world to begin a new life in America. I had just turned twelve and my breasts were beginning to ache from growing.

We said our good-byes to Grandmother, who had lived with us, and to many aunts, uncles, cousins, and friends who had been an integral part of our life in Korea. As the bus pulled away from the terminal to the runway, we bowed and cried, and held in our memories the vanishing sight of Grandmother shaking her white handkerchief.

It was October 5th, 1971. Our father had gone ahead of us to set up a house and a store in New Jersey. His decision to move his family to America came when he retired from the Korean Air Force. He had toured America several times as an officer and was lured by the vast land, the material wealth, the opportunities, and, most of all, democracy. He believed in the American system; if he worked hard enough he would succeed. Unlike in Korea where, without good connections and right status, hard work didn't necessarily bring security, let alone success.

Father explained to Grandmother, who wanted him to work for his politically powerful and socially well-established cousins, that he did not want to bow to anyone to live his life, which was often the case in this tradition-bound and class-conscious society. With this resolve he decided to start a business, a retail store in America. As with many immigrants, my father had no experience in the dream he wanted to follow, just sheer desire and will.

The uncertainty made my parents nervous, but my older sister, Marina, fourteen, and my younger sisters, Lucy, ten, and Rosa, eight, and I couldn't wait to get to America. To us America was the magical land of Disney World, Charms candies, Hershey's chocolates, and the Sears catalog. The American movie *Parent Trap* and the dubbed television shows *Family Affair* and *Father Knows Best* promised us that we were going to a country where everything was plentiful, orderly, and fun.

In fact, the very first story I heard about America was that Americans were so honest and law-abiding that once, when a man found a watch in the park, he wound it and left it on the bench for the owner. Not only did that finder not keep the watch, but no one else passing by paid any attention to it because it didn't belong to them.

Nothing had prepared me for the America that was awaiting. It would be a long time before I emerged from this chaotic transition with any sense of who I was. The ten-thousand-mile stretch over the Sea of Japan and the Pacific Ocean to the Atlantic Ocean was how far my spirit and emotions had to journey in order for me to find myself.

❧

At first, everything seemed as we had imagined. Father had rented a Tudor house with an apple tree in the backyard and a wooden fence in the front. It was on a tree-lined street in suburban New Jersey with all white neighbors. The supermarkets were filled with more rows of goodies than we could count, and the department stores were dizzying with a variety of clothes, handbags, shoes, and makeup as we had never seen before. The roads, which were well paved, went on endlessly, lined with big signs, buildings, and houses. We knew how big the country was when the McDonald's in our neighborhood had a sign for having sold one million burgers. One million!

Marina and I were enrolled in junior high, and Lucy and Rosa in grammar school. The initial whirl of attention—our photo in the school paper, the introductions in classrooms, and many hi's—faded quickly, as did the easy smiles of teachers and students, and we began facing many difficulties. We were the only Asian students—in fact the only students of color—in the entire school. Since an English as a Second Language program did not exist yet on the East Coast, we were put into the lowest-level classes where the students weren't very motivated or helpful. The speech therapist who was assigned to us treated us as if we had some speech impediment rather than a language barrier.

Our solution to the rising problems was to learn English as quickly as possible. I wanted to have a smart retort for the boys who taunted me and my sisters with "Ching-chang, chong-chang," explain to our neighbors about why we gave them Ritz crackers wrapped up in tin foil for Halloween, and tell my classmates that Korea was not a primitive country without shoes and television. More than anything, I wanted to help my parents at the store in Newark.

My father had decided to open a wig store. At the time, many of the wigs sold in America were made in Korea, and his brother-in-law owned one of the factories in Seoul. The store, Black's Wigs, was located in the heart of Newark and most customers were Afro-American women from around the city, including the ghettos. In time, I would come to understand the history of Afro-Americans and their life in America, but then, the store in Newark was the only window I had of this world.

The first time I saw a black woman over three hundred pounds waddling into the store sweating profusely, my heart pounded fast. She filled almost the whole store and my parents looked small and helpless. The large woman tried to explain something, and when my parents didn't understand, she got angry, yelled at my parents, called them "Chinks," and left the store. My knees buckled under me, and although my parents tried to look calm for my sake, they too were shaken up.

Eventually my parents would get to know their customers well, and know how to deal with some who were mean, but the regulars who came to the store for more than a decade became good friends with Mother. They exchanged hugs and recipes. (We still eat collard greens with smoked ham with our Thanksgiving dinner.)

In the beginning, though, the whole store experience was unsettling. My father was out of his perfectly pressed Air Force uniform, picking large afros among rows of plaster display heads while explaining to black women about wigs. Father, who knew English fairly well, had trouble understanding his customers. My mother, who hadn't worked a day outside of the home, now brushed, styled, and sold wigs to these people using the few words of textbook English she had learned in Korea.

Our busiest days were the days when the welfare checks came out. The customers came in droves on that day, especially if it fell on a Saturday, and splurged on wigs. Often the money came out of their bras and underwear, which my parents then hid in the basement of the store until they went to the bank. All the wigs were priced one cent short of their real prices, $3.99, $4.99 (we soon learned this is how America markets sales merchandise), and with sales tax, the prices inevitably went up, which surprised some customers who weren't used to paying tax. When they reluctantly took off their wigs to try the new ones on, their hair looked nothing like the wigs we sold. It was matted down or braided underneath, a tangled secret they shared with us.

As I learned more English, I tried to help my parents by listening to our customers carefully, to every inflection, tone, word, and sentence, but I still didn't get most of their street language. Nothing we read in school, heard in our neighborhood, or watched on television gave me any clue. This city, which was only twenty-five minutes away from our town, might as well have been in a different country. In the Father Knows Best neighborhood we lived in, we did not talk about my parents' business.

Even though the wig business was successful, my parents suffered exhaustion from a seventy-hour-a-week work schedule, theft both from customers and employees, racial discrimination from some black customers and white neighboring store owners, and even physical harm from the local thugs. I still remember the color of the blue-black dusk when my mother was brought home in an ambulance with a swollen face and bruised arms from having been beaten up. She'd refused to give the cash box over to the two black teenagers who stepped in when she was left alone for a few minutes.

While the business success gave us a new car and a home in an idyllic-looking white neighborhood (which I later recognized was actually a

Jewish neighborhood), for me the facade of America rapidly slipped away. The underbelly of "the land of opportunity" showed itself. It was a young country driven by materialism and technology more than tradition and history, with a segregated racial/class structure that isolated immigrants and members of minority groups.

Often, I felt like a hidden link between the black world my parents inhabited at work, the white world of my school, and my Korean home.

Even at home I did not feel comfortable and safe, but was overwhelmed with new responsibilities. All our life, we had lived within the walls that surrounded our house under the supervision of our grandmother, mother, and domestic help. Mother was home when we returned from school and our responsibilities were to do as best as we could in school.

Overnight, my older sister and I had the duties of the three women who had supported us. We went to school and struggled with our new life there, then came home, did homework, supervised our younger sisters in whatever ways we could, cooked dinner, and waited for our exhausted parents to come home. There was no longer a wall around the house that protected us from the outside world, or a mother who was available to guide us through everything.

I was learning a new language in a new culture while going through puberty with little support either at home or at school. My strongest allies were my sisters, with whom I could share most things. With the beginning of my menstruation, at the age of thirteen, I was initiated into womanhood but in a completely unfamiliar territory.

As I grew older, in my teens, I became more aware of the beleaguering difficulties of having to live with two different sets of values and codes of conduct. Often what was "right" for one culture was "wrong" for the other, and what was accepted in one was rejected by the other. It wasn't possible to assimilate—to make similar—the two cultures, Korean and American, whose fundamental values and philosophies were opposite.

At the heart of the Confucius culture which I came from were the virtues of filial piety and loyalty. The family unit was the core unit and individuals were sacrificed for the harmony of unity. For females it meant we were to be the best daughters, sisters, wives, mothers, and grandmothers, and serve the male members of the family—sons, brothers, husbands, fathers, and grandfathers. Their welfare came before ours. The idea of living for oneself by self-assertion and self-expression was diametrically opposed to living for others by sacrificing oneself. I felt unavoidably torn apart between the values of my mother-culture and the new, adopted one.

On the one hand, I knew talking about myself, especially in public, was simply impolite, if not embarrassing, and communication with others should be done indirectly through the channels of mediators, so as not to shame anyone. Even then, there was appropriateness as to how one spoke with the person depending on the relationship. Relationships in Korean culture were strictly hierarchical. Teachers and elders, for instance, had absolute authority over students and the community, and were treated according to their status. A student bowed his/her head when a teacher spoke.

Yet, in school, one of my teachers admonished me for not being respectful enough to look into her eyes when she spoke, and students disregarded me when I did not speak up out of politeness and consideration. The word "I" took on a kind of importance that made me uncomfortable, and the sense of separation from "we," the family, was ungrounding. The honor of my silence was sometimes taken as stupidity, rather than virtue.

Painstakingly I learned that it wasn't possible to speak up and be silent at the same time, or think about the welfare of myself and others simultaneously, or be submissive and assertive in one breath. In essence, I could not meld together the two cultures or find a happy medium. Rather, I dealt with the demands by pulling out a different identity from the compartments of myself as I needed.

❧

By the mid '70s, more Koreans had immigrated to and settled around our area. My parents and we started going to a Korean church regularly, which became the main place for socializing with other Koreans. Around them, I tried to be the "good" Korean girl I was brought up to be, and when in school, I observed how to be more Americanized by being assertive, independent, and "free."

The identity issue became particularly pronounced after I entered college. At least while at home and still an adolescent I was anchored in my parents' culture, but two hundred miles away, there were no parents to remind me of the beliefs and values I came from. I tried to become a full-fledged American by delving into the mainstream. It was the late '70s and my roommate and friends were partying to the Grateful Dead, among other '70s bands. I learned the lyrics even though I wasn't sure about their exact meanings and followed my friends to beer parties and bong parties, and tried to be as lost in them as possible. They now have terms for what I was then, "banana," or "Twinkie," yellow outside and white inside.

The "America" I delved into was a small liberal arts college in Pennsylvania where the majority of the population was upper-middle-class white Anglo-Saxon Protestant. Until then, I did not fully grasp that the Jewish neighbors I grew up with weren't part of the majority, or that WASPs were the segment of the white race/class in a position of power. There were four Asians and fifteen Afro-Americans in the body of sixteen hundred students, who stuck out like sore thumbs. The more self-conscious I became about being a member of a minority, the more I wanted to blend into the majority.

Inevitably, though, I would have to go home and be reminded of my Korean background. There was my mother with strands of curly wig hair stuck on her shirt, rushing around the kitchen to make me Korean food. Her hands were chapped, and the nails chipped from washing dirty wigs, using hair spray, and styling six days a week. My parents didn't have to remind me that all their hard work was for their daughters, so that we could be educated well and, more importantly, marry well.

The usual generation gap between parents and children tripled when there was also a cultural/language gap, which made it often impossible for us to understand one another. They knew very little of what went on in our American schools, and were appalled at the mention of female students being allowed to drink alcohol on college campuses and the reported percentage of female students having premarital sex. They were very clear about what they expected from us. We were to marry a Korean man and stay a virgin until then.

The double standard that applied to Korean society was particularly painful for Korean-American females who immigrated as children. On the one hand, we knew what Korean-American males expected even in America: submissive, subservient, well-educated, feminine women. My sisters and I were expected to marry Korean-American males, especially twenty years ago when there weren't very many interracial marriages for Koreans. On the other hand, we saw how some of our American girl-friends had the freedom to choose their future with much more ease than we could have even imagined. They had different boyfriends before marriage, moved away from their parents, explored their career options, and even decided whether they wanted children or not.

Back then, only a few Korean females were brave or brazen enough to go against their parents and the accepted norms of Korean society and marry an American. Most submitted to their parents, who either pleaded with them or threatened to disown them. They would even-tually marry a hapless Korean man with a lot of degrees and complain about the lack of romance.

As in other cultures, Korean males had a different standard from females. They were free to become as "liberalized" as they wanted as long as they married a Korean girl in the end. They smoked, drank, partied, had American girlfriends, then went back to Korea to find a "pure" wife. Korean-American girls weren't their safest bet. There were so few eligible Korean-American males that when those we knew or were friends with went back to Korea for a wife, we were disgusted and disappointed.

❧

The Korean-Americans of my generation were few and far between when I was growing up. I never did find a group or a niche I felt I belonged to. To find a person who came to America around the same time as I did, at a similar age, from approximately the same social class and background, and who had common interests, was not easy. By the time I transferred to a university in Boston my junior year, I had in fact become Americanized enough that I did not want to be clumped in with those Korean students who tended to stick together. Other Koreans who were outside of this circle were hard to meet unless they were in my classes or the clubs I joined. Yet, I was not Americanized enough to feel at ease with Americans either.

I was always busy assessing what the social codes were for different persons or groups of people. Clearly, one of my roommates, who was a Jew from Brooklyn, had a set of expectations, rules, and holiday different from the Caribbean black roommate who was educated in England before coming to America. They were different from the Waspy dorm-mates from my previous college, who were different from the Italians who lived "down the hill" in my parents' hometown. Coming from a homogeneous culture, I was spinning from trying to figure out everyone's social codes, moral values, and even the norm. I remember going to see Woody Allen's movie *Zelig* around that time and thinking I was just like the main character, who took on the traits of people he was with and became one of them.

I became exhausted, frustrated, and even angry from trying to fit into different sets of expectations and feel accepted. The result was that my personal, familial, and cultural boundaries blurred into one another, and I was lost. In fact, my life became so complicated at one point that when I went shopping for a pair of shoes I could not decide for whom I was buying the shoes—the Korean church people, the preppy American friends, the ethnic American friends, Korean-Americans at school, and so on. I gave up and went home empty-handed.

❧

There were two things that would help me to find myself. My love for literature, and the opportunity to teach under a remarkable woman who put me on my path toward becoming a writer.

Through a fortuitous chain of events, I was hired as an English teacher at a Catholic high school. Even though I had majored in English, I never expected to do anything with it since it was not easy for me to get through the courses. I tried to major in other areas, like the sciences and political science, but kept returning to literature. I knew I came alive when I read what I could only vaguely hope to express, and in sharing the stories in the books, I didn't feel so alone. I did try writing about the things I felt passionate about, but was too discouraged by my lack of command of English to pursue it wholeheartedly.

At the age of twelve, I started writing poems and short stories in Korean, but I wasn't learning any more Korean, and my English wasn't good enough to describe the complex emotions I was beginning to experience. I remember sometime around age fourteen visualizing what I wanted to express and consciously leaving out the words because they were inadequate. My journals, which are filled with Korean, Konglish, bad English, and English, chronicle the frustration of this language transition.

Sister Marion, the principal who hired me, saw through my accent and the color of my skin right to my love for literature and the seriousness with which I would teach it, and believed that a twenty-two-year-old Korean-American could teach high school English. I never studied as hard as when I was teaching, and in the process I understood how powerful literature was. This inner-city Catholic high school was ethnically diverse with first- and second-generation immigrants who were both native and nonnative speakers: Hispanics, Ukrainians, Italian-Americans, Afro-Americans, Irish-Americans, Asian-Americans, and Eastern Europeans. In the stories we read together and shared, we found universal themes that we could relate to: family tragedies, personal triumphs, nations in war, the war between good and evil, the relationships between mothers and daughters, fathers and sons, the displaced people of the world, and the beginning of life and the end. We were able to transcend our cultural and racial differences and connect in the unity of who we were.

At Sacred Heart, each day the entire school started with a silent prayer and then recited the Lord's Prayer. For those few minutes we came together as one, whether we were Catholics, Protestants, or Buddhists. We were universal in our spirituality even if we were from different religions. In the same vein, I saw that we were one in our humanity even if we were from different cultures, thus I was able to move beyond the boundaries of the two cultures I lived with and search for my own truths.

This was the beginning of my spiritual journey that would later enmesh with my creative journey. I learned through the example of Sister Marion how to treat my students equally, not the same since no one was the same, but equally. I tried to see each of them within her cultural context with the compassion I wished I had received from others, especially when I was a teenager.

With Sister Marion's encouragement, I pursued a graduate degree in literature. Although by the time I was finished with the degree I had left Sacred Heart and was married, it was the beginning of my writing career. After receiving my master's degree, I finally felt confident enough in this language to write what had been brewing in me for two decades.

❦

I started writing my first novel in 1990, four years into my marriage. This was a pivotal part of my journey in defining myself further. I had married a Korean man who came to America to do his graduate studies. He was open-minded and receptive to changes, much more so than some of the Korean-American men I had dated whose ideas and values were stuck in the Korea of their childhood. Still, when we went to Korea for our Korean wedding and stayed at his parents' house, I saw how steeped he was in Korean culture. After all, he had lived there for twenty-four years.

My husband tried hard to make me, his Americanized wife, feel comfortable at his parents' house, which made his mother cry and ask me why her son was acting like a guest in his own home. I barely made it through that week. It was June and hot, but I wore a heavy apron over a long "home dress," and put on socks since no new bride was supposed to show her bare feet. Their polished wooden floor was slippery and I was sliding every which way, somewhat like the way I felt about myself when I was with them.

We didn't return to Korea but once in our ten years of marriage. I felt badly, but I could not play the role of a good daughter-in-law for any length of time. Usually I was exhausted and sick after my in-laws' visits to America, and felt I just couldn't be myself no matter how hard I tried. I ended up acting for them.

As my novel progressed, the gap in my marriage widened. When I wrote, I wasn't concerned about who I was supposed to be, or what role I had to play, or whom I needed to please. I wrote as my heart dictated, and I began to hear "the still, small voice" within me. Initially that voice scared me so much that I tried to silence it by clinging to the marriage and changing myself to fit the life I had, but it became unbearably painful, not unlike wearing shoes two sizes too small. But, even as I fell into despair, my writing grew strong. This process allowed me to separate myself from everyone else around me—my family, my husband, and my friends. I was finally becoming "me." I knew somewhere within me that when I finished the novel, my marriage would be over, and I would be at a very different place.

❧

Writing, then and now, for me is a way to get to the truth about myself. In this respect it's been deeply spiritual. The process of writing this essay made it clear once more that underneath my cultural identities, roles, and definitions of myself, I am simply and foremost a human being, "born of spirit and water." The events and conditions of my life were given to me as tools to understand my humanity better. In this light, "becoming American" was a way for me to probe further into the complexity of human nature.

❧

Much has changed since I first came to America. There are now one million Koreans living in this country, and in bigger cities like New York and Los Angeles, "Korea towns" have been growing. I remember when there was only one Korean grocery and one Korean restaurant in New York City. English as a Second Language programs are implemented in many educational institutions across America, and with the 1988 Olympic Games held in Seoul, the world finally became aware of this country that has grown remarkably since the war in 1953. For all these reasons, perhaps adaptation has become easier for the recent immigrants.

The changing times also show in my family. One of my sisters married a Caucasian from the Midwest who learned to speak Korean and converses in Korean with my parents. I have left my marriage and moved out to Seattle after the publication of my first novel, *The Long Season of Rain*, which is about a girl coming of age in Korea in the '60s. I am now working on a second book, *Between the Bodies of Water*, in which the protagonist comes to America and starts her journey of coming into her own.

Being Korean-American and a woman writer in the '90s, and living in Seattle are now simply conditions that I live with, the meaning of which will continuously change.

Sometimes when I am staring out at the Puget Sound, which stretches to the Pacific Ocean, I can see the passage of my journey and know that I am finally at home, within me.

Disassembling Helie

HELIE LEE

MY PARENTS CROSSED THE LARGEST OCEAN to come to America so
that their children could one day live in a nation where we would not
be judged by our lineage, the God we worshiped, or the kimchee we
ate. America promised us children our childhood, something my parents
were deprived of in their own country—South Korea—under the harsh
colonial occupation of Japanese masters. In America, the Korean War
that had ripped apart their country and families wouldn't haunt our
play. We could eat strawberry *ice cakie* all year round, sleep in pillowy
beds with legs, and wear cowgirl outfits.

I was four years old and my sister, Julie, six, when my mother dressed
us up in matching yellow dresses and knitted bonnets to get on a plane.
We were leaving our home in Seoul. Ever since my father was a young
soldier and saw his first John Wayne movie, he was determined to get
to America, the land of big cars and gorgeous-looking food. But everyone else had seen the movies as well. The U.S. forces had imported
Hollywood films to entertain the hungry and jobless masses. Everyone
wanted to get to America, but only those with official government business or student sponsorships made it out.

My father refused to accept his refugee fate, and when his daughters
were born he gave us American names, ignoring the snickers of relatives
and friends. Sharing his aspirations, my mother secretly searched for a
way. Through hushed rumors, she had heard that the Canadian gov-

ernment was accepting Asian immigrants in celebration of its one-hundredth anniversary of independence. At the time, in 1967, the Canadian government hadn't yet established an embassy in U.S.-occupied South Korea. It took several more weeks of inquiries before my parents discovered that the British embassy was acting on Canada's behalf. Immediately my father applied; his application number was five hundred, but less than one hundred applicants passed the requirements for immigration. However, conversational slangs learned from American GIs and my father's technical skills as a radar specialist qualified us into the country.

In order to make the move, my family sold everything. My father was the first to leave for Canada to secure a job and a place for us to live. I vividly recall standing on the windy landing holding a crushed flower as he scaled the steep metal steps that ascended to a glistening spacecraft. He was wearing a tan trench coat, cinched around his slim waist, with the collar flipped up, looking very handsome. The next moment he magically disappeared. Four months later, our turn came. My mother led my sister and me up the same rickety metal steps. At the top, we waved our miniature Korean flags at *Halmoni* (Grand-mother) below. "You're Korean. You'll always be Korean ladies," my mother said firmly, her eyes puffy red with tears.

I nodded obediently, not knowing the meaning of her words until I actually saw how different being Korean looked. Our straight, jet-black hair pulled tightly into side ponytails, flopping like elephant ears, stood out amongst the waves of bright-colored locks that sprouted, already curly, from people's scalps. They had sandy brown, emerald green, and blue eyes that seemed to have fallen from the sky. I kept wondering what the world looked like through blue eyes? Emerald green? Was everything prettier?

I instantly liked our new home. Instead of the sticky rice I was used to eating every morning, noon, and night, our French-speaking neighbors offered me sweet jelly-filled sandwiches shaped like golden half-moons. The unpainted shanty structures of Seoul and the armed soldiers in olive-drab uniforms didn't clutter the streets. I slept in my own bunk bed with knobby legs. Pastel pink and waves of ruffles warmed my dreams. It was the kind of bed that little girls like Shirley Temple slept in. My parents wanted me to have whatever she had, though they seldom bought anything for themselves. My mother even permed my hair in our tiny kitchen, giving me damaged frizzies instead of adorable bouncing curls. But I didn't care. It was my crowning glory. It made me look more like "them."

My parents, however, kept gazing toward America's promise. They held on to their wishdreams of the land of the free which were filled with large-screen images of Sandra Dee in *Suddenly, Last Summer* and having *Breakfast at Tiffany's* with Audrey Hepburn. A year later, in 1969, after the birth of my brother, David—named after King David— our family of five finally migrated south of the border with our Salvation Army dishes and only three hundred dollars in our combined pockets.

Sunny southern California was our intended destination. My father chose it after reading in an almanac that the average year-round temperature there was in the pleasant seventies. It was never hit by monsoon storms or got oppressively humid. He also learned that a large population of Koreans resided in an area called *Eh Ay* (L.A.). After some searching and the use of an English/Korean dictionary, my father managed to rent a two-bedroom unit in an apartment complex near Vermont Avenue and Pico Boulevard. He had originally applied for the single, but there was some kind of code against so many people living in a one-bedroom. My father thought it was an odd law. He grew up sleeping with his five brothers and sisters in the same cramped space, and no one complained.

In that neighborhood, you could smell a bouquet of strange spices and listen to folks arguing and laughing in exotic tongues. It was the first time I tasted napkin-thin tortillas and Indian curry, and saw *ajumahs* (middle-aged aunties) wearing fiery saris that revealed their paunchy bellies. Where was Shirley? There was one girl, Patty, who lived on the second floor near the emergency exit. She had the same blond hair, but it was stringy and usually oily, and her clothes were unwashed and dirty. Patty taught me how to make butter Popsicles. She'd take a bar of hard butter out of the refrigerator and stick a wooden chopstick I'd given her into the center and lick it until it slipped off the stick. My mother thought it was a good idea. She'd heard that butter and milk and processed cheese were good for our bodies. It'd make us grow tall and meaty so we could fit into the already-made department store clothes. But they had this funny, sour odor that made people stink, and I knew where Patty's stained hands had been.

We didn't stay there long though. My parents didn't want us to mislearn English. They worried that we'd mix up our *r*'s with *l*'s and *v*'s and *b*'s like they did and cripple our chances at success. They wanted us to speak the language as well as a "native" person. That meant white. Never mind that authentic Native Americans weren't white, but brown and olive like us. So we moved from neighborhood to neighborhood—a total of five times before my thirteenth birthday. Eventually we settled in an orange tract house cushioned in the San Fernando Valley, where there were plenty of bagel shops and only one Chinese restaurant. My parents specifically picked the area because the local public high school had produced students with some of the highest SAT scores in the state.

While my parents worked long, grueling hours, six days a week, to pay off the mortagage on our suburban home, I mastered microwaving hot dogs and packing my own lunches. I understood at a young age that it was my duty to get straight A's and enter college. A college degree was insurance against owning a grocery store. Without supervision, I never missed a day of school; I was never tardy. I paid attention to my teachers and studied hard from the textbooks that taught me much more than English and mathematics. In history class, I discovered that the "founding" feminists with sunken eyelids had lifted my sentence issued at birth as a woman. Their organized marches and bra bonfires raised my stock equal to any son in America. I was no longer cast as a second-class citizen and fated to servicing a husband by the age of twenty-five. Suddenly, I had options, as many options as there were cereal boxes at the supermarkets. I wanted to try them all, try them twice, feeling that I would not be penalized but, rather, rewarded for my spunky spirit.

I balked at my uncles and male cousins sitting like stuffed Buddhas at the low dining table as their sweaty-faced wives refilled their *soju* shot glasses and cut their meat. Jabbing their kimchee-stained chopsticks at my defiant face, they accused me of being an unnatural girl. In their slanted, bloodshot eyes, my refusal to submit to a woman's "natural" instinct to get married and birth a dozen babies went against nature. I wasn't a "real" woman. I was a freak. "You don't care about future? You change thinking or no Korean man want you," they warned, clucking their tongues against the roof of their mouths.

That was perfectly fine with me. I wanted to distance myself, to be out of their reach. Nothing attracted me to their patriarchal culture which demanded I kowtow to Confucius' sexist commands even while on majestic American soil. I knew I deserved more than what Korean men offered their indentured wives. I knew firsthand how "American" guys treated women. They didn't judge or sneer or call me demeaning names: "rotten fruit," "woman-child," "unnatural." They didn't shame me because I spoke remedial Korean and my entire recipe repertoire consisted of microwaved hot dogs, packaged ramen, and sticky white rice. They were enchanted by the fact that I could even roll off a few choice phrases in another language, that I had an electric rice cooker (and a spare in case it broke down).

"American" guys didn't come with ancestral baggage and archaic expectations. They gladly serviced me. They opened doors, rose when I approached a table, and offered to cut my meat. They weren't turned off by smart women who liked to debate and discuss. They affirmed my intelligence, didn't see it as anything strange. They weren't concerned with losing face.

When I entered my twenties, I noticed my parents no longer watched the old John Wayne movies, nor did they insist I eat processed cheese. The fridge was filled with marinated anchovies, oxtail stew, and ten different varieties of kimchee. The potent smell of garlic and red pepper invaded the homogenized milk and the strawberry ice cream tasted fishy. The television was constantly fixed on Channel 18, the Korean station. My parents pleaded with me to sit down next to them on the couch, munch on some toasted dry squid, and view the news being transmitted from Korea. They knew I could barely follow the words. In our house my siblings and I spoke English and my parents spoke Konglish—a "lowbrid" of Korean and English.

It was all so schizophrenic. First they pushed me to acculturate and to follow the American way and then in the next breath they pressured me to try to speak better Korean and to join the Korean Students' Association at UCLA. They wanted me to get rid of my tan and worn cowboy boots and act more ladylike so I could catch a respectable Korean bachelor brandishing a designer degree. "Did you know Joseph at 'Harbard' Medical School? We gib Joseph mommy your number." I looked at them like they were crazy.

The world had modernized, integrated, and they were still stuck in the color-coded past. I wasn't going to be swayed there. No amount of guilt or threat to ship me back across the Pacific in a nailed crate branded "Made in Korea" was going to convince me to bow my head and conform. I was never going back to Korea. I was American and I had the documentation to prove it. We had all traded in our maroon passports for navy blue ones when I was in the fifth grade.

"You Korean. You one hundred percent Korean," my mother would say, trying desperately to sear her words into my consciousness. Her panic escalated when I turned twenty-three and was still dressing as I pleased and tanning at the beach. She constantly compared me to her friends' dutiful daughters who carried Louis Vuitton handbags and let their parents match them up with men.

My father loved to regale me with long emotional stories about *the* war—mothers separated from their children, children starving, soldiers being blown up—expecting it to trigger a teary response. But I felt nothing. Not because I was incapable of feeling but because the stories sounded like folktales to me. My chest didn't ache nor did it swell when I saw our family's book of records that went back five hundred years, generations and generations of Lees, my name included. Just the mention of a Korean kid scoring a perfect SAT score in Kansas or a Korean athlete winning a Ping-Pong championship or the sight of a Hyundai on the road would ignite my parents' pride as if it were their own kid, their sister, their car.

I didn't understand their fierce pride, having been so long removed from the distant shores of Korea. They were more traditional than recent immigrants, fresh off the boat. It was as if the clock stopped as soon as they deplaned. I found myself wondering what was so great about being Korean. What was so great about being an identifiable minority? Why wouldn't they let go of their past?

To placate my parents, and simply to escape, I decided to Sojourn to my birthplace, something I'd sworn I would never do. My parents were thrilled. They prayed fervently to Jesus Christ, their white savior, that I'd come back triumphantly with a picture-perfect bridegroom. That was the furthest thing from my mind as I packed my faded 501 jeans, tight tanktops, boots, and a glossy photo of my freckle-faced then-boyfriend who was of Scottish descent.

The moment I landed at Kimpo Airport in Seoul, I was aware of how much I felt like a misfit. All my life I had tried to blend into the dominant culture and couldn't because no amount of peroxide or eye surgery could make me white. And finally, when I was in a place where everyone looked like me, I still stood out. It was upsetting. I took it for granted that I'd feel a sense of freedom. I thought I'd blend into the landscape. This wasn't the case. People stared at me with raking eyes. I became conscious of my American-girl swaggering body movements and inappropriate dress.

Collecting my courage, I traveled to the demilitarized zone on my own. I touched the high barbed-wire fence that stretched across the belly of the peninsula, which divided the country in half. I visited thousand-year-old temples and regal palace gates that had withstood modernization and centuries of battle. I met with distant cousins who welcomed me with outstreched arms into their homes and unwove heroic tales about my mother and *Halmoni* during the war. How *Halmoni* had led her young children out of communist north to the UN-backed south, ditching air raids in the process. How my mother, at the age of thirteen, saved the life of her baby sister.

I listened with such an overwhelming, insatiable thirst that when I returned to the States a year and a half later, I began to ask my parents and *Halmoni* (who had immigrated to the States some time after we did) all about the past. The past, which was no longer a time gone by, a dead weight. I now saw that it held ancient treasures. And the more I delved and discovered, the more I felt myself being steered toward a future I had never imagined for myself. I began to write. I didn't even know I could write. My family helped me knit stories into a bound book using *Halmoni's* voice. As her powerful words moved through me I was able to reflect and meditate on the delusional life I had fashioned for myself. I could feel my sense of self rising. This sparked a newfound awareness and excitement. After the book *Still Life with Rice* was published, I became a spokeswoman on Korean culture, traveling to various college campuses across the country. "Be proud. Embrace your legacy," I spouted to young Korean-American students donning extra-large Nike attire from head to feet. But the whole time I was lecturing, I had very little real understanding of what that self-concept meant. I was merely talking the talk. I hadn't fully embraced my own identity. I still gravitated toward guys who looked more like Brad Pitt and Antonio Banderas than Russell Wong or Chow Yun-Fat.

Twice, I came close to marriage with "American" guys. After all, I never declared that I would never marry. Of course I wanted to build a secure home and live happily ever after. I was just reacting to all the perennial pressure and bungled matchmakers who thought they could ask for (and collect) a hefty price for my head because I was now a published author.

I tried hard to march both of my relationships down the church aisle, but they ended more bitter than sweet. All the things that impressed my boyfriends about me in the beginning began to bother them. They got sick and tired of eating sticky rice all the time and complained about kimchee breath. They wanted to eat Italian, Mexican, even Pan-Asian, which really isn't Asian food at all. They thought it was weird that I wanted to dig the wax out of their ears with a teeny metal spoon like my mother had done for me as an expression of her affection. They felt crowded when I began each sentence with "us" and "ours" instead of "yours" and "mine." In their blue eyes, my desire to be with them all the time made me weak and unattractive. I was no longer the strong, smart, beautiful woman they fell in love with. They wanted to be in a relationship where both people were driving but on the same road in their own cars.

I didn't understand. I had my own car.

My parents, who were my lifelong constant role models, were rarely apart. They shared one closet, one banking account, dipped their spoons into the same soup bowl, and never used the word "boundaries," unless referring literally to geography. From the instant they held hands, they were committed to a mutual future. All personal needs and greed were relinquished and they became one well-functioning unit. It was unspoken that certain sacrifices had to be made for the survival and strength of our family. Independence and selfishness disturbed the household. What was mine was yours: clothes, cars, and prescription medicine. We used what we needed, but always sparingly. Growing up, none of our bedroom doors had locks and we weren't required to knock for entrance. These things were familiar and comforting to me. But the guys I had loved wanted their own soup bowls and wanted me to pay for half, even though they ate more.

I really didn't understand. I was devastated to find a different version of the same sexist thinking about what a woman's role should be. It was agonizing to accept the end, let go of what I had worked so hard to nurture. I wanted to believe they'd never leave me. In the boxed-in world I came from, couples stayed together through thick and thin, forever. My grandparents survived the Japanese occupation, two wars, imprisonment by North Korean communists, and starvation. My parents made it through immigration, discrimination, and all other types of gaping cultural differences.

I kept wondering about these men. What was wrong with *them*. What was I doing to *them* that was so horrible? Why did they give up on *us* so easily? Then it painfully dawned on me that I had been choosing the wrong guys. Attraction was based on race rather than the content of a person's character or compatibility. I was no better than the freaks who pursued me because they wanted their geisha-girl fetish fed. Worst of all, I had rejected men who looked like my father—my father who had never abandoned me or let me down. When my mother used to work late at the garment factory, my father took over the cooking and cleaning after his long commute home from his electrical engineering job. He taught me how to ride a bike and roller-skate fast. He was the one who told me if I studied diligently and got good grades, I could become a Ph.D., diplomat, or whatever I wanted to be. When I started writing my first book, he was there to help me every step of the way, excavating research material, translating tapes, and enduring my endless mood swings.

I was consumed with shame. My actions had been saying "Fuck you" to my father. "Fuck you" to the group of men that he belonged to. More than anything, I wanted to stop being so hateful and make amends. That was when I consciously decided to seek out an Asian man.

This decision was scarier than the time I was caught in the middle of a tear-gas demonstration in Seoul or the time I was accosted by Soviet guards on the train to Prague. I struggled with my fears. They were very real, but it wasn't about deferring to a man or having my feet bound. I had too much attitude for that to happen. I'd give 'em Helie. What spooked me was the incestuous feeling of dating a brother, and the unknown—especially the unknown. Inexperienced, I had bought into the stereotype of small penises and inadequate foreplay. Would I have to give up sex and passion? Passion fed my writing. I never saw my father kiss my mother or reach for her tenderly or heard moans seep out through their bedroom door. The romantic dramas I happened to catch on Channel 18 were juvenile and clumsy and badly written. My Asian girlfriends didn't discuss their sexual encounters with their Asian boyfriends like my white and African-American girlfriends, who freely shared in explicit detail.

Michael was the one who actually sought me out. We met back at UCLA. He was also a Korean-born American. His family had immigrated to the States later than mine, when he was ten. We kept in contact through the post-college years and after his move to Hong Kong to work as an investment banker. At his invitation, I flew to Hong Kong to spend some time with him . . . just to see.

My fears were quickly forgotten. Michael was a great lover, the perfect fit. We laid in bed drenched in sweat, talking late into the night about marriage, children, and the future. We skipped over the whole dating phase and moved right into being an old, familiar couple. We finished off each other's sentences and dipped our spoons into the same soup bowl. Without having to go into a long diatribe about Korean history, cuisine, or any explanation of *han* (guilt), he understood everything. With him, I could finally shed my decorative albeit heavy armor. I didn't have to perform stupid dog tricks to be accepted. Together, I believed, we would make a strong partnership centered on *jung*—an infinitive connection.

My parents loved Michael. It would have been so easy, but once the euphoria settled, it became painfully evident that our relationship wasn't working either. We both wanted it to so badly and yet our cultural and generational differences still proved to be unbridgeable. We were riding in the same car, but fighting to drive on different roads. I tried for a long time to fit into Michael's frame and just be a silent passenger because I refused to accept the death of another relationship. I was so terrified of being single again. Voices inside my head kept marking off the time, squeezing it. "Thirty. Thirty-one. Thirty-two. Thirty-three." And I kept thinking about my parents. I didn't want to let them down. I owed them this one thing after everything they had sacrificed for me.

At thirty-four, I am still single. The realization knocks me off my feet every now and then when I pass by a couple or a pregnant woman. Everything I thought I knew and was passionate about in my fun, fearless twenties is all mixed up in my head. It was naive of me to think I could just unilaterally wipe out my ancestral heritage and then reinstate it at a whim. It was naive of me to think I had come full circle when I started dating Michael. I failed to see that somewhere in between being Korean and being American, there was a place of identity for me.

Today I'm at a point in my life where I no longer wish to be someone other than who I am. It has taken me a long time to get here. I know somehow there's a way for my split halves to fit together. But I can no longer rely on denial or scattered faith or a wedding band to make what is not working in my life work. Just recently I began therapy. It sounds weird to say "my therapist." The admission gives me an uneasy cramping in the pit of my stomach, where I hold all my secret worries. In my family, you don't flash your problems. It's shameful. *What would people think?* You deal with it quietly and internally so as not to draw attention to yourself. We have done it this way for centuries. But it hasn't worked and isn't working for me. After the breakup with Michael, I suffered a major depression. I slept a lot, buried under the covers, humiliated. And, when I finally did emerge from my darkened place, no one knew I was lost because I wore an unmovable, protective mask. I coped.

But coping isn't enough anymore. I want to live fully.

I've made a determination to look honestly at myself, at the real reason why I have resisted intimacy with Asian men. The possibility that they might bring me closer to myself was terrifying. But the problem isn't with them—the boys, the guys, the men. There's this subconscious, lingering sense that I, as a female, am not good enough. This is the most important journey of my life. This is my process of becoming. I need to look at the hurt and rage at a very deep level, even at the risk of disassembling Helie. Only then will I taste wholeness as a Korean, an American, a woman in this society. Only then will I be able to celebrate my heritage. And be free.

Becoming Midwestern

KYOKO MORI

A FEW MONTHS AGO IN LAKE GENEVA, WISCONSIN, a librarian asked me if I felt "more and more American these days." *I've lived here for twenty-two years*, I thought. The question was particularly disappointing because we were at an annual convention of the Wisconsin Library Association, where I had been invited to read my work as a Wisconsin author—my graduate degrees are from the University of Wisconsin, Milwaukee—and I now live and write in Green Bay. The material I read made many references to these facts. The librarian who asked the question, however, assumed that after all these years I was still slowly adjusting myself to "being in America," that living here every day was not something I took for granted, the way she must take it for granted. Even though all of my writing life has taken place in the American Midwest, I was still considered to be a foreigner whose identity and allegiance were at some formative stage—more and more but not fully American.

I felt defensive enough to give a snide answer. "I don't know what it means for anyone to feel *American* or *un-American*. I'm not sure if *feeling American* is something that happens to people in degrees, as in *more and more*." The question made me defensive for the same reason that another often-asked question does: "When you first came to this country from Japan, what was the hardest thing for you to adjust to?" When people ask these questions, there is something they want and expect to hear. The stories they are waiting for—of a brave but disadvantaged immigrant woman trying to understand an unfamiliar language, missing the customs and the foods of the homeland, overcoming one "culture shock" after another—have nothing to do with me. I resent being expected to tell such stories because I have none to tell and also because, even when they are the true stories for many first-generation immigrant women, there is something self-congratulatory or condescending in most listeners' attitudes. The stories of immigration are often heard by non-immigrants in the spirit of "I am so lucky that I was always an American." They are the adult, quality-of-life versions of "those poor starving children in China" for whom we were supposed to eat all the food on our plates.

The city where I spent my first two years in the Midwest—Rockford, Illinois—is not far from Lake Geneva. It's a medium-sized, industrial town an hour and a half north of Chicago. When I went there, I was twenty; I had decided to transfer from the college I was attending in Kobe, Japan, to its sister college, Rockford College. The day I left Japan, I knew that I would never go back there to live. There was no future in Japan for a woman from my upper-middle-class milieu who wanted to be a writer more than she wanted to be a nice suburban homemaker. Even though I only had a student visa at the time, I was determined to live my adult life in the States. I had been bilingual since I was a child. Many of my friends in Japan were Americans. I had already spent a year in Mesa, Arizona, attending high school as an AFS student. I was prepared for being in America. Being in a small town was another matter.

All the way from Chicago's O'Hare Airport to Rockford, the bus went through flat stretches of cornfields. Sitting in the back with my two suitcases, I began to cry. I had grown up in a big city among tall buildings, busy storefronts, and crowded residential neighborhoods. The vast, flat landscape outside the bus window inspired an almost existential fear: I imagined giant hawks coming to carry me off. Things didn't look much better when the bus arrived in Rockford. The college was on the edge of town, in the middle of cornfields. Nearby, there were a few gas stations, a Stop-and-Go, a Dutch Pantry where you could get weak coffee and greasy doughnuts, and a motel that was supposed to look like a Swiss chalet. For the first two weeks, the girl from the

Bronx and I marveled at squirrels crossing the road right in front of cars. I walked two miles to the nearest magazine stand, looking for the magazines I was used to reading in Kobe—*New Yorker, Atlantic Monthly, National Geographic.* They only had *Good Housekeeping* and some car and hunting magazines. This is what I have to tell people who ask me about my hardest adjustment when I came to America: There was more American culture in my Japanese city than in a medium-sized Midwestern city like Rockford; I missed the magazines, movies, paintings. Back home, I hopped on the train and went to museums if I had a few hours in the afternoon. From Rockford, it was a two-hour bus ride through the cornfields back to Chicago, where I stood in front of paintings by Georgia O'Keeffe and Mark Rothko in the Art Institute on weekends and cried—relieved, finally, to see something familiar.

But I did not mourn the life of going to museums, coffee shops, bookstores, and concerts in the big city I had left behind. It was a life I would have lost, had I stayed. One by one, my friends in Kobe got engaged to the sons of their fathers' business associates. Soon, they sent me their wedding pictures—their faces painted white with rice powder, their heads covered with the traditional lacquered wigs, my friends scarcely looked like themselves. Their elaborate weddings involved three, four changes of clothing. The last pictures showed them leaving the reception in prim dresses and pillbox hats that were oddly *retro*, making my friends look like Japanese Jackie Kennedys. They seemed not only an ocean away but also decades away, stuck in some time warp. Their days of going to museums and concerts with girlfriends were long over now. If I had stayed, I'd have been alone anyway.

At Rockford, I found a home in books. I continued to read the writers I had been reading since high school: Jane Austen, the Brontës, Edith Wharton, Sylvia Plath, Emily Dickinson, Walt Whitman, J.D. Salinger, Ernest Hemingway. In what might be called "the life of the mind," I had been an immigrant long before I left the country and went to Rockford. My reading and thinking self had immigrated to the world of English and American literature during high school because the Japanese authors we read seemed so very cerebral and authoritarian. Even the people who were considered to be eccentrics and nonconformists—

Mishima, for instance, or Tanizaki—wrote books that were ponderous with big ideas and dark, heavy symbolism. In their work, I did not find the moments that rang true to me—as when Holden Caulfield is upset to see an obsenity scrawled on the wall, or when Emma Woodhouse offers Jane Fairfax her carriage because she is ashamed of the selfish and stuck-up way she's been behaving. Though I didn't feel completely at home in the city of Rockford, I felt rooted in the books I read in my classes at the college.

In Rockford and Milwaukee, I studied creative writing as well as literature. In my writing, too, my immigration had been long under way. Back in Japan, I had attended a private junior and senior high school where we studied English with American teachers, whose teaching method emphasized giving detailed and specific feedback on our writing, instead of the vague words of wisdom that their Japanese counterparts tended to give. As a result, by the time I was eighteen, I knew more about writing in English than I knew about writing in Japanese. One of the reasons I left Japan at twenty was that I wanted to study creative writing, which is not taught in Japan, in Japanese or in English. Because all of my formal training as a writer took place in an American setting, and because I only write in English, I always thought of myself as an American writer—a writer who has learned much from contemporary American literature and expects to be measured by its tradition. I could not think of myself as a Japanese writer because I don't indentify with the Japanese literary tradition and I don't write in Japanese.

The story of my immigration is also a story of becoming an adult. I've spent the last twenty-two years in the American Midwest: two years in Rockford, five years in Milwaukee, fifteen years in Green Bay. In that time, I've experienced the big events that make up the lives of many American adults: pursuing and completing advanced studies, finding employment, getting married and divorced, buying a car, buying a house. I have been an American citizen since 1984: I've voted, paid taxes, signed petitions, volunteered in a local election campaign. I have only experienced these events—events which are marks of full adulthood—in the American Midwest. Maybe that's why I'm miffed by people asking me if I feel American. As an adult, I have never been or felt anything else.

Another important fact of my immigrant life is that except for my five years in Milwaukee, I have lived in small Midwestern towns where people think that some store or someone's house is "clear across town" if the trip there takes more than twenty minutes by car. Most people in Green Bay come from Green Bay—they did not grow up somewhere else and move here. It's a big event for someone to relocate from the east side of town to the west side. There have never been many people of color in any part of Green Bay. Most people are third- or fourth-generation European immigrants—their grandparents or great-grandparents came from Holland, Sweden, Norway, Germany, Poland, Belgium, Czechkoslovakia. This is Willa Cather country, though the people themselves may not be very aware of their own ethnic heritage. Many families started as farm families and then became working-class people in the paper mills, and now, in what is called "the service industry." Along the way, they came to think of themselves as having always been "American." I don't fit into these people's preconceived notions about Asian women as war brides or refugees. I am forced to confront the gap between the stereotypes people have about me, on one hand, and who I think I am, on the other. My neighbors might not remember which country their grandmother came from, but if I had children and grandchildren, they would always be asked if they thought of themselves as American.

So I don't think of myself as American in the unquestioning way that people around me think of themselves. No one of color can do that, living in Willa Cather country. But certainly, I don't identify myself as a citizen of any other place. I'm not one of those people who argues that countries don't matter, that we are all citizens of the world at large, fellow residents in the international global community. Undoubtedly, that is true on some level, but most of us want to classify and identify ourselves in a more *micro* sort of way, and I am no exception. Reading a newspaper is a good test. I go through the international news with a sense of intellectual and civil duty: As an educated person, I ought to stay informed. An article about whether the city council is likely to give a go-ahead to the new bike trail in my town or one about some altercations in a bar between two county board members who have always hated each other—now, that is real news. My eyes skip everything else and go to those headlines.

A further way I can identify my American citizenship is to say that I am an Asian-American or a Japanese American. These are classifications that are important to me. Several years ago, I was part of a group in Madison called Asian and Pacific American Women's Alliance. We got together once or twice a month to have dinner, organize presentations and readings, raise money for special events. I felt a sense of belonging with women whose backgrounds were similar but also varied: Some of us were first-generation immigrants, others were third or even fourth; many of us taught at colleges; all of us had other issues we were deeply committed to, such as reproductive choice, environmental protection, or gay rights. We were a good community because we were similar and different. I was sorry when many of the women moved away and the group dispersed. Being with these women gave me a stronger, more immediate sense of being Asian-American. Maybe that's how an identity based on who we are differs from an identity based on what we do. If I were to live in a town where no one else runs, my sense of being a runner would be just as strong and immediate as when I belonged to a running club in Milwaukee. But my sense of being Asian-American feels a little more abstract when I don't have an Asian-American community to belong to.

The Japanese part of the Japanese-American is important because I discovered Japan by being an American as an adult. When I lived in Japan as a child, being Japanese was something I took for granted at times and rebelled against at other times. In the very Westernized big city where I grew up, what remained Japanese were the male-dominated expectations and attitudes that underlay every marriage, family, and other personal relationships. These were the very things I wanted to reject because they threatened my ambition to become a writer instead of someone's wife and mother. But when I left Japan and was not threatened everyday by these oppressive aspects of Japanese culture, I began to remember the things I loved and was nourished by: the flowers my mother and grandmother grew in their gardens, the Buddhist altar where my maternal grandparents burned incense for the souls of their ancestors, the mountains and the sea of my hometown. Sometimes, we have to leave a place to realize the impact it had on us. We make a place our own by the act of leaving it. Living in the Midwest and thinking/writing about Japan has done that for me.

Now, I am on the verge of another departure. I have just accepted a five-year teaching appointment at Harvard. After twenty-two years in Illinois and Wisconsin, I will be moving to Boston. I already know that I will miss the corn and hay fields where I've learned to identify the various kinds of sparrows. My existential fear of open spaces is long gone. I have come to love the landscape of the Midwest and its various natural elements. I've learned the names of the wildflowers that grow in ditches near cornfields. If a hawk comes swooping down, I can tell if it's a red-tailed or a Cooper's. Walking through the woods on the bluff of Lake Michigan, I know this isn't my native country—but neither is it for most people who now live in Wisconsin, so the land seems as much mine as anyone else's. Maybe in Boston, I'll walk along the Charles River with my binoculars, hoping to see the same blue herons and killdeer and pintails I'm used to seeing here.

The Midwest has left an imprint on my work. Many of my poems were inspired by walking, running, bicycling, bird-watching, and gardening in various parts of Wisconsin. Although my first two novels were set in Japan, many of the characters and events actually originated in my experiences as an adult here; the novel I'm currently working on is set in Milwaukee. My last book of essays has a subtitle: *On Being a Woman Caught Between Two Cultures.* The two cultures I refer to are the Japanese culture of my childhood and the Midwestern American culture of my adulthood. As a reader, too, I've come to appreciate the portrayal of small-town Midwestern characters by authors like Garrison Keillor and Jon Hassler. Though I don't share their ethnic and religious backgrounds, I understand their characters' complete acceptance of their own and other people's eccentricity. In the small towns in the Midwest, people are not obsessively driven to psychoanalyze themselves or each other. If someone behaves in an odd way, people around him or her would politely accommodate that behavior so long as it's not malicious. This polite but ironic acceptance of human frailties is at the heart of these authors' comic gift. It's something I've come to identify with both in life and literature and will surely miss.

A move across five states at forty-two feels just as large—perhaps even larger—than a move across the ocean at twenty. When I left Japan, I was only leaving a place I had been born to. I didn't have a sense of ownership or attachment that comes from having chosen a place. This time, I'll be leaving a place I chose a long time ago, for a place I am choosing now. I'd like to think of the upcoming move as Part Two of my immigration. An immigrant is a person who is able to move on and be nourished by the place she has left as well as by the place she has arrived in. Just as I needed to become American to also become Japanese, moving out east will complete my settlement in the Midwest. As an immigrant, I'll know how to let go and hold on at the same time.

Recalling a Child of October

IRINA REYN

SINCE MY ARRIVAL IN AMERICA, acquiring outsider status has always
been easy. A couple of weeks ago, I was visiting my former Russian
literature professor at Rutgers University. Three other Russian girls were
waiting for him outside his office. While waiting, they entered into a
conversation, during which they realized that they were all recent immigrants. They were speaking in Russian. Eventually the topic turned
to "Americanized" Russians. It was obvious from their dismissive tone
that the girls had contempt for these "Americanized" Russians. "They
think they're so cool because they came when they were ten or eleven,"
one scoffed. "Yeah, but they're not Russians. Not really," another replied. "They refuse to speak Russian and only hang out with Americans." "But," the first chimed in, "they will never be Americans no
matter how hard they try." The girls quickly looked over at me.

I knew then that standing apart from the group—this particular one
or any other—would be a theme that would play itself out for the rest
of my life. If those three girls represented my Russian culture, I was
definitely not a part of it. They intimately knew a country I have not
stepped foot in since I was seven. Recognition of this fact brought about
a familiar mixture of anger and envy. It seemed as if their identity had
been fully established, while mine may never truly be. I realize that until
I reconcile my interwoven allegiances, I might always be the one leaning

against a canary yellow wall, pretending not to hear the clipped cadences of conversation swirling around me.

Having so few scraps of memory from my first seven years in Russia, I try to will myself to remember important moments. It is as though by fleshing out those pictures in my mind, I am shaping them into a foundation solid enough to hold up my identity as a Russian-American. I most fear forgetting the details of my childhood. Without them I will never really know myself. The images that flick through my mind are brief random snatches of time—mushroom hunting in the woods, nightmares of the witch Baba Yaga, burning-hot miniature milk bottles lining my back as a treatment for a cold—but none are as vivid as my first day of school. On the evening of August 31, I went to bed feverishly. The following day was one I had heard about from parents and grandparents, from *Spokoinii noche, malishi* (Good night, children), the one television show I watched from 8:30 to 9:00 P.M. every night. It was a day talked about in hushed whispers with my friends in kindergarten, and fictionalized in books I could read as well as ones read to me.

It was 1980, the first day of school in Moscow and I would be in first grade. That day, the first day of school, was anticipated as much as, if not more than, a birthday. Families would escort children to school with flowers to hand to their teachers. Parents would greet each other gaily in the schoolyard assessing their future compatriots at rallies and other school functions or greeting friends and parents from the past year. The day was celebrated as a national holiday. Most importantly, the uniform could finally be worn. The special one for holidays. It was the customary black dress with a white pinafore, not the everyday black pinafore. It would be laid out on the back of my chair, perhaps on the backs of the chairs of all the seven-year-olds in the Soviet Union.

I still remember tossing in my bed until I saw hints of daylight edging through my lace curtain and finally resigning myself to the excitement of the day. I recall getting up and fingering the starched material, tracing the lace of the white pinafore with my fingers, pinning the white bow clumsily on my head, which with short hair was no easy task. Patiently sitting in my wooden chair, I waited for my parents to awake and enter the door to my room, sweeping me up in the chaos of the day. Having no camera at home, I was taken to a professional photographer to commemorate the day. The result was an unsmiling girl with her head cocked to one side, her hands folded on a book, the background a blending of solemn tones, shades of black and gray.

No other first day of school—not my first day of third grade in Brooklyn, my first day of junior high in Queens, or my first day of high school in New Jersey—would ever feel the same to me, have the same sense of rightness. I was a child at home in the world, in the place that made sense and belonged to me. I was supported in all my actions not only by my parents and peers but by the communist state, which at every step was always there, urging me on proudly, telling me that what I was doing was perfect, exactly the way it should be done. In November of that year, I was an *Octabryonok*, something I knew was to be treated with pride, not only because I was wearing the white pinafore, but also something to do with the formal nature of the occasion: the principal's voice during the rally that day, the poster of Lenin pointing his finger at me, the accentuation of the authoritative horn above all other instruments. Only later would I discover that I was taking part in an initiation ceremony enfolding me into the communist state. As an *Octabryonok*, I, along with countless schoolchildren across the country, was symbolically celebrated as a child of the October Revolution, when the Bolsheviks, led by Lenin, overthrew the government and seized the country in the name of the "people." The reason the victory of the October Revolution was celebrated in November is that Russia accelerated their calendar two weeks ahead to comply with the rest of the world's.

In the school auditorium, we first-graders were soberly pinned by elder classmates with a red star on which a childhood picture of Lenin was emblazoned. We were to wear these stars displayed on the left side of our uniforms at all times. With my status as a citizen of the state secure, I was flushed with triumph and the knowledge that I was enveloped in a community. What I didn't know on that same November day was that at that moment my parents were already making all the necessary plans for our move to the United States, to New York. After being on a two-year waiting list, they, along with thousands of other Russian Jews, were finally allowed to leave. When I was told this news the following February, I shrugged and went ice skating with Olga from two buildings down. America meant nothing at all to me. I had no concept of its place in the world or its relationship to my country. I doggedly went on with my routine, disregarding the great change that was about to take place.

I bid farewell to my friends from Moscow and my Ukrainian summer dacha in a daze, half-listening to my mother's promises that America would have boxes of fifty crayons and dolls with long hair and extensive wardrobes. Growing up in a provincial Ukrainian village, my mother always dreamed about crayons herself, turning over in her mind the smooth surfaces of things she would reinvent. Putting me to sleep on the few nights before we left, she regaled me with fictional descriptions of the sparkly new place we were going to, then played an English lesson on my record player. "Apple, *yabloko*," I would hear a man's deep voice say before anxiously drifting into an uncomfortable sleep. "Apple, *yabloko*."

Our first apartment was in Flatbush, Brooklyn, in a one-bedroom which I shared with my parents. We continued the life we led in Russia. Most of our entertainment centered on food: salad Olivier with its mayonnaisey peas, potatos, and apples; warm borscht with a white island of sour cream in the middle; piroshkis, crumbly and doughy, emitting a garlic potatoey warmth. Perpetual toasts were made to the adults, to children, to America—the clinking of glasses amidst cigarette smoke and loud conversation with the backdrop of a Persian rug hung on the wall. Our apartment was a confused fusion of the old and the new—*Charlie's Angels* and the Smurfs melded with my Russian records, Judy Blume slowly eclipsed Pushkin, Blondie and Madonna drowned out Alla Pugacheva. My parents were all too happy to let the transformation take place—it would allow me to slip painlessly and naturally into this new culture. Suddenly, my parents turned to me to construe this new world for them. I reveled in my power, child turned patient teacher.

They would sit amused, listening to my erudite deconstruction of why Chachi was the sexiest boy in America, or my authoritative translation of an episode of *All in the Family*.

I remember so little from those two years in Brooklyn before we moved to Queens. But I remember the unfamiliar feeling of fear when I went out of the apartment alone. There would be lines of elderly people sitting on their rainbow beach chairs on Ocean Avenue, looking at the passersby and gossiping. I remember facing the bullies during lunch period at school who tried to wrestle pizza out of the children who were easy prey, the coziness of a decorated tree on New Year's Eve, drooping heavy with hidden caramels in its folds. During the first year in school I frantically tried to hide the fact that I could not speak English. In the first month of third grade I took to doodling instead of writing, passionately believing there was a possibility my teacher would not realize my essay "What I Did Last Summer" had suddenly become a series of interlocking ovals in my able hand. Despite my parents' concern that I would never speak English fluently, by the end of my first year, in third grade, I had already won the spelling bee. That did not stop the kids from calling me "commie" every chance they got.

Upon first hearing this slur, I was perplexed at its meaning, and asking my parents produced no answers because they were equally confused. Apart from technological competition with the U.S., my parents were not taught to hate the Americans. So I had nobody to explain this heady insult that would not completely disappear until college, mostly because the children themselves did not know the meaning of their own words. It was only during glasnost and the Gorbachev period that people around me became aware of the need to shift their thoughts and language. Over the years my definition has evolved for Americans around me. Since my childhood corresponded with the end of the Cold War, I was at first viewed with suspicion by other children, in high school with dismissal, and in college with fascination in my assimilated otherness.

I enjoyed school, especially English class, but never understood American children's loyalties and friendships, which seemed to me to be arbitrary and ephemeral. I was awed by their command of space, but sensed that once claimed, the space was not to be shared. I was not able to formulate the impression that American children are raised with a certain degree of confidence, independence, and self-reliance, that the degree to which relationships are needed seemed to be alleviated due to their ability to maneuver smoothly in their environment. Being born of a collective country, Russians' friendships take on the covenant of family and the relationships tend to be full of earnest ardor and vehement devotion.

Not surprisingly, my shyness and intensity drove people away and I tended to gravitate to other immigrants like myself, who felt the same displacement. Yet at the same time, I believed that English was empowerment and studied it worshipfully. I sensed the power of language in classes and on the playgrounds. I noticed the way the teachers leaned toward the more articulate students and recognized the status of those children who straightened their spines while eloquently retorting to an assailant's affront. Instinctively I knew that having control of English was one of the few chances I had of not being swallowed up here, both as an immigrant and as a female.

Eventually, I got the fifty crayons, in a shockingly yellow box with all those decadent colors arranged in such an orderly way, edges so blunt and beautiful. I caught the fever of childish consumerism, begging for a Cabbage Patch Kid and a My Little Pony, whose pink tail I combed lovingly three times a day. However, asking for things made me feel guilty, because I could not separate myself from the feeling that money should not be squandered needlessly. Spending quarters on the arcade was an anguished enticement for me and when I gave in, the minutes of Pac-Man ended up being devoid of pleasure.

Only when I came to America did I encounter a culture that allowed for indulgences, that assured us that it was okay to buy something for the sheer pleasure of its purchase. Being accustomed to the ceremonial quality of the gift, the sudden surprise of a new object in my hands, I was thrilled with the constant possibility of procurement. But internally I carried the acute tension of desire and limitation, of guilt and fulfillment. An annual temptation was a nearby carnival, whose booths glittered with the fortuitous promise of America itself—getting something for practically nothing. For only a handful of change, it was possible to win an enormous striped yellow tiger! However, after a few dollars my only prize was a stuffed forest green foot which I immediately christened Charleston and slept with for a few years before it got lost. I used to scrutinize that foot, hanging in my room on a thin gold string, and wanted to weep for its pathetic uselessness, for its unworthy creation. I felt it was my duty to love this displaced stuffed appendage.

In America, people clamor for belonging and acceptance, but it seems so much simpler to remain jagged and edgy. A duality exists within me that permeates every aspect of my life. My Russianness wants so badly to be like everyone else, but as an American I am proud of an insight into another world that I somehow have a claim on. This split divides me until everything in my life is defined by its relation to its opposite. Yet I can never say I am a citizen of both countries. That is the uniqueness of the Russian-American experience. Russian Jews left with a bittersweet taste in their mouths, something I may have been too young to experience, but the residue of which was always visible in the adult conversations.

This residue was particularly evident in their relieved Thanksgiving toasts, the unfamiliar glow of a Sabbath candle and sporadic memories filtered through a cloudy lens. Russia is a country that requires passionate devotion to the motherland, but as Jews my parents were always relegated to the sidelines. They knew nationalism was something they could hardly afford. So they came here not with a lifelong passion for all things American but rather with mixed feelings. They viewed the move as an escape to a land of opportunity or at the very least fairness, where they could get what they worked for.

A few weeks ago, I brought home a photography book that compared original photographs of Stalin's Russia to the ones which Stalin doctored before showing them to the masses. I found it fascinating to see how important people who were later shot and killed for being "enemies of the people" had literally been erased from the photographs with awkward gaps left in what had once been their place. I wondered how it would feel suddenly to discover the suppleness of history. How do people reconcile living in a country that deceived them for seventy years while at the same time coaxed them into a fervent love of their homeland?

My parents sat well into the night looking at those photographs of executed people. They did not know who Trotsky was before coming to America and never wondered why their employers forced them to go out to Red Square and cheer with red flags when a foreign dignitary arrived. It is while listening to these stories that I feel the most American, and Russia becomes a distant and unwieldy thing, its relevance relegated to books, television, and memories.

It is with these contradictory feelings that I view a return to Russia in the near future. I know I need to go there to understand fully myself, but I am so afraid to be disappointed by the place, by the people. But what makes me most frightened about going back is the prospect of feeling no warmth there, no home, as though the country would wearily and dismissively say to me, "Why did you come here? Go back to America. There is no essence of you here." I fear that when I visit childhood friends and relatives, we will sit across a wooden table and they will see only a plumed, foreign creature eyeing them wildly.

I know I cannot return to my country of birth idealistically thinking I will be enveloped in its history, greeted as one of its own. Being a severely economically depressed country, there is no indulgence for humoring my nostalgia. I am often advised not to interact too intimately with Russians when I visit for fear that I would be viewed with envy and bitterness for my comfortable lifestyle. Apart from the "New Russians" who greatly profited from the recent capitalistic surge, most Russians are barely scraping by. Being pragmatic by necessity, my relatives would not understand my not working in a practical vocation like engineering or computer programming, but instead living single in Manhattan, with no prospect of a family of my own before me, a self-indulgent writer. I know how lucky I am to have the luxury of commodious analysis without the personal suffering.

New York is teeming with Russian immigrants, and I always overhear snippets of conversation on the subway, in the Century 21 department store, in the produce section of the supermarket. My instinct is to join the conversation, invite myself over for dinner as though they are all my relatives. "I'll bring cognac, take off my shoes," I imagine telling them in explanation of such a seemingly rude self-invitation. "I'm Irina." (For no doubt someone in their family has the same name.) I am half-surprised they don't know me or acknowledge my relation to them.

So what do I have left of Russia? Despite the pervasive Russian imprint on the Brighton Beach community in Brooklyn, I am a stranger there. The area belongs to Russians who, in their desire to patch together a past, have created a society, which, like me, has evolved into something completely different. The lavish Russian nightclubs cater to a taste for ostentatious wealth and larger-than-life entertainment I don't really share. But I make the pilgrimage for birthdays and anniversaries, still a bit in awe of the dancers in complicated sequined costumes re-creating mythical scenes of an older, more familiar Russia near tables overstuffed with food, something that most of Russia will never see. Russians gather to be among their own people, but the longer they are in this country the more removed they are from Russia itself. It is the closest thing I have to a residual instinct, though, being there among my family friends and relatives who have formed a group of their own—neither Americans nor Russians—but the émigré circle, who speak with authority about a country that is changing without them. And so the country doesn't belong to me, doesn't want me, and I struggle with that knowledge along with a residual fear that I am American now and all pretensions to another culture are just that.

However, if I want to know what I would be like had I been born in America, I need only to look at my eight-year-old sister. Leading a fully American suburban existence in New Jersey, she has never needed to dream of fifty crayons. She has two rooms in the house, every Disney video, and dozens of computer games. She goes to school with the same friends, has sleepovers, and goes trick-or-treating every Halloween. She slips easily between worlds, proudly singing the lyrics to the newest Backstreet Boys song, while at the same time knowing how to use Russian to bring about a pizza delivery. She is a child who knows her own power, shrugging when complimented, quick to display her sharp memory. My visits to my parents' house confuse her—she knows she has a sister in "Manhattan" but is jealous of my relationship to "her" parents. Over the dinner table her large brown eyes carefully regard my absorbed parents, whose hands are guided by this visiting sister. Perhaps she senses a bond from which she is excluded, a journey she was not a part of, and it makes her irritable. In private, with her friends, she is proud of an "old" sister whose shadow occupies space in the house, whose name she is mistakenly called by daily. But I envy the ease with which she navigates her world, her insouciant reaction to her environment, her confidence about her place in it.

I was home this past September when she got out of bed to face her first day of third grade. She languidly got up, brushed her teeth, scanned her closet for a suitable outfit. She finally picked out navy blue Guess? sweatpants and a deep red Guess? sweatshirt with the words "Guess? For Girls" emblazoned on it. Then she patiently waited for my mother to brush her long brown hair and ran downstairs for a bowl of Cap'n Crunch and milk. Grabbing a Lunchables (with pepperoni pizza and a Rice Krispies treat), she grabbed her electric blue JanSport backpack and hopped out the door waving to her friends in the silver car in our driveway. I look out the window affectionately at the girl that could have been me—but wasn't.

On Becoming

NELLY ROSARIO

A WOMAN BORN IN THE DOMINICAN REPUBLIC and raised in Brooklyn, New York, is expecting her first child. Having lingered in many communities but remaining firmly rooted in none, having named and renamed herself, she is like a stamped travel trunk. She needs to constantly rub the compass in her belly and look within for her true North. This woman has flat feet. Always a nauseous feeling of vertigo, disoriented on the land where she feels both native and foreign.

Balance is often difficult for this woman, but she keeps traveling. Sometimes she sits in her Brooklyn apartment horrified that she lives in a country where scientists fiddle with genes and black men are still dragged to their deaths. Other times she finds herself exhausted on a plane back from a summer stay in Santo Domingo, glad (and surprised she is glad) to finally see the island of her birth shrink away through the window. Where's home for this woman? She can't completely control the world around her; she herself must become home.

After twenty-seven years it's still hard for me to believe that I am that buoying woman full of new life, flat-footed, wanting the right shoe to keep balance and walk my own path. Who the hell am I, really, I ask all the time, and with more probing, who do I want to ultimately become?

To become anything involves a process of gradual transformation from one state of being to another. Caterpillars become butterflies. Children become adults. I spend most of my life in a state of constant transformation. My views of the world change with the calendar dates. One year I like my wardrobe, the next year I'm disgusted. I'm not satisfied with myself for too long, wanting new beginnings: a new haircut, a change of address, more schooling, increased spiritual growth. So I fumble through life in this haze of changes, leaving a trail of discarded husks. Occasionally, in moments of intense reflection (and writing), I go back to one of these husks to sniff it, to see if some of my original essence is still there. I'll try one on for size, maybe take pieces of it to graft onto the newer me. Still, many times I feel outside of myself, as if I live my life in third person, the struggle being to turn the "she" into "I."

This struggle's not a simple matter of replacing pronouns. It's the tough process of breaking through the outer shell and inwardly becoming that "I." The fact that I was born at roughly 23°30' north longitude 30°30' west latitude and was raised at 38° north longitude 97° west latitude easily generates a laundry list of who I'm supposed to be: a "Dominican-York" in spandex, probably raised in Washington Heights, a spitfire Latina torn between "Old World" submission and "New World" rebellion, a Hispanic American sponsored by Budweiser. The list could be longer if I only paid more attention.

But I don't. Ironically, it's in the very country that has generated this list (and fiddled with genes and dragged black men to their deaths) where I feel I have the luxury of becoming "I." These United States, where individualism is Word, has allowed me the privilege of breaking away from that woman who was supposed to live with her parents until marriage (virgin), who was supposed to study at a local college instead of going away, who was supposed to keep her hair long and ultra relaxed.

For a long time I fiercely fought the idea that I'd become American (a term itself so slippery, so transitory, that no geography, no anthropology, no obsessive essay can stuff it into a neat category). Living all my life in a country where anyone with a dose of melanin is considered marginal, I have willingly, if not defiantly, used many other cultural/racial labels for myself outside of the mainstream. I've labeled myself a Dominican woman, an Afro-Dominicana, Latina, Afro-Latina, black woman, Caribbean woman, woman of African descent, woman of the African Diaspora, woman of color.

I used and still use these labels before resorting to "American" or the oh-so-dreaded hyphen, "Dominican-American." My resistance to "American" also has roots in the efforts various ethnic groups historically put into obliterating their own culture. to fit into mainstream (white) United States.

Okay, I've done my share of frantic Dominican flag-waving worthy of a Fifth Avenue parade in mid-August: Goddammit I'm Dominican, baby! I am merengue. I like *plátanos* and fried cheese. My Spanish is song. I like sand between my toes. I love drama. I love parties. Visit my home and I'll offer you a million beverages. I'm sun-drenched and superstitious. I'm obsessive-compulsive. I'm beautiful. I'm hardworking and self-reliant. I'll die without family. I'll die without jokes. I have a martyr complex. I'm political. Raunchy. Resilient. *Dios, patria, libertad!*

Again I've become a list.

Where does Dominican end and "I" begin? Sure, within each culture there are differences. This combination of qualities is not solely Dominican (though some may say it's pretty damn close), but I do wonder where stereotypes end and the heterogeneous identity or self begins. Then within each family there are differences. So what is there to be said for national psyche and personal idiosyncrasy? Though I've lived here since I was three months old, I became a naturalized citizen at the age of twenty-two. I was born in 1972 in Santo Domingo, Dominican Republic. I was conceived and raised in Brooklyn, New York.

Papi came to New York in 1962, a year after the end of Rafael Trujillo's thirty-year dictatorship. The opportunity to travel abroad opened up to those beyond the rich, and Papi grabbed it with hopes of improving the economic lot of his parents, his siblings, and himself. Mami arrived five years later, leaving behind a rural upbringing for a shot at better work, and maybe an education. They met each other here, and despite the drudgery of sweatshops and odd jobs, managed to begin a life together.

Twenty-three and pregnant with her first child in a country she was still adjusting to, my mother later went to spend her last months of pregnancy with her mother-in-law in the Dominican Republic. As the last of my organs developed, she sat eating mangoes in the shade of my grandmother's porch, always with too much spit in her mouth. Now in my last weeks of pregnancy and with less spit in my mouth, I wonder how she must have felt away from the chill of New York, knowing that once she had me she would have to return. I've never bothered to ask her who she imagined she would become in the United States, who her children would become. Mami, what went through your mind as you held your three-month-old baby in your lap and the island shrank away through the airplane window?

Soon we were four siblings being raised in a predominantly working-class Latino neighborhood on the Southside of Brooklyn. Like many immigrants and their children, we lived in two worlds. Each of us in the family found individual ways to navigate between the varying degrees of our Dominican and American selves—including my parents. During tax season it's Papi who does the taxes for folks for whom English is still a nightmare. My siblings' music collections include bachata, hip-hop, reggae, merengue, R&B, and salsa. My mother has read Danielle Steel, V.C. Andrews, Jackie Collins, and some American classics—in Spanish. My own eyes cross when I'm looking from both Dominican and American perspectives. The vertigo comes from being simultaneously nearsighted and farsighted, a feeling of seasickness, my compass awry. Even my parents' vision of this land has changed.

My parents' American Dream in the '90s is fresher and more proactive than their dream during the '70s. Making lots of money here and returning to the Dominican Republic to build a house and live happily ever after has been replaced by investing in the well-being of their family here in this country. They've sweat thick drops to channel resources toward their children's education, and service in our Brooklyn community. The United States is their present reality and priority. As naturalized citizens, they're still helping steer the gears of America. They—we—are here to stay.

But where else would I be? I've lived here all my life. I've studied and worked here, and even conceived new life here. I will not cheat myself of an America I'm continuously helping to shape.

My race politics, to many a Dominican stateside and abroad, are amusingly American: African-American, in particular. A quickness to embrace blackness or African heritage is in direct opposition to Dominican pride in hybridity. "We are a mulatto nation," says current president Leonel Fernández with a comfort that comes from not having to prove whiteness or accept blackness. Though the Dominican Republic is a racially heterogeneous nation, its strong African presence can't be simply dismissed with deflated statistics and powerful hair relaxers.

Having been raised in the United States has allowed me the legacy of black consciousness left behind by past generations. Like every other person of color, I grew up colonized: "bad hair" complexes, trying not to smile too widely to keep my nose "in check," taunting my brother with the darker skin. Whiteness and blackness were relative, their meaning changing as I got older. Growing up, we Dominicans were the blacks and Puerto Ricans the whites in a Latino community that replicated the United States' racial polarities. White status came with lighter skin, automatic American citizenship, and English fluency, sometimes at the expense of Spanish.

In the United States "culture" and "race" seem to be Siamese twins. High school peer and intellectual-bully-on-the-down-low Dana Hale forced me to reconfigure what I identified as. Dana herself was a contradiction. She preached blackness à la Malcolm X in green contacts lenses and peroxide hair. I wasn't Dominican, she maintained with authority, I was black—our only difference being that our slave owners spoke different languages. Black not only meant race but also culture (the Siamese twins), whereas for me black referred to race, not necessarily culture. I considered myself Dominican, not black in the sense of African-American. "Latino" and "black" didn't have to be such oxymorons. I refused to accept blackness on African-American terms, as if they had a patent on the concept.

"See, that American imperialistic streak is where they're just like their white counterparts," I'd say to Pan-African friends in college. Dominicans—or more specifically "black folks who speak Spanish"—were an anomaly to many African-Americans. In my dorm room I hung a Dominican flag, as did other children of immigrants, not only to remember but also to educate. I gravitated toward the black diaspora on campus instead of the Latino groups, which were really cliques of Latin America's well-to-dos who wouldn't be bothered with either Chicanos, Nuyoricans, or any other American derivative thereof. I wanted to simultaneously share my urbanness, my blackness, my Latinaness, my Dominicanness, and all the other "nesses" I was still discovering. In addition to a heavy workload freshman year, I further splintered myself as a member of the Black Student Union, the Caribbean Club, the Hispanic Society of Professional Engineers, and any Pan-African group activities. I'm sure this country's fixation on racial/ethnic categories contributes to making many a poor soul suffer from multiple personality disorder.

Returning to my Brooklyn neighborhood after college, I found myself having assimilated very American idiosyncrasies. I didn't feel as "Latina" with a prestigious white college degree under my arm and a very Afrocentric view of the world. At the local bodegas I was sometimes spoken to in English, then met with surprise when I answered in as Dominican a Spanish as I could muster. I was reactive at family gatherings when I heard slurs worthy of David Duke. My words had little credibility. Who gave a damn that I was in defense of our own blackness? Who cared that the black struggle in this country has allowed us fairly comfortable bus rides and somewhat reduced the number of times a cop's club grazes our heads? I was just this Americanized post-college kid with too many black friends and other imported ideas in her kinky head.

Some of the other imported ideas in my kinky head took away a lot of my "femininity." I was literally too headstrong. Love of books and sports and going places and an appetite for learning were not "girlie" enough for most of my extended family. A part of me, though, was very much subservient—the well-behaved A student who never challenged authority figures. Summer trips to Dominican Republic—where the cultivation of feminity can be almost clownish—has made me most aware of how the United States has shaped my idea of feminity.

My cousins (the "hair and nail cousins" as coined by writer Julia Alvarez) hated the slackness of my jeans or my refusal to wear my hair straight. Well, I hated having to be accompanied by a male relative or acquaintance wherever we went past sundown. I hated having to limit my comments on politics in conversation with men. I hated the incessant "psssssst" coming even from the mouths of ten-year-olds. I hated the rigorous exhibition of our bodies for foreign consumption. I hated claustrophobic discussions with other women about clothing, hair, men, men, and men. I hated the complacent martyrdom of women humiliated by their husbands' infidelities. I hated constant questions about boyfriends and marriage and children. I hated male chest thumping, for everything from driving a car to eating a piece of fruit. I hated to hate.

Being raised here, then, has brought me into conflicts with my parents. Though they raised me to be educated and hence, independent, the result later proved to go against their own traditions. They were uncomfortable with my wanting to study away from home, to travel, to have boyfriends (premarital sex), to move out on my own. Along the way they've eventually supported my decisions, but I was always left with a feeling of guilt, of having betrayed them and broken from tradition. For them, American women aged before their time because they lived wordly lives. "There's a difference between being liberated (*la libertad*) and being a 'libertine' [*el libertinaje*]," my father would say, shaking his index finger at me, the specter of illicit sex always hovering.

Well, with delightfully illicit sex now behind me (and, hopefully, still more ahead of me), I'm entering the realm of motherhood. In a few weeks, I'll bring a new soul to this world. Will I be an "American" mother or a "Dominican" mother or both? Which elements of each woman will I draw from? Whether or not I choose to be the one to wash dishes and cook and clean is of consequence. The name my partner and I choose for our child is of consequence. It may determine whether this soul will be defined by the double hyphens, Dominican-Puerto

Rican-American, or whether American will be a sufficient term to contain her or his rich cultural and racial background. Every action in my life responds to where I have placed myself—including my writing.

The very language of this essay is an eye-cross. Not simply English, but English with American idioms and conventions. My writing has many times been a struggle to find the right word, the right turn of phrase to articulate an idea, emotion, or experience that may have originally occurred to me in Spanish, or emerged out of a very Dominican place in me.

I shuttle the world in my head from Spanish to English and vice versa. Spanish to English has helped me find more interesting phrasing for my work, consequently filling my writing with enough hiccups to keep an editor's knuckles cracking. English to Spanish has helped me fill in the parts of my Spanish that haven't matured beyond high school composition. Consequently my Spanish, however fluent, is littered with Anglicisms.

I can't say I'm fully comfortable in either language. When speaking to native Spanish speakers, I hold my breath after blurting out a word fashioned out of English when its Spanish equivalent fails me. I don't feel my Spanish is "educated" enough. My relationship to the language is not academic as it is social and religious, and very much a part of my childhood. I've been told that in Spanish my voice takes on a softer, pleasant, sometimes subservient timbre. The language does represent for me love and constraint, passion, warmth, and at times self-oppression. Self-oppression from obligatory Sunday mass, from parents with many rules for children growing up in New York, from a country where children and women are told too often to shut up.

English, on the other hand, feels so much more liberating, cruder. I curse more, demand more, invent more. Though the language to me is colder, not always as colorful, it's more elastic. Black English, in particular, allows for more movement and expression. Yet around those who chew English like gum, I still find myself faltering. There are so many words in my vocabulary with which I am intimate as a reader but not as a speaker. I understand the meaning of "episiotomy," yet my pronunciation of it is phonetic, and the discreet listener will repeat the word properly for me before taking another sip of calcium-rich juice at the birthing center.

With my siblings I speak English. Spanish used to be a way of tattletaling. "Alex, *no digas malas palabras.*" With our friends, too, English is the language of choice. Spanish used to be for us too right-off-the-boat, not hip enough. Spanish meant trousers and pointy shoes instead of Lees and fat-laced Pumas.

Lees and fat-laced Pumas were the cornerstones of hip culture for us. As we get older, the meaning of culture and what we choose as our culture becomes more complicated than clothing and music. We are all in transition, becoming something else, giving birth to new selves. Now is a time to nurse new life. It's a time for me to soak my feet and calibrate my compass. I'm still at 38° north longitude 97° west latitude.

The real question for me isn't "Have I become American?" but "Is this discussion already passé?"

Now Is the Time to Try Something —But Have I Got Nine Lives?

UTE MARGARET SAINE

RECENTLY, IT HAS BEEN BOTHERING ME to ask students the appointed question of Spanish chapter one, "Where are you from?" *"De dónde es usted?"* To express it, you use the verb *ser*, one of two words for "to be," and which implies the permanence of one's origins. Yes, I am a professor of Spanish. Puzzled, my southern Californian students squint at me, wondering which house or apartment, town or village, to designate. Or did I want the whole list? Their birthplaces? Some have a faint notion where their parents lived then, however briefly. Did I want to hear where they now live? Never mind, they've just moved in, or are on their way out, on to bigger and better things. . . . They're all migrants! I usually settle for "Where are your ancestors from?" although that entails a whole slew of country names and continents.

It's appropriate in the United States that one's ancestors come from somewhere, that people's surnames echo a multitude of nationalities and languages. But what's in a name? Going beyond the name is often considered inappropriate. Most second- or third-generation immigrants don't visit their old-country town and relatives, don't speak their language, don't know about their history or current affairs. Yet it seems the less concrete the origins they can lay claim to, the more they glorify their ancestry. A friend with a supposedly long pedigree abruptly halted

165

research upon discovering that his earliest forebear was a horse thief. To date, assimilation and peer pressures have created a sameness imperative that runs counter to our country's immigration history and makes first-generation immigrants feel underappreciated.

Genealogical research rarely provides more than names and dates. Because of limited knowledge, indirect immigrants assume that, say, Birmingham or Essen are homogeneous and somehow better places to be from than Oaxaca or Benin. They are unaware of Celts, Teutons, and Romans among their ancestors, to name just a few, of Sicilians in London, Andalusians in Paris, the Polish in Essen, and Magyars everywhere, unaware moreover that persons from Birmingham and Essen hark back to rural villages, in infinite historical regression. A spirited Prague friend speculated that she owed her tiny feet to the Huns. We ought to applaud her. Only when we accept the diversity of our roots, when we stop tearing each other—and ourselves—apart about the relative merits of ancestry, can we begin to define ourselves as a country whose unique potential lies precisely in its cultural cornucopia. This goal, worthy of the next millenium, is one to which I plan to contribute.

Yes, my otherness is infinitely more crass than that of most Americans: I'm a foreigner, I might as well be from Mars, according to the U.S. government, which calls me "alien." When I was new in the country, I saw a young woman wearing a T-shirt with the bold letters FOREIGNER. Ah, I thought, she took the bull by the horns and labeled herself with so many scarlet letters. We were both disappointed when she revealed that it was a rock group—though what a revealing name.

Except for stays and travels abroad, I lived my entire life in Germany until the age of twenty-one, then came directly to the United States. So far so simple. But what does it mean to be born at the end of World War II, in the country of the main perpetrator? To be raised a German, and, inexplicably to my parents, within months of coming of age, opt to emigrate?

My war experiences as a toddler were almost cozy. Tucked into the friendly if subdued village crowd assembled in the factory basement during bomb alerts, I would absorb the heart warming glow of the open furnace. The January 2, 1945, Allied bombardment of Nuremberg ten miles to the north, which destroyed the historical inner city, was to me mere firecrackers, like bursting coals in the furnace we sat around as if celebrating a perpetual New Year's Eve party.

Hitler wanted Germany to go under, with him. The government made no provisions for food, clothing, let alone anything else. Dire poverty made our village women revert to spinning wool upstairs in the inn, laughing and telling stories in an ambiance we might find in German romantic stories, one hundred fifty years before. The Brothers Grimm would come to spinning rooms to collect fairy tales from women. Once, in our front yard, several women and a few men trampled down shredded fresh cabbage in a huge barrel to make sauerkraut. They didn't do it out of joy, or to preserve a historical custom, as people might nowadays in places such as Old Williamsburg, with other people watching, but because they had to. Exaggerating certain elements of folk culture and placing taboos on others, the Nazis had destroyed what little remained of it after a (nineteenth) century of Industrial Revolution. The postwar generation gladly desisted from these fascist charades.

Postwar was written all over my childhood. I wore almost no shoes until I entered elementary school. This suited me fine, since I adored roaming pine forests, meadows, and creek edges, and they declared me the savage in the family. To my dismay, none other than the great Goethe had written a ballad where a huge church bell chases and suffocates a girl who likes to roam. One pair of shoes, which I was made to wear on festive occasions, arrived in a CARE package sponsored by Mother's sister Emmie, who emigrated to the U.S. in 1913. Laced, light brown, but far too big, I avoided them whenever I could. Worse, other shoes were too small and I still remember the pain. Today, my soles are covered with calluses, useful except for getting into tight shoes.

I cannot remember whether my first orange—chewing, slurping the pulp while kneeling over a chair—also emerged from a CARE package. Frugality was everywhere. Grandmother and Aunt Luise, who both partly raised me, saved every thread, which I still find engaging, both environmentally and artistically. Aunt fed an extended family of eight with her "defeat" garden: beans, different cabbages, lettuce, carrots, spinach, rhubarb, apples, plums, pears, and, of course, cherries, red and black currants, raspberries, gooseberries, and most herbs. She taught me about plants, treating them like pleasant acquaintances with welcome surprises destined for our benefit. Thanks to her, I'm able to learn about the flora wherever I live or travel. Along with geology, which I avidly follow, this creates an instant bond with new surroundings. For Aunt and myself, it became a garden of victory, after all.

Although we lived in the country, there was not enough food. Farmers were besieged by "hamstering" city folks trading valuables such as jewelry, precious fabrics, and cameras for flour, milk, and eggs. It was said that in those days they had Persian rugs even in the cow barns. In our family, Mother sallied off on bike, always returning with plenty, while Father baby-sat, reading us fairy tales—equally important food.

We lived in the United States occupation zone. One of the first jokes about Americans, before I even knew what that was, told of an Army private dispatched to check the black market. Chancing upon an elderly woman with a suspiciously inflated bosom, where she had stashed away several pounds of flour, he tapped against it. There rose a revealing puff of white dust. "Ah, milk powder," he exclaimed, leaving her alone. I was not sure I understood the joke, but the American seemed friendly. Obviously, this was long before I became allergic to sexist jokes, but it very well describes these nervous times, when—according to Martin Walser's 1998 autobiographical novel *Ein springender Brunnen* (*A Surging Fountain*), which I'm currently reading—men named Adolf dropped their first name and irate citizens made Party members wear signs inscribed "I was a Nazi" for several weeks.

When the "nonfraternization" policy was wearing thin, an American couple once came to fish in our river. In Germany, fishing rights are limited to the person who pays the yearly county fee for a stretch of river. That was Grandfather, and we children felt intensely possessive of the Schwarzach. But Father sent me across the narrow bridge to present them a bunch of garden flowers. The lady promptly reached into her purse and gave me my first, unexpected Hershey bar. We kids liked American soldiers not only for the chewing gum, a novelty, but because tanks left ruts in the meadows, which made catching frogs much easier.

I felt an odd silence in those days, a cloud of something unsaid, bottled up and ready to explode. I wrote a poem about the garden by the river, with Mother mending, embroidering in cross-stitch to have everything nice and pretty, and intruding, that inexplicable silence. Germans minded their own business and worked and worked to forget, to "again be someone": by the mid '50s, this became the German "economic miracle." Raised in an authoritarian manner, they were slowly learning the ways of democracy. Discussions were about rearmament, with fifty percent against. Persuaded by the United States, who wanted Germany in NATO, Chancellor Adenauer created the German military. Reunification, the other subject, was promoted as the instant goal by the Rightists, notably the refugee organizations, and commemorated in sad nostalgia by everybody else. Until well into the '70s, patriotism was claimed exclusively by the Right. Even the first stanza of the national anthem was dropped, because the Nazis had interpreted the words "Germany above all" too literally.

Besides the river noise, the only way to stanch the silence was music. Because our house was tiny and Father only dared enlarge it after Grandfather's death, we children slept behind a partition off the living room. The piano was placed against it. After the good-night kiss, Mother would play mostly Chopin and Father would play Schumann, Beethoven, Bach, and Schubert. Schumann was his favorite composer, and when he played during the day, he would tell the composers' stories. Soon I was to take lessons, first from a schoolteacher, and my access to music became even more personal. When I was seven, Aunt would begin my sessions of Schubert's lieder, always accompanying me on the piano. In the "Erlkoenig," the erlking's spooky pain made me feel sadder than the dying boy in his father's arms.

Weekends were spent with the extended family. The grandparents, aunt, and one uncle's family lived with us in the compound, but on summer Sundays, many aunts, uncles, and cousins would flock to us from the city. Saturday, Grandmother would bake a yeast coffee cake and Sunday, cook for some twenty people, often with fish Grandfather caught as one course. Father had an old kayak, in which as a student he had traveled down the Danube to the far border of Hungary. Without supervision, we would carry it upstream and leisurely row down. In an old willow that was bent almost horizontal over the river, which had a big head due to basket weavers' prunings, we would play house and, when attacked by "Indians," slide into the river. I watched early spring inundations, which turned the valley into a lake about to flood the cellar, from a platform one foot above the water's edge, inventing a great sea voyage, as strange objects, plants, and dead animals floated by.

I have found this fascination with water in another landlubber, the Rimbaud of "The Drunken Ship." My first geography lesson was that "the Schwarzach flows into the Rednitz, the Rednitz into the Regnitz, the Regnitz into the Main, the Main into the Rhine, the Rhine into the North Sea, and the North Sea is part of the Atlantic." The eels caught in fish traps, whose skin we pulled down in one piece from a horizontal cut on their necks, spawned in the Sargasso Sea. I was aware of Robinson Crusoe. And I had an "aunt in America," whom I would soon write in broken English. In our hallway, there was a handsome framed world map. If we had a question about geography, we ran to it.

When I was five, my bed lamp fell on my sea grass mattress. Father saved me in time, but the mattress continued smoldering for another day, turning blacker and blacker. At the age of four, I discovered that a year before me, my mother had a stillborn baby girl named Ute. This caused me anguish: What was my real name? Was I dead or alive? I have recently preferred Margaret, my second name from both grandmothers.

In my youth, courtesy was forced down children's throats as if they were adults, while at the same time we observed with dismay its ever-present erosion, hypocrisy, in adults. I, however, kept them reasonably at bay after Grandmother unwittingly revealed an amazing trick. Once, when Mother asked me to set the table, Grandmother, who had to work at fourteen, pleaded: "Let her read, there is nothing better." From that moment, I was rarely seen without my nose in a book. Daydreaming.

Dying persons were never informed about their state, nor were children told important things they could grasp. When I was seven, Mother took me to the hairdresser's. Pretty soon I realized I was bleeding on my head and screamed bloody murder. Mother had my ears pierced without telling me. I have written, and found, another ear-piercing poem by Spain's contemporary poet Juana Castro. Is it a coincidence that both countries lived through fascist periods? I felt violated and soon lost the pale blue earrings shaped like forget-me-nots, so that the holes grew shut again. Years later, my fiancé would pierce them anew with a heated needle and some alcohol. I dutifully wore earrings as a young wife, but only became enamored of them after divorce. My German girlfriends comment that they could not wear them—meaning such florid clunkers as mine—and I feel like saying: You lack-of-freedom-bunch-of-bonsai-poodles. But instead, I count the blessings of the relative tolerance, or shall we say indifference, of United States folks, but also their joie de vivre, augmented by that of recent immigrants. Maybe I am still compensating for the repressions of my German youth—which, of course, have long disappeared there.

Invalids in streetcars, war memories everywhere. My first encounter with the word *art*, so important later with its aura of freedom and authenticity, happened when Grandmother showed me a calendar with the heavy black lines of sparsely colored woodcuts. "Painted with the mouth, painted with the right foot," she intoned, pointing to some captions. Art, it seemed, was a heroic endeavor.

On turning ten, after the rhododendron bloomed profusely, I received a one-volume children's encyclopedia, which I devoured and, like Minerva's owl, regurgitated in mini-lessons, a favorite form of expression of mine to this day. But happiness was shattered when, after a stiff entrance exam, Mother placed me in a strict girls' boarding school with obligatory church attendance. Five years without nylons and Coca-Cola, indispensable goods United States culture had so quickly and enticingly showered us with in the '50s. Obligatory long hair and aprons on weekdays, until fourteen. Sharing the frustration were girls from all over Germany and abroad, some of whom I still visit and write to. Perhaps not surprisingly, many of my German girlfriends from this and later schools emigrated, like myself, to Italy, England, Brazil, France, and, of course, the United States. In order to escape repression, particularly of gender. When Mother suggested that, despite baby-sitting my second brother, I would never become a good wife, housewife, and mother on account of my good grades, my camel's back was broken: I silently vowed not to spend my life under her inquisitive eyes.

At thirteen, barely ten years after events, I quite accidentally saw a Danish film about a concentration camp. It was one of the greatest shocks of my life. It seemed to me that I now understood the rampant silences in the wrong places of my childhood. The collective crime obsessed me. I would resort to a double strategy: read all I could about the Third Reich, in the increasingly indispensable bookstores, and on the piano play only Bach's *Well-Tempered Clavier*, pure music, since Beethoven, Mozart, and all the rest were tarnished by the narratives the Nazis had attached to them. Today I understand the involved generation's silence as one of the clichés of history: the archbishop of Durango, Mexico, asserted concerning the Cristero rebellion massacres, that "all that happened was so deplorable that it is better that history be written fifty years after, when no one of us is alive" (source: Agustín Vaca).* Or, as Theodor Heuss, first West German president, phrased it, more than collective guilt, Germans ought to feel "collective shame."

What made things worse was that one of my less favorite aunts reminded me during a visit of what a cute two-year-old I was when saying a poem at the *Bund der Mütter* (League of Mothers) festival in 1944. She proceeded to recite what I had mercifully forgotten:

> *In summer when it's warm and dry, too,*
> *We save our mothers the socks and the shoe,*
> *For socks and shoes cost a lot of marks,*
> *So barefoot like geese we walk to the park.*

***Los Silencios de la Historia*, a study based on the oral histories of women from the Mexican Cristero movement.

Bullying people, the women on the home front, into saving resources, in order to ship more to the soldiers! With a chill I recognized the frost boils of Stalingrad in this poem, whose doggerel-cum-propaganda I have tried to preserve in the translation.

Actually, my family had not behaved too badly. Grandmother and Aunt continued befriending a woman who successfully hid her Jewish husband in the cellar until after Capitulation. The fascist major reprimanded them, but at least refrained from searching the woman's house. Ironically, it was Grandfather, the self-taught socialist turned enterpreneur, who ordered Father in 1937 to enter the Party, "so that nothing would happen to the company." And Father, the jovial polymath, demurred, joining a minor association of car owners called NSKK. Maybe it meant little that in the dozens of Third Reich–era postcards I later read at Aunt Emmie's, my parents, engaged until 1939, had not once written "Heil Hitler," but it reassured me somewhat. Emmie, however, was puzzled about Mother's many boyfriends, who, upon my closer graphological inspection, turned out to be Father's funny Bavarian aliases. After the war, his Jewish friends visiting from Brazil, Flatbush, and Nahariyya agreed that fighting the regime after the "Night of Broken Glass" was to court the death of one's family. That didn't satisfy me completely, and my parents and I had some long conversations.

In the summer before university, I discovered the Provence, its light, the semi-aridity, which fascinate me so much in California. I had fallen in love with literature and resolved at first to study German. Unfortunately, the critical focus on the past I sought was nonexistent before the 1968 student uprisings, which were to mark me profoundly, both in what went on in the United States as well as in France and Germany. Restlessly, I turned to French, perhaps the Gallic spirit would exorcise my demons, and was fortunate to learn Spanish daily for a year from three delightful Spanish women students. In the end, I assuaged my frustrations by marrying a pleasant American fellowship student, with whom I decided to emigrate, despite the fact that France, Spain, and Latin America were my countries of interest.

❧

As a 1963 immigrant, I slipped in under Germany's huge quota with a laughable intelligence test and an instant green card. Those were the years of the brain drain. In the U.S., impatient Germans like myself studied sciences or became German professors. I wanted to be different. I also felt that in German I had an unfair advantage over my husband. I lived with my friendly in-laws for a year, like an overgrown, now-American teenager. Checking the recently purchased library of fascist Germanist Joseph Nadler, on the fifth floor of the Rice University library, I found the vilest racist cartoons. Then Kennedy's death on the radio, here, in Texas.

During my first vacation, a short trip gave me a new inspiration: I irremediably fell in love with Mexico and its cultures. One year later, we ended up in a most stimulating intellectual climate, Yale, where after another year of library work, I began graduate study in French and Spanish. My new interests were anthropology, pre-Hispanic studies, twentieth-century architecture, and cinema in every shade, shape, or form. I was impressed by how lightly U.S. intellectuals wore their erudition and how casual academic language was, as compared with those in Europe. Our first son was born and I would have been happy, if the increasingly lopsided household chores and child-raising—in a couple that had vowed to be equals—were not making me fall further and further behind. Nineteen seventy-one allowed me to live in Germany—near the French border—for a year and my second son was born in 1973. From my friend Hanna Demetz's thoughtful book *My American Daughter* I learned that U.S.-born children of immigrants were Americans foremost, yet I managed to take my kids to visit Germany frequently, so that they speak German and are well acquainted with the country and our family.

Career disparity increased after 1975, in California. Though I lost no time to qualify for teaching Spanish, I became more and more dispirited, too depressed to write, to take care of my children. After the divorce, during which I lost my sons for several years, I was able amid the worry to devote myself entirely to writing for the first time: the silver lining? Articles appeared, but poetry still came in German, strictly for the drawer: I didn't feel up to becoming Josephine Conrad. My younger son and I followed up several stays in France with Berlin during the fall of 1989, experiencing the nascent utopia of reunification. When friends and family urged me to stay, I realized I was wedded to California. In 1991, friends invited me to join them in founding the writers' organization PEN Orange County, and we have met monthly ever since. I decided then to write poetry in English, which resulted in *Bodyscapes*, published by Pacific Writers Press in 1995, as well as translations, articles, and several books of poetry in progress.

California has become the place where I feel at ease as an immigrant among immigrants, where I can choose to—as José Marti said—"throw in my lot with them." I admire and enjoy the resourcefulness and resilience of immigrants from rural Mexico, their vibrant culture, from saints' fiestas to *pan dulce*, but also California's cosmopolitan ties to the rest of Latin America. I admire U.S.-born Latinos, who may be the first indirect immigrants in U.S. history holding on to both cultures—and who are better off for it, emotionally and spiritually. Without Latinos, California and the Southwest would be a lot less attractive. Working hard to increase Spanish enrollment at a local college, I established a program for students to study and live with a family in Mexico. Accompanying them allows me to intensify my contacts with that culture, writers, and migrant towns. Locally I promote exchanges between students learning Spanish and native speakers of Spanish who wish to improve their command of English. It is amazing how many professionals all of a sudden have decided to study Spanish. My classes give them a great variety of conversation and culture, and personal answers to the eternal question "How do you say?"

Multicultural California—after efforts now and in the future to make it real—is for me the antidote to Nazi Germany. That is the California I am privileged to help lift into the twenty-first century. Like a cat, I seem to have several lives, simultaneously. And my aim is to find ways to transmit this exciting, vital multiculturality I have experienced, to the other past and present "migrants" here in the United States, so that our differences may converge in a polyphonic chorus of celebration.

Whispered Histories

ROSANNE KATON-WALDEN

SOMETIME IN 1948 WHILE MY FATHER was trying to convince my mother to marry him, he promised that they would live in America. "Ruby's children will be Americans!" he said to her grandparents. My mother could only have said yes to such a proposal. There was nothing for her in the Blue Mountains village of Highgate. She was a dark-skinned illegitimate child, born out of a love affair between Victor, the fifteen-year-old son of a wealthy mulatto government official, and the thirteen-year-old daughter of their black maid.

According to family lore, this scenario followed: When Victor's people heard a rumor that the "little gal," as they called my mother's mom, was living in another village squiring a baby that looked just like their son, they sprang into action. One day after the "little gal" left her shack to get some water, my great-grandmother went in, confirmed the baby's resemblance to her family and took it. My mother only saw her mother one other time, on the eve of her departure for America. That's all I know. She claims not to remember anything of note about their meeting. I grew up in a culture, in an era, where children were given few details, if any. We children lived in a vacuum of whispered histories, the truths of which seemed ominous. We were always too scared to ask.

My father knew that moving my mother to America was not going to be easy. The people at the American Consulate were famous for rejecting dark-skinned applicants for immigration. However, Daddy was a man with a plan. A bureaucratic plan. He'd been to America before; he knew the rules. He decided to plan the birth of his children around his ability to secure a pair of U.S. visitor visas, good only for a couple of weeks of travel on the continental United States. After two blessed tries resulting in my older sisters, Jackie and Genia, (this plan had no downside) my father was able to perfectly time my birth with a trip to America. I was born in New York City, in Jamaica Hospital (where else?). My parents and I immediately flew back to Kingston to wait out a long, tedious paperwork odyssey. It was a joyous time: I was an American, and Daddy was able to demand officially that my family move with me to live in the country of my birth. It took until mid-1955. I was nearly four years old when we came to America.

THE SOUTH BRONX

741 East 181st Street. The Katon family lived on the sunny side of the street. Literally. Every day we baked in the sun. Not allowed to set foot off the stoop, there we would stand, squinting into the Bronx sun, in polished Mary Jane shoes, matching starched dresses (my mother sewed all of our clothes) and Shirley Temple curls (which looked more like rat tails than anything that ever adorned Miss Temple's head).

I had some vague awareness that we were no longer living in Jamaica. But I believed that the South Bronx was tethered to the island of Jamaica as securely as my soon-to-be-born sister Connie's umbilical cord was attached to its amniotic sac. At that point I didn't realize that we were actually living in the magical place called America. I thought we were still en route. I believed this because I thought I had never seen a real American (not even in the mirror). I had never heard anyone look out of the window and comment, "Oh look, there goes an American guy!" When my parents talked about our neighbors they referred to them as Italian, Polish, and Irish. I am embarrassed to say that we Katon kids thought The Bronx was America's vestibule.

My big sister Genia and I spent days playing the same "going to America" game. She played the rich lady; I was her maid. She walked around our apartment pointing out what needed to be packed to go to America. My role was to stuff that item into a pillowcase with the knowledge that what was left was mine to keep in The Bronx. She blathered on endlessly of all the Americans she was going to meet. I was always jealous. Her pretend boarding of a Pan American airplane was my cue to weep inconsolably. We were sure that Americans never returned to The Bronx.

The South Bronx of the '50s was an underclass immigrant enclave. Besides Italians, Irish, and Polish, there were a smattering of Jews. Working folk, the kind whose children watched their parents' teeth disappear at the rate of one per year. Skinny folk, just one generation removed from the old country. Brokendown folk, pitching pennies into church fountains. Those immigrants, walking the streets of their new land, expecting an upturn in their fortunes through either an intervention of the deities, or luck.

The only other "colored" families, on this densely populated city block, were those of the building superintendents. Daddy owned the little duplex building we lived in. It backed up to the city dump. Sounds of the mechanical garbage trucks often lend a soothing soundtrack to all my early memories. Daddy moved heaven and earth to pay the mortgage on time. He was constantly out of work so I don't know how he managed. Once, a city worker came by to inform my father that we qualified for welfare. Daddy turned down the offer when he discovered he would have to give up ownership of our house. (Jamaicans didn't believe in renting.)

"Home" was the center structure in a trio of tiny two-story duplexes. The apartments were under five hundred square feet. No one ever bought the buildings on either side of us; the windows remained boarded up; their only inhabitants, rats and roaches. Our place was the last of the row houses built around the turn of the century. Now we were surrounded by 15-story apartment buildings built before World War II, and brand-new federal housing projects whose occupants were only sometimes on relief. I remember that when the projects were new, all of the tenants were white. That was partly because even though you had to be poor to move in, you couldn't be *too* poor! You had to have a steady job.

In pre–Civil Rights Movement America, Negro and Puerto Rican men in the cities had a hell of a time finding jobs. Outside of the "supers," no colored man expected steady work. They hustled daily or weekly labor, catch-as catch-can. Colored moms with children old enough to go to school worked as domestics. This still left most colored families below the financial cutoff to get into the projects. It wasn't until the 1964 civil rights bills that the cutoff was eliminated. Suddenly, all white people, even those from the wrong side of the tracks, became equal. They left for the greener pastures of the suburbs. When the projects refilled, it was only with minorities.

Daddy was always hunting for a job. He was under five feet tall and over fifty years old. He dyed his hair with Miss Clairol and lied about his height. But in Daddy's shadow, we all felt diminished. Daddy made all of the family decisions. He purchased everything that needed to be brought into the house, even my mother's sanitary napkins, as Mom was not allowed to handle money. There was a long list of things Daddy forbade us to do. We were not allowed to talk to "them." Everyone who was not Jamaican was "them." Poor white people were "Them" with a capitol T. Rich white people were "They." They lived in mansions and were movie stars. They didn't like people of color. They felt the same way about poor white people. They controlled the world. Daddy never said if we could talk to rich white people. He never expected we would come across one. The only white man I ever saw let into our house was Mr. Anthony, the numbers runner. He always arrived in a suit and tie.

Daddy was a race man. We kids just thought he was out of sync with the world. Much to our dismay, he forbade the straightening of our kinky locks. He liked to give us used encyclopedia books from God knows where, for our birthdays. By the time he died, when I was fourteen, our bookcase had an encyclopedia from A to Z. Each book a different color and shape. Each from a different publisher.

Daddy liked to read the *Daily News* and recite the Shakespeare and Longfellow that he had learned at the University of The West Indies, which he'd attended as a youth. He had been adopted as a baby by the Katon family. His biological family had consisted of an Afro-Latin father and a Syrian mother. (A typical Jamaican Cocktail.) His biological father had been killed just before he was born and the Afro-Caribbean middle-class couple that lived up on the hill asked to adopt him. He resembled his adopted mother so much no one who knew the family suspected that he was not their child. His adopted mother Frances was a pip. She was a back-to-Africa type—nearly a century before back-to-Africa was cool. She was of the same generation of Jamaican intellectuals that produced Marcus Garvey. Frances taught Daddy to love his African heritage, all the while never mentioning to him that he was adopted. My mother always said that he was the only light-skinned Jamaican who liked dark-skinned people like herself.

Daddy told us children very little about his past. He told my mother even less. Still, we knew that he tried to make us girls the the grandchildren of the woman who loved and raised him. His Frances. We also knew of the rude awakening he received when Frances died. He was only eighteen. His adopted father quickly remarried a woman who threw Daddy out of the house while revealing to him for the first time that he had been adopted. It was because Daddy remembered the urgings of Frances that my father then visited America for the first time. He came by steamship to Ellis Island and lived in Harlem through the depression.

As the story goes, Daddy worked for the *Amsterdam News* as a writer and poet. He once wrote a story that was published on Christmas Day. It was about a Santa Claus in Jamaica traveling on a donkey, bringing toys in a burlap sack. Daddy always carried a clip of that article. An old yellowing reminder of who he'd once been and what he'd once done, folded up in his wallet.

I imagine Daddy as a young man in Harlem, a dapper little guy, wearing a biscuit hat and a bow-tie. The man loved Harlem, which is why his sudden departure remains such a mystery. We do know that he had been mugged. He was beaten up so badly he almost lost his voice box. He traveled back to Jamaica, lived a while in Costa Rica, sat out World War II in Kingston. All before he met my mother.

Mommy was thirty years younger than Daddy. I am sure that some people in the neighborhood thought Mommy was the oldest of the Katon daughters. We spent all of our time in the house. Daddy felt he was paying a mortgage of two hundred dollars per month to have a roof over our heads, so why should any of us want to leave? Since Mommy couldn't go out, she played America with us. She gave us iced sugar water and told us we were drinking soda. We believed her when she said that raw oatmeal was a snack advertised on TV—an appliance we were too poor to own. We carved bowls of corn-meal mush with knives and pretended it was pie. Beet juice was renamed Kool-Aid. Mommy made up America for us as she went along. I remember that she didn't realize what the radiator was until she sat on it one day while it was hot. My mother knew no one in the States outside of us. She had no one to run to when my father's white-hot rages turned violent. We would all hide with Mommy in a closet and wait for the storm to blow over.

My oldest sister, Jackie, was still in Jamaica awaiting her papers. To this day I still can't get a straight answer from my family as to why she didn't arrive in America until she was thirteen years old, five years after Mommy, Daddy, Genia, and I came. After Connie was born, Juanita and Freda-Jean came and rounded out our family. We ranged in accents from the older sisters Queen's English, to baby Freda's New Yorkese. My mother used to beg us to read to her so she could marvel at the fact that some of her children had American accents.

There must have been a slew of tenants who rented our downstairs apartment, but I swear I can only remember one family—Eddie Williams and his mother, Dorothy. They had moved from the Deep South where Jim Crow was alive and well. Eddie was ten years old when he moved into the house and he had that dazzling smile one only imagined to be attached to the square jaws of astronauts or fighter pilots. Eddie was the color of bitter-sweet chocolate, coffee and fudge. Things I had never tasted but knew smelled delicious. His mother, Dorothy, worked as a domestic. Her claim to fame was a sixth finger on her left hand. Eddie was smart and funny and I never understood the injustice of his being assigned to the 6-4 class for slow learners. Still, Eddie graciously shared his knowledge with me, the seven-year-old shrimp who had been skipped into the fifth grade. He drew a checkerboard and, with bottle-top checkers, taught me how to play my first "American" game. He made a deck of cards with crayons and paper in order to teach me how to play War and Go Fish. When his toes poked out of his shoes, and the soles flapped as he walked, he bragged to me that his footwear was air-conditioned.

I could not believe my luck. A true gentleman had appeared in my little world and I didn't even have to leave the stoop to talk to him. If there was an imbalance of power in this relationship between the daughter of a paranoid landlord and the son of the always-late-with-the-rent tenant, Eddie never let me know he felt it. Eddie saw my world, the North, as a constant opportunity for future success. His optimism was contagious. For the first time I dreamed about my future as an American. All of the men I have loved have had to measure up to my seven-year-old self's vision of Eddie Williams, with only my husband Richard coming up to the task.

A bit before my tenth birthday my father got what looked to be a steady job as a machinist in a small plant in Jamaica, Queens. In the 1960s, Jamaica, Queens, was the ultimate destination for Jamaican immigrants. It was something like Chinese people coming to New York and settling in Chinatown. Even my mother, who knew no one, had recently found some old girlfriends from her home village who'd now bought a house and lived in Jamaica, Queens. Daddy announced one day that he was about to buy a house in Queens—on the edge of the much desired Jamaica. We all spent the day traveling by subway, bus, and finally taxi to close the deal.

A grinning white man with one leg and a wife with her hair done up in pin curls and a scarf greeted us and pointed out the many features of the tiny attached row-house. I didn't care that the rooms were the size of closets and that this new place actually felt smaller than our apartment in The Bronx. There was something promising about it. I even saw a deep purple crocus peeking out from under the muddy snow on the lawn. When my family moved to what quickly became a racially isolated Negro ghetto, we truly felt that we were now Americans.

If my parents had ever wondered what all the screaming and fuss was about during the civil rights struggle, the wondering ended when we moved to Queens and they saw firsthand how neighborhoods with a majority black population were neglected by the powers that be.

P.S. 136 was seven blocks away from our house. I didn't know why we had not been allowed to walk the two blocks to my school in the Bronx, but now my sisters and I were allowed to walk over seven blocks to this school in a neighborhood that was still largely unknown. A population that looked like us must have been deemed safer. P.S. 136 had recently gone through big changes. In the space of one year, the school went from eighty-five percent white to almost one hundred percent Negro. The teachers, all of whom were white, looked stunned and acted as if they were shell-shocked. For example, my teacher, Mr. Worthington, arrived promptly at 8:40 each morning, pulled a cumbersome black-and-white television out of the closet, turned it on and proceeded to take bets on seasonal sports games. That was all we accomplished every day. Sometimes he let us read the funny papers. Other days, we told each other jokes. When my father heard about this, he was horrified. With the full knowledge that such nonsense would not be tolerated if there had still been white children at the school, Daddy searched around and found an integration program. The next semester, my sister Genia and I integrated Woodside Junior High in Astoria, Queens, Archie Bunker's old neighborhood.

Paying our dues, crossing picket lines, and ignoring the slings and arrows of mean-spirited, pint-sized thugs really taught my family what being American was all about. In the nightmare of those times, we kids knew that increasingly in the Caribbean, people who looked like us were running their own countries. Negro and colored people were being elected to office and making decisions as well as their white counterparts in America. Sometimes better. Certainly better than those Southern Dixiecrats we watched screaming like lunatics at old ladies lining up to vote in Mississippi. We had gone to school in an integrated setting in the Bronx, but it was nothing like what we encountered in Queens.

"Don't bellyache," our parents told us if we dared to complain. "Go to this school and learn." They knew that come what may, *their* American kids were up to the challenge.

THE DISTANCE

One morning, Daddy could no longer lift his right arm above his head. Three months later, he was dead. The head nun at Mary Immaculate Hospital, where my father died, recognized the glazed look in my mother's eyes as that of a newly widowed woman who had never held a job in her life. She promptly offered Mommy a job in the hospital cafeteria. Mommy worked there until she retired twenty-five years later. She learned how to cash a check, shop for the family; she managed her accounts so well that she soon bought a bigger house on a better street in Queens, still only blocks away from Jamaica. We were—and continue to be—so proud of Mommy's career. With my sisters' support, she didn't skip a beat.

After Daddy died, I shed my family like a snake sheds its younger skin. Sheer dumb luck landed me a job as an actress. Negroes were beginning to appear in television advertisements. A white talent agent was sent to my neighborhood to find the "right" Negro teen to appear in a national commercial for Metropolitan Life Insurance. After being spotted riding my bike, I was hired. In eight hours, I earned more money than my Daddy had ever earned in a year. The handwriting was on the wall. Daddy's world was being rendered obsolete by the sacrifices that were being made by Rev. Martin Luther King, Jr. and Malcolm X. How Daddy adored the early speeches of Malcolm X—as if he still the young student of Grandma Frances. I'm so sorry that Daddy didn't live to see the changes that came to pass.

The word Negro was dropped from my dictionary and I rechristened myself an Afro-Caribbean-American. I found that adding Caribbean into my identity stopped me from getting beat up for not speaking what would, many years later, be called "Ebonics." "She's not trying to sound white," people would say in my defense. "She's from the *Caribee-an.*" I was the first of my family to travel to Manhattan on a regular basis.

At first for auditions and acting jobs, and later for high school. I attended the High School for the Performing Arts, the same school featured in the movie, *Fame*. I remember buying my first *New York Times* for ten cents and marveling at all the interesting information that was available. I would buy the paper each day and read every single article, including the obituaries. Eddie Williams was right. I saw that my world was a constant opportunity for success, and I wanted to experience as much of it as I could. So I set out to do exactly that.

I toured the country in theater productions and even landed a play on Broadway. I became somewhat of a stock player in Norman Lear's innovative political television sitcoms. I continued to act in television commercials. In fact, to this day a cola ad of me riding a bike (we never stray too far from our beginnings) and wearing a dashiki plays hourly at the Smithsonian Institution. I traveled the world as an actress, appearing in films and working on movie crews. I was a *Playboy* centerfold (Sept. '78)—their "Black American girl next door." At one point, I dropped into communal life and tried to become a resident Black hippie until I realized that my natural habitat was concrete. (Most American asphalt is, after all, imported from Jamaica.)

Through all this, I didn't yet feel completely American. Since America didn't seem to fully embrace people like me, I felt that America didn't deserve me. Thus, I let my identities float. What I discovered in my search for a way to belong was that I had a talent to blend in, unnoticed, with the darker, poorer underclass of whatever place in which I was visiting or living. Among those people, I never had to be the "other." When my husband and I first met, at a poetry reading being given by the First Lady of Nicaragua, he assumed that I was Nicaraguan, a member of the darker, English-speaking people of their Atlantic coast. I didn't realize that even at home, as myself, I was never really the "other."

Then one day it dawned on me that to be American is to enjoy the right to reinvent oneself. In this way, I have always been an American because as an identity, as a brand name, America is still forming. As a concept, it is still malleable. I am helping to shape it, just as my parents helped to shape it. They became citizens so that they could vote for

Nelson Rockefeller and Jack Kennedy. When they cast that first vote they knew for sure that they would not leave the United States for any reason in the world. It was their home. And through all my wanderings, I must have also understood that it was my real home because I have never missed an election. I have never missed the opportunity to take part in the dream. The one that Daddy promised my mother and her grandparents. The dream of America.

Reluctant Citizen

ANNETTE GALLAGHER WEISMAN

> *Hardly anything else that happened to me was*
> *as important as this: that I left one country and*
> *came to another. That an ordinary displacement*
> *made an extraordinary distance between the word*
> *place and the word mine.*
>
> *Eavan Boland,* Object Lessons

I'VE SEEN THEM ON THE NEWS, desperate people taking desperate measures to reach our shores: the United States of America. I've felt both sympathy and shame as I've watched parched, exhausted bodies being airlifted from makeshift boats in shark-infested waters. I've also watched dispirited families who've barely had a glimpse of the land of affluence before being herded back across the Rio Grande by U.S. marshals. Some of these émigrés may have been given asylum, but most I knew would never achieve their dream: to live permanently in the United States.

In 1977, I married an American—a slam dunk for citizenship. I remained, by choice, a legal resident, a status that permitted me every legal right except the right to vote. My feelings of shame in watching those emigres struggle for survival was because I had what they wanted—a green card—yet it took almost twenty years before I would officially give up one country for another.

It seemed to me I should feel passionate about becoming an American, but I could not. Swearing allegiance to this country instead of the place I still, in my heart, called home was like changing religions or cutting off a limb. Part of me resisted such a drastic move. I wasn't fleeing from some despot, or pursuing a dream, nor trying to support a family. I wanted to live here without having to abandon my country of origin by becoming someone else: an American. The problem was my love for Ireland; my Irishness had been taken away from me once, I did not want it to happen again.

Yet in a sense I had grown up with Americans. The first television show I saw as a child, in Dublin, was *The Lone Ranger*. Unlike Britain's British Broadcasting Company, the newly formed Radio Telefís Éireann had in the '60s filled much of its air time with American TV shows. I watched everything from *Bonanza* to *Hawaii Five-O*, and even named our dog, Paladin, after a western series.

My view of how the average American lived was largely based on *Father Knows Best*: that perfect family with perfect teeth and not one hair out of place. Even small details of their lives intrigued me. For instance, instead of mail (which we called post) being dropped through a small opening in our front door, Americans had a big box on a stand at the end of their driveway. Everything about America seemed bigger, and maybe better, but I had no desire to live there. It didn't occur to me. I was happy to watch Americans on television, happy, too, when John F. Kennedy came to visit his ancestral home, but he never inspired thoughts about leaving Dublin. Years later, a few months after my marriage, Bob and I moved from New York to Colorado. And it was then, only then, as a young wife sitting on a crate waiting for the moving van to arrive that I noticed the mailbox at the end of our driveway, and I realized I was now part of the American dream—the one I'd watched on television. We subsequently moved to other places in the Midwest; yet I never felt at home. In short, I never felt American.

My Irish sensibilities are hard to define, it's more a feeling that's ingrained to my very core. Though I don't sound or look particularly Irish, I connect instantly with someone who has an Irish background. Even second-generation Americans will have that mischievous glint in their eyes, or a look of melancholy that could make one cry, and, especially when times are tough, a wry sense of humor. While I don't bear any grudges, I bear the wounds of my forefathers, who for hundreds of years had their land, religion, and language forcibly taken from them.

Oddly, other than making plum puddings at Christmastime and a few other holiday rituals, I don't have many Irish customs to remind me of my family and my Irish roots. I've eaten more corned beef and cabbage over here than I ever did in Ireland. While my mother cooked Irish recipes such a colcannon (a potato dish mixed with cabbage or leeks, milk, and plenty of butter), and on special occasions Dublin Lawyer (lobster pieces mixed with cream, flamed in Irish whiskey, and put back in its shell), she loved to create her version of international cuisine. Our family often had dishes such as chicken cacciatore, shrimp creole, or Indian curry for dinner, and for dessert, maybe trifle or baked Alaska. We weren't rich, but we ate well.

In fact, the aroma and taste of food is something I associate with Ireland: the hot, buttery potato pancakes my mother made for me after school; the raspberries and blackberries I picked in the Dublin mountains that spilled over the basket of my blue Raleigh; and the rich smell of coffee and exotic teas that would emanate from the portals of a well-known restaurant, Bewley's of Grafton Street.

I didn't join any Irish organizations when I first came to this country, feeling wary of any group that sets one apart. With blond hair, blue eyes, and no language barrier, it was easy for me to assimilate; I could be from many places. The same reasons that made it easy, however, also caused an identity crisis within myself. My Dublin accent isn't the brogue Americans are used to, so they often think I'm English. When I tell them I'm not, I'm Irish, they apologize, thinking they've offended me, when I'm simply stating who I am. Once, on Fifth Avenue, I heard a woman with a Dublin accent pass by and almost ran after her . . . to say what? I don't know. But I was so used to thinking I should sound like an Irish Spring commercial it was a relief to come across someone like me: a middle-class Dubliner.

Though the reasons for my reluctance to become an American are complicated, they all stem from this: the afternoon in May when my mother came into my room and sat beside me on the bed. Before she could say "We're moving to London," her shoulders began to heave in epileptic jerks and she cried uncontrollably. I had seen my mother cry before, from frustration, anger, sadness, but nothing like this: sheer gut-wrenching misery. I put one arm around her, and with the other hand picked at the tufts of cotton on my candlewick spread, not sure what to say. When she'd calmed down, she told me very little about the situation, but enough to know that our departure for England was imminent. Later, I asked, "Will I not be going to France this summer?" At seventeen, I had been looking forward to being an exchange student and couldn't believe what she had told me: that my father had gone bankrupt and we had to leave Ireland. "No, pet," my mother said. "But you will, this is only temporary."

Of course, it wasn't temporary. Neither were the drastically different circumstances we found ourselves living in for the next few years. My father, who'd taken a job as an elevator man at the Dorcester Hotel, in Hyde Park, eventually found work as a manager of a printing firm; actually several of them, as one after another shut down. But, in midlife, he couldn't find a job in advertising again. And from then on, he never had much leisure time at all, working well into his seventies, till he was literally broken, stooped over and short of breath. My mother, Kay Gallagher, was personal assistant for twenty-one years to four consecutive ambassadors of the Ethiopian embassy. Like my father, she worked well into her seventies, until she died of cancer in February 1997.

After several moves, my parents settled in southeast London with my sister, Susan, and two brothers, Brian and David, who are much younger than me. By that time I had a flat of my own in Chelsea, so I never lived with them. My sister bought the house a few years ago, but with both our parents now dead, the only place I still consider home, other than Cincinnati, is Ireland.

Yet I have been technically British most of my life. Other than my new American passport, the only one I've ever owned was British. A passport wasn't necessary to travel between England and Ireland, so I didn't need one until I went to Italy in my early twenties. The trip with my boyfriend was relatively spur of the moment. According to a 1947

Act of Parliament, I was entitled to a British passport because my paternal grandmother was English. I got one partly for the sake of expediency and partly because a British MP, Enoch Powell, was making racist comments at the time about repealing the Act to keep various Commonwealth subjects and undesirables, such as the Irish, out of England. I was happy to inform him, when I met him once, that I was Irish, and so was my boss, Patrick Cosgrave, a senior officer in the Conservative Research Department.

I was by no means "a true blue," and was becoming by default more English than I intended to be. Patrick, who wrote erudite articles for English journals such as the *Spectator*, was formerly the London correspondent for Radio Telefís Éireann. I had been his personal assistant, cajoling well-known people such as British Members of Parliament, for him to interview.

I liked working for Patrick and was flattered when he asked me to join him. I hoped, being Irish, he would be able to influence British legislation to provide socio-economic fairness for all in Northern Ireland, a struggle perceived incorrectly as solely warfare between two religions, and not based on inequities in areas such as housing and voting rights, of which the Protestant minority had the upper hand.

The Conservative Research Department, near the Houses of Parliament, was an extraordinary place. Edward Heath, the shadow Prime Minister at the time, had an office on the top floor of the building: an elegant house, not a skyscraper. Sometimes I'd see the "Iron Maiden" herself, Margaret Thatcher, trudge up the stairs, brown bag in hand, to have lunch with him. Another iron lady, an old dowager type accompanied by her bullmastiff dog, kept a strict eye on us "girls." She was "displeased" when a secretary pinned a movie headline on the wall behind a handsome, if somewhat narcissistic, junior officer, which read, "Patten: Lust for Glory." The officer was Christopher Patten, who would later become Governor of Hong Kong.

Apart from becoming confusingly British, I also adopted a new name, or rather reacquired my given one; like obtaining a British passport, it made the most sense at the time. I was christened Annette Frances Gallagher, but when I was too young to remember my mother started calling me June. Annette had been my father's choice and I don't think my mother really cared for it. That, coupled with the fact I was born in June, seemed to warrant the change. So I grew up in Dublin as June Gallagher. Other than an occasional reason to fill out an official form, I forgot about my real name.

When I worked at *Vanity Fair* magazine in London, there were a couple of Junes already on staff. Upon discovering my name was Annette, the editor, Audrey Slaughter, asked if I would mind being called that. I didn't see a problem at the time and said no, naively thinking it was like having a pet name. Later, as I interviewed people and covered various events for the magazine, I found it impossible to revert to June.

This change of name had repercussions regarding my identity that I didn't realize till much later: in effect I became two people. I asked friends and relatives in Ireland to call me Annette, but that didn't work; they couldn't, or wouldn't, remember, yet by now more people knew me by my "real" name. I discovered in trying to eradicate June completely I would, in a sense, be wiping out my past life in Ireland, which I didn't want either, so I gave up. I had to reconcile myself to having two countries and two names.

My emotions regarding who I was were complicated a bit further by my marriage. At first I retained my maiden name. While it's logical to pronounce the second "g" in Gallagher, it is silent in Ireland, so when mispronounced it sounds like a different name to me. Also the combined Gallagher Weisman is a bit of a mouthful. I did, however, substitute *G* for my middle initial *F*, in a somewhat pathetic attempt to retain my Irishness, identify at least to myself who I am.

Language is another area of confusion. Sometimes my husband doesn't understand something I say, and asks me to speak "in English," which annoys me. One would think it would be more difficult if English were my second language. But there are subtler differences in language between English-speaking countries than spelling alone. I am always translating in my head from Irish English to English English and, finally, to American English. If English were my second language, others might appreciate the effort I make to accommodate them, rather than assume I'm the one who doesn't speak English properly.

Apart from grammar, there are expressions and even names of common items that vary, yet sometimes two out of the three countries use the same terminology, so I have to remember which ones. For instance, the English and Irish usually say "courgettes" for zucchini, the Americans and the English say "spring onions" for scallions. I have gone into a store in England and asked for a sliced pan and no one knew what I meant. It means sliced bread, probably a derivative from the French word for bread: *pain*. And on and on. I try not to use expressions such as "I have to get my skates on," which means to hurry up, but sometimes my Gaelic grammar returns without my being aware of it. And I will, if hardly ever, say something like "Will I not be going to France?"

The Irish poet Eavan Boland tells the story of moving to England as a young child and saying to a teacher, "I amn't getting on the bus." I felt empathy for her, knowing it was an Irish way of speaking (a contraction for "I am not"), and could almost hear the chill in her voice when the teacher snapped back, "You're not in Ireland now." Eavan also spoke of the map on the wall at school that was a history not her own; she wanted to remember Irish places and events before she forgot them—"To ask where exactly was my old house? Its brass One and Seven." Neither did I want to eradicate my history: my name, my country, my language. When I went to school, the Irish language was a compulsory subject from first grade on. I resented it at the time, because I also took Latin and felt one dead language was enough. Like most languages that are rarely used, I can't speak it conversationally, but I can pronounce it well and understand some of it. In fact, the sound of Irish is always in my head and on my tongue: it's in everything I say and write. Just like my accent it's inherent, and not something I can eradicate completely, even if I wanted to. Sometimes though, I wish I were the Hollywood version of my nationality, with red hair, freckles, and a strong brogue, so I wouldn't keep confusing people and ultimately myself about my country of origin.

Unlike author Frank McCourt in his memoir *Angela's Ashes*, I did not have a miserable childhood. My memories of growing up in Dublin did not contain scenes of pitiful deprivation and destitution, at least in a material sense. His experience was not mine, nor remotely similar to anyone I knew. Like McCourt, I was educated in Catholic schools, but there were several lay teachers who were not Catholic, including a Jewish elocution mistress, Mrs. Weingreen, both loved and feared by all. And the nuns never beat us, except one who was known to rap the knuckles of piano students with a ruler. I have grown weary, frustrated, and irritated in general by the ignorant, country-bumpkin, pigs-in-the-parlor kind of image that books, plays, and movies continue to foist on the public, as if it were the norm.

Not that I think Ireland is perfect. Far from it. I didn't need to fear murders and burglaries, we kept our doors, like most people, unlocked, but when one lives on an island an insular way of thinking prevails. The Catholic Church back then was in effect the Monarchy of Ireland, revered and looked up to by the majority. The Church strongly influenced the behavior of Catholics. Not that that was bad—being kind to one another is a good thing—but intolerance of one's fellow man isn't. Women who were pregnant out of wedlock were shamed and had to go to England for an abortion if they wanted one. Contraceptives were unavailable, as those were against the Church's laws too. Homosexuality wasn't even discussed, and women claimed to walk into doors, rather than admit their husbands beat them. I didn't know anyone who took drugs, so I led a fairly sheltered life until we moved to London.

Unlike Northern Ireland, however, there was no religious animosity in the Republic and I had both Protestant and Jewish friends. I wasn't raised to be racially prejudiced either. However, I rarely even saw anyone of color, other than an African or Indian student walking in and out of Trinity College. But when my family moved to London in the mid-'60s, the first man I dated, fell in love with, and slept with was black. A man who'd grown up on an island too, Mauritius, off the coast of Africa in the Indian Ocean. He had the added cachet of speaking French, and I was smitten by his looks and charisma.

Sometimes we have no control over events that shape our lives, nor realize the implications of decisions we've made. That's what happened to me: I already knew what it was like to have two names, two languages, and ostensibly belong to two countries. I wanted separation emotionally from the second country I'd lived in, England, before I could contemplate a third. And something deeper than that. It isn't that I'm anti-English: some flag-waving extremist whose pride in one's heritage has caused this emotional angst of separation from homeland. I'm not much interested in parades, have never drunk green beer, and abhor terrorist acts. There's just something in me that says I'm Irish, how could I be anything else?

I had had no choice in the matter when we moved to England: one day I was a happy high school girl in Dublin, the next I was a necessary financial component in helping to support the family, so that any of my airy-faerie ideas, such as college, art school, or finishing schools abroad were not feasible. I think that's the main reason it took me so long to become American: freedom of choice. Now that I was free to choose one country over another, I would do so when I was ready. Finally it happened like this:

When my father died, unexpectedly, I couldn't find my passport. While I had been thinking of becoming an American increasingly over the years, the quickest thing to do in time for his funeral was to get another British one. Unfortunately, my green card was in the one I'd mislaid. Nothing, however, would stop me from attending my father's funeral. So I left Cincinnati without re-applying for the card that would secure my re-entry into the United States. On my return, I was ushered into a room with the proverbial lightbulb over my head and interrogated by two immigration officials. I had three options: pay a fine and be deported; renew my legal residency status and pay a fine; or become an American citizen. There was only one logical decision, I realized then, it was also the one I truly wanted. The officer asked how long I'd been married and seemed more amused than surprised by my reluctance to becoming a citizen, saying, "British people always take the longest, My mother-in-law took as long as you did." I was about to correct him and say I wasn't British, I was Irish, which would have been ridiculous considering he had my passport in his hand, but realized it didn't matter anymore: I had resolved to become an American.

I had to commit to citizenship before I could go home, so after signing some papers I was given a date to go down to the Immigration and Naturalization Service. Among the forms I'd been given to fill out was an example of the test I'd have to take. On my way to the interview my ten-year-old son, Patrick, quizzed me in the car; I was afraid I might forget the names of the American presidents and various aspects of the Constitution. The exam was easy. I only wavered when it came to my signature; I paused for a moment, and then wrote: Annette Gallagher Weisman.

Along with people from thirty-seven other countries. I became an American citizen on December 13, 1996. I remember that the presiding judge was a woman, there were witnesses from the American Legion, and two Boy Scouts read a poem. And finally, a woman lawyer from the Philippines gave an eloquent speech about how she still retained her heritage, though she was proud to be an American. Ironic. But I was now at peace with that inner struggle.

As I took the oath, I was struck for a moment by the words "I will bear arms on behalf of the United States . . ." Wait a minute, I thought, but nobody else seemed to flinch, and the pledge continued. I could hardly hold up the proceedings, but I continued to think about it. I knew I would have fought for Ireland if it came to that; providing it was a just cause, I could do no less for the United States.

Just like living with my husband before we got married, I discovered that becoming a citizen, as opposed to being a legal resident, has a palpable heft; in my opinion, the piece of paper does matter. Despite denials beforehand, one does feel more committed after the oath whether it's to a lover or to a country.

When you truly love, you allow for idiosyncrasies and weaknesses. That's how I feel about Ireland. I will always love it despite its insular ways, now much improved since it has been included in the European Economic Community and is no longer suppressed by or financially dependent on England. Unlike a person, however, Ireland didn't leave me, I left it. If you've ever relinquished someone or something that meant a great deal to you, then maybe you can understand my feelings of abandoning Ireland. Part of you remains with that place, or person you loved, and in return they've added a new dimension to your life. You're no longer your original self, but a hybrid made up of as many places or people who've mattered to you. As writer Luc Sante once said:

"I have become permanently 'other.' The choice I am faced with is simple: either I am at home everywhere or I am nowhere at all . . ."

That is how I felt for almost twenty years; if I couldn't be Irish, I would be "other." But, as in marriage, I've found that I want to forsake all others. I want to be loyal to the country I'm in, which I still have difficulty calling mine. I owe it that. I am now consciously trying to look at things from an American, rather than a European, perspective, without losing, or clinging to, my Irish heritage.

I attended a ball game a few months after becoming a citizen, and sat with my family enjoying the whole American scene: the guy going up and down the aisles yelling. "Hey, beer. Beer here"; the instant camaraderie of complete strangers as they passed someone's money along to the vendor; the peanut shells on the floor; my daughter, Samantha, cheering, looking all-American in her blue jeans and baseball cap; Patrick's intense look of concentration and Bob's unsolicited coaching advice to the players far below; "the wave" of fans to encourage a little action on the field.

I remember that day clearly. That was the day, I first put my hand over my heart and sang the words to the national anthem instead of looking down at the ground as I used to do, feeling embarrassed. I was at last united with my family. I had finally swum ashore to join them.

Unbecoming American

MITSUYE YAMADA

FOR YEARS AFTER MOVING TO SOUTHERN CALIFORNIA from New York with my husband and our three young children, I felt that I was just a resident here, not an inhabitant. One does not become an inhabitant until one feels rooted, until one begins to blend in, and until the landscape becomes one's natural habitat. As we drove through miles of vast desert spaces into the Southwest from New York in 1960, the stark landscape had little appeal to me. We were moving to my husband's new job in California. Towering palm trees greeted us as we approached the "civilized" areas kept green with imported water. Our nine-year-old daughter exclaimed, "Are we in a foreign country?", and indeed, everything seemed to grow to gross and untamed proportions on this land. At our new home in Sierra Madre, a suburb of Los Angeles, I stepped out the back door and saw that the blazing sun had dried up the grass and most of the plants except for one startling presence: an eight-foot century plant guarding the back door. A lizard skittered across one of its long sharp tentacles writhing wildly in the hot sun. For a second I flashed on the miniature version of this plant which I carelessly tossed into the garbage while packing. It sat demurely on my New York kitchen windowsill for years, but now exploded into a monster plant and was ready to take its revenge! I jumped back into the house and slammed the door.

Although in time I learned to appreciate that the true desert plants, such as this century plant, thrive on little water and take a hundred years to grow to maturity, in the beginning as a new immigrant to southern California, I resisted adjusting to my new environment. I considered myself a sojourner, a temporary resident, and became more psychologically isolated than ever.

Several years ago when I was asked to participate in a panel of "California writers," I realized this desertlike land where I had felt most alien now owns me. Here is where I recognized, finally, that I must have felt displaced in every other place I had ever lived in: Seattle, Fukuoka (Japan), Minidoka, Cincinnati, Chicago, and New York. With that recognition, I have come to know who I am. Here is where I could now say, "I am a poet, a woman, an Asian American." I have adapted to the rhythms of the desert and have become a California poet. At what point in one's life does a transplanted alien become a true inhabitant? How does she finally become symbiotically connected to the land she occupies?

I think of how my mother came to create her own "community" while living in the United States for seventy-eight years. When she died, several months short of her ninety-eighth birthday in 1997, all fourteen of her grandchildren and a few of her great-grandchildren traveled from coast to coast to Seattle, Washington, for her memorial services. They sat one evening exchanging what one of them called "Grammaisms" with each other. Although only two of the grandchildren spoke Japanese (her language of preference), she had no trouble communicating to them her high expectations of them as well as her displeasure over their behavior, dress, or haircut. She actively participated in the lives of her four children's growing families and kept us all very much aware of our ancestral ties to Japan. My three brothers and I, following what has now come to be seen as a path taken by most Nisei (second-generation Japanese Americans) who lived through the internment experience during World War II, scattered throughout the country, married, and raised our children in primarily white neighborhoods. But no matter where we were, in the suburbs of Seattle, Chicago, Denver, New York, or California, she came for extended visits and settled in with ease in our homes and neighborhoods because she brought with her her own culture: her language, rituals, customs, and food. Because she seemed, through all these years, to fiercely resist assimilation, my children would ask her if she ever considered going back "home" to Japan to live and she would answer, "Of course not. America is my home because my children are here." I marveled at my mother's ability to make our collective homes her portable "community."

On the other hand, for me, every move to a new geographical area was a wrenching experience. I moved often since leaving our home in Seattle. Although I am, by most standards, a thoroughly assimilated Japanese American, I have felt displaced no matter where I was. Both my mother and I became U.S. citizens in 1955, when the McCarran-Walter Immigration and Nationality Act of 1952 made it possible for us to do so. She in Chicago at age fifty-six, and I in New York at age thirty-two. She moved from the state of being "unnatural" to becoming "naturalized" with great jubilation. She and her friends celebrated their new standing as Americans for days.

I was a bit more circumspect about taking advantage of a new law that granted me citizenship but was racially discriminatory to Asians in the Asian-Pacific Triangle. When I told one of my friends that I was now a U.S. citizen, she said, "Oh for heaven's sake, I thought you already were. How come you weren't?" The comment and question made me not want to tell anyone else because they reminded me of how little most "ordinary" Americans know of the racist nature of their laws and underscored the unfairness of these laws that deprived my parents and me of U.S. citizenship through all these years. My mother had no such reservations. She continued to be as Japanese as she always was, but reveled in her new status as a U.S. citizen. I reasoned that the difference between us was that I had greater needs than she, emotionally, socially, and intellectually. My mother came to accept the world as it was handed to her and seemed not to be fazed by contradictions in her life. I, having been educated in America, demanded more from American institutions and was continually frustrated when they did not live up to my expectations. Whatever it was, most of my life I struggled to find a place I could call "home" until we moved to California.

I grew up in the 1920s and '30s in Seattle, Washington, a land of little sun and much rain. I lived there during most of my childhood years before World War II, which were, by most standards, relatively benign and happy ones. Yet, because of the circumstances of my birth, I, unlike my three brothers who were native-born American citizens, was often reminded of my "foreignness" when I was growing up. I must not do or think as they do, I was often told by my parents, because I was *nihon umare* (born in Japan). How this "happened" was part of my mother's story, often told and retold, of the "hard time" she had raising us all alone without family support in this country. My father, overwhelmed by the thought of the birth of a third child, decided mother would be better off in Japan with her family during her confinement. She set off for Japan (it used to take two whole weeks on a boat, she would say) when she was six months pregnant, Mike, her older son barely two and a half years old, and Tosh, the younger son, only ten months old. A month after my birth, Tosh, then fourteen months old, became seriously ill with encephalitis. She was forced to return to Seattle with him for medical help that was not available in Japan at that time, leaving me with a nursing mother and Mike with our fraternal grandparents. Because of Tosh's long convalescence, I joined my parents when I was three and a half years old. Mike came to join us much later when he was eight years old. Joe, the youngest son, was born when the family was finally all together. So we were a family of three American-born citizens and three noncitizens.

The ineligibility-to-citizenship status of the three of us made my parents feel unwelcome in their adopted land, but with the birth of their American children, they were resigned to staying here. She was determined that I, the only Japanese citizen among her children, should be brought up a properly educated Japanese girl. Otherwise, she often told me, "you won't know who you are."

I was sent to Japanese language school on weekdays after American public school, and on weekends, taken to flower arrangement and tea ceremony classes at the Japanese Community Center. I was enrolled in a Japanese dancing school and given calligraphy lessons by a "master Japanese calligrapher" who came to our home. It seemed to me that my brothers, who only attended Japanese school with me, did not have to take their lessons as seriously as I did and often cut classes with impunity. When I had the temerity to complain about this to my mother, she explained that my brothers were, after all, American citizens. And besides, she would say much to my puzzlement at the time, "they are boys." I was to learn years later that my oldest brother, Mike, who spoke only Japanese when he joined our family at age eight, was having his own adjustment problems at school, but to me in those years, the boys always had more freedom than I did.

When I was sent back to Japan at the age of eleven, I learned that I was a displaced person there as well. In the small village in Kyushu where I was left with my mother's relatives, I was completely baffled by the country dialect that my relatives spoke. The language I learned in the U.S., the carefully cultivated Tokyo dialect my mother taught my brothers and me, was a source of much merriment to my cousins. I was enrolled in sixth grade with special circumstances in a girls' school because my training at the American Japanese-language school in Seattle ill-prepared me to compete at my grade level in Japan. Hours of private tutoring by the teacher after school hours were not enough to help bring me up to par with the other students. I sat in on the classes without participating and was encouraged to mingle "for social intercourse with girls of my own age." But through my cousins, I had learned that my speech was a stilted formal Japanese of deference spoken only to mothers and teachers, not at all suitable for casual conversation with one's peers. Needless to say, I hardly opened my mouth, except to respond *hai* or *iiye* (yes or no) when spoken to during recess and lunch. The girls were generally kind, including me in their games, assuming that I was a painfully shy American girl who didn't speak Japanese.

After a year and a half of schooling in Japan, I returned to join my parents and brothers in the United States, much relieved to be back in familiar surroundings. That short period of feeling like a total alien in Japan, being taunted by my cousins and sitting on the sidelines at the girls' middle school, gave me a renewed sense of my Americanness when I returned to America. I no longer accepted my parents' admonitions that I must behave like a properly humble Japanese girl. I gave up all the lessons they were subjecting me to except Japanese school. By high school, I became as thoroughly "assimilated" as I thought my brothers were. I cut Japanese school regularly, having become actively involved in the debate team and the creative writing magazine staff which met after school. Because I returned home at the usual hour as if I'd attended Japanese school, my parents only learned of the deception when I brought home a report card with an F in Deportment for my frequent absences. After the initial shock, they winked at this single (they thought) infraction because my grades were acceptable. The year of tutoring in Japan had put me far ahead of my classmates, and I did well on most tests. Moreover, I became the darling of the teacher because instead of awkward Japanese phrases copied out of the exercise book, I turned in free-flowing prose for the composition assignments. I then became a misfit among my Nisei classmates in American Japanese school.

I realized early on that my mother's determination to keep me connected to our "old country" by language and culture ran somewhat counter to her own early attempts to please my father by learning the ways of the new country. One of my most vivid memories of my early preschool days is that of accompanying my mother twice a week to the local Japanese Baptist Church to attend English classes with the Japanese immigrant women in the neighborhood. The single most influential person in the lives of the new Japanese immigrant women in the 1920s in Seattle was Miss MacNeil. To me, a five-year-old Japanese child who had just recovered from a serious illness and was probably very small for my age, she was an enormous presence. My father referred to her as "the big white spinster lady" and my mother called her "Misu Maku neelu." The table she and other Japanese immigrant women sat around in the kitchen of what must have been the parish house of the church was covered with oilcloth with green lines and faded red cherries. The oilcloth had a distinctive oil smell that I always associated for many years after with Miss MacNeil. My mother and the other women had composition books they scribbled on. The women sat at the table hunched over their tablets painstakingly copying the letters Miss Mac-Neil wrote with white chalk on a small slate with a wooden border she held in her hand.

Going to these English classes was a big event for me. I usually sat
with two other girls in the corner of the room where there were a few
blocks and some pamphlets with colored pictures of Jesus in them. We
usually sat in a row in small wooden chairs with dowel backs that pressed
against my bony back. We were not permitted to talk while our mothers'
lessons were going on. I could only sit rigidly and stare at Miss Mac-
Neil's giant brown Oxford shoes. Once when I wiggled and squirmed
so much that the chair legs made scraping sounds on the wooden floor,
my mother came and took me to the bathroom, although I did not
have to go. She hustled me back, put her hands on my shoulders, and
firmly pressed me down into the chair seat.

The best part of the day was after the lessons when they wiped the
oilcloth and spread out their *obento*. They all brought the same kind of
lunch, rice balls with pickles. The voices that spoke in halting English
phrases during lessons burst into lively Japanese sounds during lunch.
Mother told me some years later that Miss MacNeil told them to bring
sandwiches for lunch if they want to be "real American," but none of
them knew what to put between two pieces of bread. They tried tofu
and *kamaboko* (fish cakes) fillings but went back to rice balls until Miss
MacNeil started giving them cooking lessons.

For my mother, getting ready for these sessions was an elaborate
affair. The day before, she went to have her hair marcelled by her friend
who ran a beauty shop in her small apartment. Mother's thick black
hair, usually worn straight back in a bun, at least one day a week gracefully framed her face in large waves. She would wear one of her Sunday
dresses, a dressy affair with a soft bow on the V neckline, a drop waist,
and a slightly flared skirt. She wore shoes, a pair of brown shoes with
buttons at the side. I was put in a dress with little ruffles at the hem,
one of a half dozen identical dresses hanging in my closet. My mother
always used the same pattern and sewed my dresses in several different
prints and colors. And I wore shoes also, a black patent leather pair
with a strap and a single button on the side, just like Mother's, and a
pair of long white cotton stockings.

These English lessons must have lasted for several years even after I
had started school. I noticed one day when I peeked into my mother's

composition book which she left on the dining room table, that she was still writing words one at a time in laborious handwriting while I was already learning to write English in sentences in public school. This didn't seem particularly strange to me since I had never heard Mother express herself in English, not even in single words.

By this time Miss MacNeil's English classes had turned into late afternoon cooking classes. Mother no longer made rice balls or sandwiches for her lunch but instead took an empty double-decker box wrapped in a *furoshiki* and brought home fried chicken, slices of meat loaf, boiled potatoes, vegetables, or biscuits to share with the family. One day when I accompanied her to her class because it was a public school holiday, I noticed that the classroom was transformed into a colorful vibrant room. The walls were now covered with Washington Delicious apple posters and diagrams and charts with brightly colored meat cuts, vegetables, and fruit drawings on them. The women wrote recipes and information about the four food groups in their little composition books. They drew diagrams of table settings. Mother's notebook was covered with Japanese words around the sketches of table settings she had drawn. The utensils were numbered with an explanation of how each was to be used.

During these lessons, the women in Mother's class subscribed to the *Ladies' Home Journal* that had recipes, pictures of colorful table decorations, drawings of women in the latest fashions, and even a column on social manners (Emily Post, I believe). I remember thinking with pride that my mother looked almost like one of the women in the magazine, marcelled waves and all. Miss MacNeil's English classes may have been a failure, but her cooking classes were embraced with great enthusiasm. Moreover, she not only taught them to cook and eat American, but also to dress and behave American.

At home Mother practiced everything she learned in her classes, everything except English. She continued to speak Japanese to us. I don't remember what mealtime was like at home in the days before Miss MacNeil except that they must have felt normal and comfortable because I don't remember them. Suddenly eating dinner in our household became an elaborate ritual. My mother took her lessons quite seriously and cooking American meals became almost an obsession with her. She became nutrition conscious and made sure that our meals were well balanced with the four food groups represented. We ate potatoes instead of rice, except for my father, who insisted on his rice every day.

I was instructed to set the table in a formal manner with the whole set of silverware complete with napkins personalized with embroidered initials. The napkins were unused, for none of us ever got into the habit of using them. Her correcting our table manners was a source of constant irritation for us. We argued that we don't have to keep "company manners" at home and she countered that good manners have to be learned so that we would come by it naturally. "You don't want to feel uncomfortable in front of company, do you?" she would say.

One day Mother announced to us that my father was going to bring home company, a *hakujin-san* (a white person) from the office. There was a flurry of activity, polishing the silver flatware, the silver tea set, a Christmas gift that had sat on the cupboard for years unused. She spent hours ironing the linen tablecloth and the linen napkins my father had bought especially for this occasion. I helped set the table with the napkins in small round silver napkin holders.

When we heard my father's car in the driveway, my baby brother, who was watching from the kitchen window, shouted, "Papa's home! A lady's with him." It took us all by surprise. The *hakujin-san* was a lady! It was not unusual for my father to bring home guests for dinner, but they were always Japanese men and my mother cooked and served them Japanese dishes with seeming ease. In a few minutes my father and his lady guest came around the house to the front door, long enough for us to compose ourselves as we lined up by the front entrance to greet them. Normally my younger brother would have run up to him and jumped into his arms and the rest of us would follow, but on this day, my father opened the front door and stepped aside to let the lady enter the house before him. We watched silently. Then he introduced us to her. "This is my wife." The woman held her hand out, but Mother bowed her head and did not see the extended hand. "These are my children," he said, gesturing. He did not bother to introduce her to us, so we never did find out what her name was. She seemed to tower over all of us, including my father. He helped her out of her coat and hung it on the clothes tree in the hallway. She kept her cloche hat on. He then led her by the elbow into the living room. We watched this odd spectacle in silence. My mother tugged at my sleeve, a signal to stop staring and help her in the kitchen, and dismissed the boys to go outside and play. When I brought the tea on a small tray into the living room, I saw that she was sitting languidly on our sofa, her legs crossed and her arm stretched out on both sides, looking quite at home. She addressed my father by his American name, 'Jack.' They sat for a while in the living room chatting.

Mother, meanwhile, was clattering about in the kitchen. I was to peek through the crack from the swinging kitchen door, which connected the kitchen to the dining room with a partial view of the living room, to warn her when they looked ready to sit down at the table. As we prepared to serve the first course, Mother reminded me in a whisper, *Hidari kara.* She wanted to make sure I didn't forget to serve the soup and main dish from the left side. At the table, the guest said more than once, "What a charming table setting," and more than twice that "everything was just perfectly lovely."

"Mrs. Yasutake, please sit down and eat with us," she said as if she were the hostess inviting a guest to her table. My mother just stood leaning against the wall, her hands clasped behind her back and with her head bowed so low that I thought with embarrassment, "Why is she cowering?" My father was telling his guest that Mother was taking courses on how to prepare American meals. At the end of the evening, they came into the kitchen where Mother and I were cleaning up to thank us. Then, turning to my father, his guest said, "She ought to get an A for that dinner. Don't you think so, Jack?"

Soon after this dinner, I noticed that Mother stopped going to her cooking lessons, and our table at home became a mixture of both American and Japanese dishes. I do not know whether or not this one incident which I remember with such vividness had a singular impact in shaping my mother's resolve to remain herself.

What I thought was her stubborn refusal to see that I also needed to be myself kept us estranged for a number of years until I became a mother myself, moved to southern California, and became involved in the women's movement. With the women's movement and its analysis of patriarchy, "man's dominion" over not only women but over the whole planet was being exposed as a destructive force. Strangely enough, my coming to understand the desert in turn made me realize that Mother was indeed entitled to her own culture, her dignity.

For a long time for me, the desert wilderness meant isolation from the center of life, a hostile place where venomous and dangerous creatures lurk, a barren place useful only for dumping toxic waste, for testing nuclear weapons, and for exiling "undesirable" human beings. I spent a year and a half in the desert of Idaho during the first years of World War II. For us "inmates," the Idaho desert literally meant isolation and alienation; the desert was not just a metaphor for us. We were faced with the harsh realities of the desert every day: the penetrating sun and the interminable dust in our beds, our food, our nostrils.

Thirty-five years later, when I was teaching English at a community college, a neighbor and colleague, an environmental biologist, guided me into the desert wilderness and the sand dunes that opened up a new world of wonder to me. I learned that the desert is necessary for our survival, that the animals and plants that live on very limited resources share what little there is in a most amazing kind of symbiosis, and that the beauty of this land is often hidden and always fleeting. I learned of the amazing adaptive features of the animals that the desert has provided refuge for.

Through my explorations of the desert areas, I came to feel a strong kinship with this land which struggles to retain its essential character. I saw that great vast parts of the desert have had to succumb to human intrusions, but that some parts of the desert resisted development and stubbornly insists on retaining its integrity. It was this characteristic of the desert that reminded me of my mother. Without realizing it at the time, I was powerfully transformed by this place, and came to full consciousness for the first time. I came to realize that my mother and I both live in a world that means to objectify us. Gradually, I came to fully appreciate what the desert holds.

I have come to identify with the desert, as a woman, an Asian American, the "other" in white America most of my life. Now, I am an older woman who is no longer biologically fertile, a retired teacher who no longer works for a salary and therefore no longer productive in the eyes of society. I must redefine the much misunderstood desert just as I must redefine myself.

I became aware of myself as a woman in a patriarchal system, as a person of color in white America, as an Asian-American woman in the women's movement, and as a poet in a society where serious poetry was not held in high regard. I came to realize that my training in all the American schools did not teach me to write from my own mythic perspective, but from the perspective of white patriarchal America.

Finally, I've come to place my roots here with the realization that we are all displaced creatures, no matter where we are, unless we become part of the natural process on the land where we live. Survival for Asian-Americans in the past decades has meant redefining ourselves to a world that has consistently misrepresented us. It is a demand for full partnership, not as exotic plants in a foreign land, but as part of the community of humans. We Asian-Americans have, by gradually contributing our own unique culture, changed the cultural landscape of this land forever.

The Language of Dreams

BELLE YANG

I.

To speak Chinese is to inherit the memory of hunger.

On lunar New Year's eve, flushed with wine and beef from the fire-pot, Baba's eyes grow misty. I know what my father is going to say. On a cozy, full belly, he is reminded of the past on a empty belly. "Ahhh, there was that year when the locust swarmed across the provinces, eating up all the corn, the rice, the millet. What could the country folk do but cook locusts for their dinner," he would say. Or, "I remember toward the end of the Japanese occupation, all we had was soybeans. We were ravenous, but we knew not to eat too much of it all at once, because the stuff swelled in the stomach and could kill us."

I am a great believer in *ming*, Chinese for life, but also fate. Had I been born on the mainland of China in 1960 instead of the island of Taiwan, I may have been one of the over thirty million Chinese to perish in the worst famine known to mankind.

To be born in China in the twentieth century is to live life as a colossal waste: wasted plans, wasted opportunities, wasted resources. Even men and women of talent born into privilege have disappeared without a murmur in the maelstrom.

To understand Chinese means to hear the underlying layers of cynicism born of an ancient country of interminable wars, of a people who have had to contend with too little for too long. Take this adage: One thirsty monk will carry two buckets of water on a shoulder pole; two thirsty monks will carry one bucket of water on a shoulder pole between them; three thirsty monks will remain thirsty because each thinks the other two should go get the water.

I felt I was tainted simply because I was keen to the nuances of cynicism. I felt evil. It didn't matter that I was not a misanthrope, but as long as I understood what was being said, I could not escape the legacies of a culture whose optimism, and perhaps, life, was ebbing. If only I could be immune to cynicism, I would truly become American—innocent, open, sunny.

I have often envied my American-born Chinese friends who are seemingly cleanly severed at birth from the Chinese language. They learned their first words in American English, and their souls tend to brightness and laughter. When they visit China, they are oblivious to the darkness which swirls about their ears; they are protected by their ignorance. I, on the other hand, began soaking up Chinese inside my mother's belly and did not become immersed in English until I came to the United States in 1967. When I am in China, I feel every slight, slur, and nastiness on the crowded Beijing streets as deeply as flesh wounds.

Chinese is the language of memories as thick and pungent as fermented bean curd. Old, stale, fulsome. What did I want with memories?

When I pad past my parents' bedroom late at night, their heads have rolled together where their pillows meet, nose to nose, they reminisce, sotto voiced. Or if a duet of sustained breathing emerges from their open door, I know they are dreaming, in Chinese, of course.

Baba, as all obstinate souls do, dreams about the past. The Daoist uncle who rolled his cigarettes with the pages of his books after reading; the patriarch, Baba's grandfather, who loved chrysanthemums and boasted over one hundred varieties in his garden; his mother, bent over the lamp, sewing cloth shoes for him while, outside, the withered grape leaves clatter on the vine. The souls lost in the chaos of time and war flit across Baba's brow like shadow puppets.

He dreams of the treats from his childhood, the sesame-encrusted *hamatumi*, toad-spitting-honey—jam-filled cakes sold on the streets— or frozen persimmons, heavy with sweetness, spooned and eaten like ice cream. Baba's statement on his first day in America: "I'd rather die if I have only this foreigners' bread and milk for the rest of my life."

Chinese is more than an ethnic identity; it is also a system of belief, with its dogma, prejudice, and guilt-inducing credo. "What? You're not marrying a Chinese? What? You say you're going to become an American? You will always be Chinese no matter what citizenship you take up. China will always have a claim on you." In China there are Buddhists, Daoists, Muslims, Confucians, Christians among a host of religions, but each person, above all, is born spiritually, piously, religiously Chinese. There is no getting away from it.

II.

This house sitting on the sunny slope of Carmel Hill which faces the coastal Santa Lucia Range is filled with my parents' blue and white porcelains, cloissonés, antique screens carved with scenes from the *Romance of the Three Kingdoms*, a Chinese classic of intrigue and war. This is the house whose language, iconography, beliefs, and values I had raged against as a young woman. I wanted to run away from the Chinese universe I had been born into and launch into an American worldview, free of the weight of memories, only to return at the age of twenty-six, seeking refuge in all that I had once rejected.

It was all in the cliché of love gone wrong, turned violent. Lover turned stalker.

My prince charming was older by a mere six years, but to me, a student of twenty, he had all the answers. He was a rock climber, a musician, a builder. He was big, brash, and blond, and never apologetic. He was not the diminutive, myopic Chinese boys with fine, white hands I had known.

Slowly, almost imperceptibly, but with eyes wide open, I had relinquished my autonomy, my responsibility for my own destiny to a man who I believed would be my guide and protector. I had relinquished power to someone willing, capable of, and happy to manipulate me for his own purposes. Manipulation is an artful blend of abuse and sweetness; without the sweetness, who would be so blind as not to recognize abuse in all its nakedness. In time as I "grew up," as my own ideas and inclinations reared and abraded against his, he did not hesitate to apply his fists to my body so as to wrench my mind his way. I will always remember the look of intense fascination on his face—a look almost of joy—as he studied the black bruise he had left on my upper arm: it was in the perfect shape of his hand.

I did not learn what freedom was until after I learned all about slavery.

I had awakened from my drunkenness about love to a half-articulated remembering that I must return to origin to be safe again. I came back to my father and mother's house, this Chinese house.

"Look what trouble you've brought on yourself. Your life is a disaster!" my father said. He did not let me off easy. The Chinese believe your body, your life, is a gift from your parents. You must treasure this gift. I had only made a mess of the life I had been given.

My bodily soul wanted comforting, but severity was what I truly needed: a stern teacher who demanded spiritual clarity, someone who would not give solace, but make me afraid of who I had been. My father was the stern teacher.

This has always been a house of heavy expectations, of demands of excellence, where mediocrity is taboo, because to be mediocre is to know the taste of hunger, to perish. My parents had to be talented, excellent, sublime, fleet, strong to make their way out of the landscape of war and struggle to this American shore. If they were not these qualities, at least they knew to unfold their own myth: They had to believe that they were not just lucky, but luck itself.

But the irony is that in achieving America, which rendered them safe, they became insignificant. On arrival, they lost their language, the language in which they first learned to dream. They had come to America with nothing except pockets full of stories, but they had lost their voices. In Chinese, they were bards and minstrels; in English, their Chinese-hardened tongues were less than songlike.

I was confined to the house for my safety. If I managed to go out briefly, accompanied by my mother, Baba waited with palpitating heart, jumped at the sound of sirens. He was justified in his fears: My stalker had sent a hail of bullets through the office window of the lawyer who took my part, and later, had ransacked our home, taking photographs, mementos, volumes of my father's poems written in his own calligraphy.

The violence that followed me home only served to confirm my father's favorite mantra: "It is dangerous. The world is dangerous." War and the torturous path of escape had taught him this and now he found confirmation even in his time of peace.

How will you possibly manage to protect yourself? friends, the police, the court, the lawyers asked me. In the deepening crisis, it was China that offered me a haven. A place where I could disappear in the crowd of over one billion and find safety, live productively.

In the fall of 1986, at the age of twenty-six, I flew to Beijing to study classical Chinese art, focusing on the great tradition of landscape paint-ing—an art of time as well as space. I learned to cast away Western perspective and vault into the sky like the Monkey King of legend—to see the world from multiple angles (the Chinese landscape is intensely different from a Western one, where the viewer remains, still as a rock, at one fixed point).

During my three years of study, I roamed across the land, sketching, painting, looking. I reached regions closed to foreigners, to which my yellow skin gained me easy entry. I traveled the Gobi Desert along the Silk Road, where Buddhism first made its appearance in the Middle Kingdom; I dug into the yellow earth of the Great Northwest and laid my hands upon pottery, art of the late Stone Age, fitting my fingers into the clay imprints of hands left by craftsmen of some seven thousand years ago; I returned to the frozen Manchurian north to celebrate Spring Festival, the Chinese New Year, with my grandparents, whose heads were frosted white with layers of remembrance; I submerged myself in the Hunan countryside of the Miao tribes, where the only foreigners seen previously were travelers from a neighboring county.

In my wanderings across a land of vastly different temperaments, my eyes were opened to a wealth of folk art, the cultural antithesis of the lofty, scholarly classical Chinese painting I had come to study. My heart was moved by the paper cuts, the vibrant graphics of the New Year prints, the naïf paintings of the peasants, each region stylistically distinct. These were works of men and women deeply rooted in their soil, works populated with farm animals, fruits of the field and stream; they were celebrations of birth, marriage, harvest, the seasons, Heaven and Earth, youth, old age, and death. The art of the country folk swelled with candor and humor, in their very artlessness they captured life more directly than any attempt at careful imitation could ever do.

It was in the countryside where I was able to dispel for myself the myth that Chinese and cynicism went hand in hand. On a painting excursion to Hunan, I was invited inside a thatched farmhouse whose front doors were thrown wide open, never locked. Two old farmers offered me a bamboo fan to cool off with, and water to slake my thirst. The brothers all the while smoked their pipes and smiled their gap-toothed smiles at me like children. They did not ask this stranger where she was from or why she was pestering around their village. They simply provided me with what they themselves would have wished for on a hot summer afternoon.

In the spring of my third year in China, the energy I had sensed on arrival, an underlying tension, a raw nervousness, a fluttering excitement, stirring below the surface of the society, emerged and manifested itself in heady days of hope and optimism. New ideas had brought vigor—most pronounced in the cities; fresh ideas were surging from across the seas; suppressed ideas welled up from belowground. I felt as if every day I would awaken to ephochal changes. The faces that greeted me on the streets of Beijing were open and candid as I had never seen before. Graciousness reigned; gone were the sharp elbows and knees of the anonymous crowd. The leaden dullness of slouching spirits was gone; eyes sparkled. Workers stuffed their entire month's salary into donation boxes to support the struggle of the students on hunger strike in Tiananmen Square. And I was as excited as anyone.

As time progressed, the energy grew wilder, the voices of the people grew louder, culminating in the passions of "Democracy Spring." But I saw it quelled. Brutally. And in the aftermath of June 4, 1989, I saw books burned, stories destroyed. I saw artists and writers numbed into silence. Great cultures tell life-sustaining stories, but in China, small lies choked the air.

The abuse I witnessed was parallel to my own personal narrative but on a grand scale; I understood the stupid thought-control, the purposeful thought-manipulation, the insidious violence—deeply, acutely. The mechanism of fear is the same whether applied to one human being by another or by a government on its people.

To swallow your voice, to keep stories buried deeply beneath layers and layers of silence, is to live in a state of bondage. Stories are magic. Stories make us individuals. They make us free. They have power to make trouble for rulers, for a story is a world upon itself: it has its own logic and cannot be ruled at all. That is why when a new emperor comes to the throne, books are burned and fresh versions of history written to his liking are published.

Physically depleted, in spiritual exhaustion, I returned to America late in 1989, but I returned with gratitude in my heart for the freedom of expression given me in America. I returned convinced that I would firmly grasp that generous gift with both hands.

III.

In this Chinese house of my parents, I found peace, five layers deep. I continued to be confined to the house even after my three-year sojourn, for the man who wished to do me harm was still a reality of my landscape. I was forced to leave the streaming crowd that seems to know its direction. I had no clear direction and initially felt bewilderment.

My mother and father stood guard as my Door Gods, the Generals Hen and Har with their bows and arrows, protecting me from evil spirits.

Keep your mind, eyes, and heart quiet, they said. Do your calligraphy as an exercise in meditation and by the end of the year, you will know precisely what you must do. You won't have to step out; opportunities will present themselves to you at your very door.

Yah, right. What opportunities? I did not believe my parents' words, but they proved to be prophetic.

The book project grew organically, a marvelous living thing; it sprouted, developed long shoots, branched, formed thick fat leaves, flowered and bore fruit.

The stories first came as a trickle. As my mother cooked over the stove, she told me about my grandmother and how she would save the umbilical cords of her babies, wrapped in crimson paper. I was inspired to paint and write a vignette. My father, not one to be left out, got into the act, too, and began to tell stories of Manchuria in the season when the sorghum was ripe, tales of men and women who colored his childhood.

The material for the first chapter of my book *Baba* began on a dark and stormy night, no less. The power was out and it was so cold, the three of us simply crawled under the covers of my parents big bed to wait out the storm.

I've got a ghost story for you, Baba said and told a tale of widowed Grandmother Sun who lost her only child to the wolves that lived in the willows along the sandy banks of the River Liu. Grandmother Sun was often seen among the tall, ripening sorghum, parting the tassels of the plants. "Stop this tomfoolery. Quit your fighting," she would say.

When the power came on, I sat up in my own bed and scribbled down what Baba had told me. The next day I asked for more stories and he provided. They were snatches of his awakened memories—not enough detail to even consider an entire story, let alone a book—but they were so vivid and flavorful, textured, poetic, heartrending. I pressed Baba for more details.

My father and I had no natural understanding. He read Zhuangzi, the *Dao de jing*, the Confucian teachings, and tomes compiled by historians dynasties ago. His spiritual address was in China, and mine so much in the West. For Baba, retrospection and nostalgia dominated; the present and the uncertain future was filtered through the vast experience of a Chinese diaspora.

China prepared me to enter into the landscape of my father's childhood to understand the values that shaped him. I was able to tap into the original language, not only the spoken language, but the symbols, the iconography, in which his spirit was nourished, his ideas were given form. Only because I had embraced the Chinese language could I ask questions of depth that would stir him enough to carry me into the past. We are shaped by the language we first learned to dream in.

There is a particular sensitivity and emotional experience reached through Chinese—our peculiar written characters composed of word-pictures and the direct, haiku-like phrase structure. Chinese is first and foremost poetry. It is this language-poetry that makes us think or feel or dream the way we do. The Chinese language is art in that in its written form, it retains its pictorial identity. Art is as important in influencing our mental makeup as diet is over our physical makeup.

Through Baba's stories, I learned to see the child in him, the wonder in him, where once I had seen the cynicism of a tired old man who warned me incessantly about the dangers of the world. In re-creating his past through words and pictures, I made friends with the boy of eight who ran barefooted in the sandy soil, stealing watermelons on a hot Manchurian summer afternoon.

Most of Baba's tales were about my ancestors. In the long days that stretched into long years of work at my writing desk, I felt the spirit of the ancients hovering over my shoulders, guiding me, protecting me. I felt a responsibility to rescue them from the deep well of forgetting. As the past took shape with great vividness, I came to understand the chain of events that nourishes the present like an umbilical cord. Knowing the past means knowing who I am today and the possibilities for unfolding the future.

At first my father did not trust me with his stories. When he read the drafts, he was hardly stingy with his criticisms if he deemed I had the texture of the landscape wrong or history wrong. Sometimes an argument would be sparked by his nasal tone of voice or my brusk retort and Baba and I would not speak to each other for days. The Chinese say you must fight with a man to know a man, and in the long years of close collaboration, he and I certainly got to know one another well, and in time, we learned to fight productively, the tension from the arguments dissipating in a matter of hours.

In the time of private concentration, I did not step outside except to take long, luxurious walks with my parents. The three of us would go out through the back fence into Hatton Canyon, our private sanctuary, for our daily communion. During our stroll, Baba would often elaborate on the stories he had told or share a song from childhood. When it rained, we put on our galoshes and looked for water skaters in the puddles. Sometimes we returned home with pine or cypress seedlings that we found sprouting among the blackberry brambles. The heavier samplings Baba carried with pride on his shoulder as if he'd bagged a wild boar. My parents replanted them for me just outside our fenced yard. They would not likely see the trees grow to full maturity, but they were thinking of the long years ahead of me when I would enjoy myself as mistress of the house in the forest.

On some evenings, when I had completed a chapter, I would read it out loud while my parents listened, Mama's eyes closed in great concentration. The three of us would grow excited by the strange beauty, humor, and humanity of the forgotten stories, or weep for the injustices of a world at war. Baba's memories would come alive and more details were extracted from the bottom most layer of his forgetting. "Ohhh, this is too good. The world is going to love it," Mama would say, stamping her feet like a child.

I have come to believe that the Chinese food culture has been preparing me all my life to work closely with my parents. Sharing, self-restraint, respect for elders, and care for the young began at the tips of our chopsticks. In this house, where we politely slurp noodles in unison, the preferred eating utensil is the bamboo chopsticks, not the knives and forks which the Chinese consider weapons of war. Our food is bite-size, sharing from common main dishes instead of sawing away at individual slabs of meat on individual plates. With the opposite, unused ends of her chopsticks, Mama will pick up a piece of tender snow pea and deliver it into my bowl, or Baba will place the last prawn atop Mama's rice which she will decline with a "*ni chi ba*, you take it." There is no "crossing the river" allowed, which means to stretch our arms across the table over dishes in front and reaching for desired morsels in a faraway dish. We eat what is in front of us and take what our chopsticks first touch. By eating at an affable pace, it is the responsibility of those at the table to make sure that everyone has had a fair share. As a child, I was scolded for digging for green peas from the main dish and popping them into my mouth, one after another without pause, or for leaving kernels of rice in my bowl. "It's by the sweat of the farmers' brows that you're provided this rice. Do not waste it. If you do, you'll grow up and marry a man with pockmarks," my mother would say, a threat Chinese mothers have been repeating for at least five thousand years.

IV.

I was certain my writing would find its way out into the world. I felt that once I had put down the last period in my manuscript, my work was fully complete and had a life of its own. It was real. Publication would be joy, but the writing itself was red-blooded life. It was lucky I was ignorant of the hurdles to publication. Had I known of all the reasons why my work would not find an audience, I would have been too frightened to begin. As it was, ignorance was bliss. I had a beginner's mind. To the beginner, everything is possible; the expert knows too well the limitations.

With the 1994 publication of *Baba: A Return to China Upon My Father's Shoulders*, my father was finally able to shake off the paranoid feelings of danger that had dominated his life. In lending him my voice, I had made him real, an individual, someone who could not be snuffed out under boots of adversity. I had rendered him safe. I was Hua Mulan, the woman warrior of legends, who cut off her tresses and went into battle in her father's stead. It was now my father who was traveling America upon my shoulders.

Baba, at the age of seventy, looks younger today than he did in his fifties. The frown-creases have been smoothed over. The cynicism, the cold snap in his eyes, is no more. Readers, young and old alike, call him Baba when they have a chance to meet him. He likes that.

In the process of writing our family tales, and the stories of the overlooked, those who have disappeared in chaos of the Chinese maelstrom without a complaint, I had written fear out of my own life. In carrying the stories out into the world, I discovered the strength of my own voice. I, too, had made myself real, an individual. Free. Some time after the publication of my second book, *The Odyssey of a Manchurian*, I awoke one morning and felt absolutely no fear, only my soul somersaulting. The feeling was a surprise. I shouted praise: Thank you, Heaven Above, for providing me with an enemy, without whom I would never have learned about patience. He stripped me down to the essentials, reduced me to the purity of origin so I can be the kind of human being I was meant to be.

V.

What language do I dream in? They say when a person is close to dying, she is left with the ability to speak only her first tongue. I suspect I will die in this house telling bad jokes in Chinese. Some caregiver, dusting the myriad antiques my parents collected over the decades, will say of me, "Oh, she loved to somersault in the grass, and she was protective of her solitude—wrote and painted almost every day. She came to America when she was seven years old, but she said she did not truly become American until she took up her past and began telling stories of old China."

All My Relations

JOYCE ZONANA

AT A SHABBY BROOKLYN DANCE SCHOOL, *I prepare for the spring recital. I am ten, and this is my first public performance. For three months I have been struggling through my tap routines, awkward and self-conscious, but determined.*

Our group has the opening number. Costumed in black leotards adorned with colored fringe, we wear cowboy hats and bandannas died to match. As the curtain rises and the music begins, we step into line across the stage.

"O-o-o-o-o-kla-ho-ma!" we sing, "where the wind comes sweeping down the plain."

I've never seen the musical, and I know nothing about this fabled place of wheat, wind, and rain, but I am hooked. I see hawks, lazy circles, a wide expanse of prairie. The exuberant music fills me, and I join my voice to those of my classmates:

> *"We know we belong to the land,*
> *And the land we belong to is grand."*

I was sure I had finally arrived when I found myself breezing down the empty highway at seventy-five miles an hour, listening to Patsy Cline and visualizing myself in cowboy boots and jeans. The color-blocked landscape—brazen red dirt, yellow-gold fields, indigo blue sky (like an infinitely stretched, frameless Mark Rothko canvas)—branded itself into me, searing my body with a passion I had not foreseen. In the distance, tall windmills spun tight circles against the horizon. At the dusty café where I stopped, I ate chicken-fried steak and drank iced tea from quart-sized Mason jars. This, I told myself, was America, and here I was, at its center. Exhilarated, I embraced the drama of my new identity.

Just six months earlier I had been sobbing in my tenth-floor Philadelphia apartment, immobilized with a migraine after failing my driver's test for the second time. A veteran subway rider addicted to the crush of rush hour (though I lived in Philadelphia I still thought of myself as a New Yorker), I feared I would never acquire this most rudimentary of American skills. For years I had refused to drive, but now, it was a necessary adaptation to the new territory I was about to enter. After five perfunctory lessons from Sears Driving School, I was pronounced ready to apply for my license. I took my first failure in stride, but I had hoped to pass on my second attempt.

From the moment he entered the car I had borrowed from my friend Jimmy's mother, the state trooper administering my test unnerved me. Fronted by his unsmiling equanimity, I grew clumsy and confused: when he said "left," I turned right; when he said "stop," I accelerated. In this stolid man's unblinking presence, as in the presence of all those I imagined as the custodians of America, I felt my body thicken and grow dark. My hair seemed suddenly coarse and unruly, my shorts ill-fitting and inappropriate. Perhaps I should have worn a dress, I told myself—stockings, heels, makeup. It was obvious I didn't know how to play this game. Sitting beside the trooper, I could feel and smell the acrid sweat collecting under my arms and between my legs; I became conscious of the excesses of my female body—over full breasts, hips, thighs; and my fragile competence—as a driver, or as anything else for that matter—vanished. Tongue-tied and ashamed, I barely nodded when I was told I had failed.

Driving me home after my ordeal, Jimmy tried vainly to console me. "You'll do fine next time," he reassured me. But I could not be comforted. I was sure I would be eternally stymied, held back by a proliferating nation of state troopers, neatly arrayed in dull uniforms, communicating to one another without moving their lips. Helpless before them, I knew I was grounded, forever trapped on the East Coast of the United States, unable to master the rules of the road. "I'll never learn how to talk to them," I wept. "They'll never let me drive."

≈❧≈

"Do they know about Jews there?" my father had asked when I told him about my tenure-track job at the University of Oklahoma. For the previous five years, I had been applying for teaching positions, diligently forwarding my credentials to whatever college or university advertised an opening in my field. I paid little attention to where the schools might be: California, Wisconsin, Texas, Montana—they all seemed equally distant, equally unlikely. In the end, Oklahoma was the only offer I received. My childhood enthusiasm for the prairie state long forgotten, I wondered how I could survive.

"Aren't you afraid?" my father continued. "We know nothing about that part of the country."

"Yes, of course, I am terrified," I longed to confess. "Of course I know nothing about that part of the country."

But the imperative to carry out my plans kept me silent. I had to keep my courage up, pretend that this was merely another easy step in the inevitable process of fulfilling my dreams. I had just completed a Ph.D. in English literature at an Ivy League school, and what had I been doing for nine years if not working to earn a teaching position at a major state university? Jobs were tight, and my dissertation adviser assured me this was a "good" one. Looking around at my unemployed classmates, I knew I should be grateful. But in my heart, I was chilled.

Oklahoma. I envisioned a barren flat landscape, unbroken by anything except oil wells. I imagined an entire state populated by Bible-thumping Protestants, fair-haired and fair-skinned Americans who would inspect me with the bland indifference, if not contempt, of the state trooper. To move to Oklahoma from the multicultural security of my East Coast niche seemed like stepping off the edge of the planet. Yet, despite my terror, I knew I could not refuse to go.

It was not simply that I was being offered the rare chance of a "good" job in my chosen profession; much more significant was the fact that Oklahoma represented for me the ultimate challenge, the challenge of America. Though I had lived in the U.S. for thirty-five years—I was only nineteen months old when my parents left Egypt in 1951, and now I was almost thirty-seven—I had never been able to shake the sense of being permanently "other." I had no memories of Egypt, no real sense of having lived there as an infant. But I still thought of myself as just off the boat. Neither college nor graduate school, neither friendships nor affairs with people I thought of as truly American, had succeeded in acculturating me.

On the subway, dark-skinned strangers spoke to me in foreign tongues: Arabic, Spanish, Greek, Hindi. Instinctively, other immigrants knew I belonged among them, even if they couldn't identify my tribe. American customs and habits eluded me; I could never interest myself in football, and the names of popular stars escaped my grasp. When I was introduced to new acquaintances, I steeled myself for the inevitable question. "Zonana," people would ask, "what kind of a name is that?" When I told them "Egyptian Jewish," their wonder grew. "I've never met an Egyptian Jew before," they would say. Indeed, I could have told them. I was exotic, alien, one-of-a-kind—an undissolved, undigestible grain in the otherwise palatable blend of America.

It's true, of course, Egyptian Jews are something of a rarity, though not an anomaly as many people believe. Until the late 1940s, there were eighty thousand in Cairo and Alexandria: some from families that had lived continuously in Egypt for two thousand years, others whose parents or grandparents had arrived more recently. My own family of Sephardim had passed variously through Syria, Turkey, and Iraq before settling in Egypt in the late 1800s.

Although Jews enjoyed prosperity and peace in early twentieth-century Egypt, political developments after World War II changed their status—so much so that today there remain fewer than two hundred Jews in the entire country. The establishment of the state of Israel and the rise of Egyptian nationalism made life in Egypt difficult for Jews. Viewed as Zionists—and thus as enemies of the emerging Egyptian state—they became subject to private and official harassment and anti-Semitism.

My father made his decision to emigrate in 1946, after a series of incidents—bombings, looting, and the burning of a synagogue—shocked the Jews of Cairo. Although his younger brother was a leading Egyptian Zionist, neither Zionism as a philosophy nor the prospect of an embattled life in Palestine were appealing to my father. He sought a nation where he might be safe, choosing the U.S. for its commitment to tolerance. But because immigration quotas allowed only one hundred Egyptians to enter each year, he had to wait five years for a visa. And once in the States, some of his old fears returned; anxiously he watched the McCarthy trials, ever alert for signs that Jews might not be welcome.

Unlike my father, most Egyptian Jews were reluctant to leave the country that had been home; it wasn't until the Suez crisis of 1956 and the Arab-Israeli War of 1967 that they departed en masse, many of them because they were being deported. Perhaps one-third went to Israel; the remaining fifty thousand or so made their way to Brazil, France, the United States, Argentina, England, and Canada. A recent estimate puts the number that came to the U.S. at no more than ten thousand—a tiny minority among America's two hundred million. It is no wonder that I am often the only Egyptian Jew my friends have met.

Indeed, during my family's first years in the States, we knew no one like ourselves other than an old friend of my mother's and some relatives who lived in Washington, D.C. We had settled in an Italian neighborhood in Brooklyn—Bensonhurst—where there was a sprinkling of Ashkenazim from Eastern Europe and Russia. And while to the Roman Catholic Italians we were unmistakably Jews, to the Ashkenazim we were Oriental impostors—not really Jewish because we spoke no Yiddish, didn't eat gefilte fish, hadn't experienced the Holocaust.

Isolated by our history, our food, and our language—my parents spoke with me in French, though they occasionally used Arabic between themselves—I spent my earliest years with no real peers, no mirrors in which I might see myself reflected, learning to value what I saw. I threw myself into becoming, if not American, at least a New Yorker—quickly acquiring fluency in English, mastering the songs and games of the street.

But my mother had a different agenda.

"I don't care what the other children do," she insisted when I begged permission to visit a friend's house or go to an afternoon movie. "You're not like the other children. You don't have to do what they do."

I didn't know then that in her attitude toward America—*"Je m'en fiche des Americains,"* ("I don't care about the Americans") she would sometimes say—my mother was simply reproducing her own family's attitude toward Egypt. Middle-class Jews in Cairo socialized only among themselves, favoring European languages rather than Arabic. Although most of their customs (foodways, hospitality, gender and family roles) were in fact firmly Middle Eastern, their social lives remained insulated from those of their neighbors. Dark-skinned and dark-eyed, with ancestors from Baghdad and Aleppo, my mother was arguably Arab—but she regarded herself as European.

It is perhaps because their cultures were so close that Egyptian Jews made such an effort to distinguish themselves from Muslim Arabs. For if they did not keep themselves apart, intermarriage might result, and with that, the eventual loss of any distinctly "Jewish" identity. Young girls and young women, in particular, were shielded from contact with Muslims. Thus, while a native, my mother never assimilated to Egypt. And so it was no wonder that she opposed my assimilation to America. Accustomed to being "other," she raised me to experience myself in the same way. It mattered little that there were no other "others" with whom to gather; I would grow up as an Egyptian Jewish girl, despite the lack of a community within which that identity could be affirmed.

But, from an early age, I resisted my mother's desires, refusing to cook, refusing to clean, refusing, most fundamentally, to imagine my life fulfilled through marriage to another Egyptian Jew. I wanted to be American, free from the constraints of Middle Eastern tradition. So I committed myself to school, believing it would grant me access to the dominant culture. And at eighteen, after an abortive first year away at college, I rented my own apartment, scandalizing the family and deeply hurting my mother. It was the only way, I thought, to escape her control. I had decided to have sex before marriage; in doing so, I placed myself utterly beyond the pale of Egyptian Jewish identity. Eventually, I would become a lesbian—an even more unthinkable destiny. Still, even as I lived my ostensibly "American" life (loving another woman, pursuing a career, and surrounded by friends who shared my interests and values), my internalized otherness never left me. For all my efforts at separation, I continued to see the world from my mother's perspective, keeping myself apart even as I felt myself excluded from the mainstream of American life. In my heart, I was sure I would never fit in. So, clutching my English Ph.D., it became imperative that I go to Oklahoma, if only to give myself the ultimate test.

My New York friends stared in disbelief when I announced my decision.

"Omaha?" they asked. "What will you do in Omaha?"

"Oklahoma," I replied, trying to mask my fear. "Oklahoma. I'm moving to Oklahoma for a teaching job. I went to graduate school so I could get a teaching job."

"Idaho? Why would you want to move to Idaho?"

"Ok-la-ho-ma," I'd say again, but few New Yorkers could keep the indigenous American syllables straight. "Red Land," I should have said, but I didn't know that yet. The Sooner State. Indian Territory. The last frontier.

❧

Though I did not realize it when I moved there, I already knew more about Oklahoma than I thought. In the fifth and sixth grades, I had read all the "Little House" novels of Laura Ingalls Wilder, those innocent paeans to the pioneer spirit. My favorite had been *Little House on the Prairie*, the lovingly rendered account of the Ingalls's homesteading experience in "Indian country." Filled with sensuous evocations of the land, the book seduced me with its unabashed romance of the West, giving shape to my solitary fantasies of nomadic freedom and independence.

In the opening chapter, Ma, Pa, Mary, Baby Carrie, and Laura—the slightly naughty, inquisitive, and rebellious girl with whom I identified—set out from the Big Woods of Wisconsin. After a long journey by covered wagon, the family crosses into the red dirt prairieland beyond Kansas. The book clearly names this region "Indian country," but for years afterward, I always imagined it as Kansas. It wasn't until I was exultingly living in what I liked to call my own "little house on the prairie" that I found a copy of the book and read it again.

In fact, the Ingalls are illegal white settlers in what would later be called Oklahoma, "sooners" gambling on the success of the Dawes Commission. Set up in 1893, the Dawes Commission sought to persuade Indians to abandon tribal land titles. But, occasionally—if only temporarily—the Indians prevailed against the U.S. government. So it is that after a year of painstakingly building and furnishing a log house, digging a deep well, and planting crops, the Ingalls must leave, setting out, at the novel's end, for yet another unpopulated "country."

" 'The only good Indian is a dead Indian,' " blusters one of the Ingalls's white neighbors, but Pa has a different opinion, teaching his family to respect the natives. At one point, Laura takes Pa's consideration for the natives a little further than he had hoped. " 'Will the government make these Indians go west?' " she asks, when a group of hungry Indians camps near their homestead.

> "Yes," Pa said. "When white settlers come into a country, the Indians have to move on. The government is going to move these Indians farther west, any time now. That's why we're here, Laura. White people are going to settle all this country, and we get the best land because we get here first and take our pick. Now do you understand?"
>
> "Yes, Pa," Laura said. "But, Pa, I thought this was Indian Territory. Won't it make the Indians mad to have to—"
>
> "No more questions, Laura," Pa said firmly. "Go to sleep."

Oklahoma, I quickly discovered when I moved there, was indeed Indian Territory, the state that still has the largest Native American population in the U.S., a place where the native presence is palpable, permeating the open landscape. Early on, a native colleague invited me to an intertribal pow-wow, deep in the country. I had by then obtained my license, and so I drove alone, down empty dirt roads, to find the busy gathering. Throughout the night, I watched in awe as Kiowa, Comanche, and Apache Indians drummed, danced, and sang beneath the huge sky.

And on one of my first weekends, I drove the ninety miles to the Wichita Mountain Wildlife Refuge, near Lawton. The Wichitas, an ancient range of worn granite and limestone mountains, rise abruptly from a seemingly endless expanse of uncultivated prairie. Held sacred by the Kiowa, they were considered by the Plains Indians to be the center of the world—like Delphi to the ancient Greeks. Here, pale green sage and dark twisted scrub oaks cling to the mountains' rough sides; huge red and gray boulders balance miraculously above sheer cliffs; clear pools glisten amid narrow canyons. It is a still and solitary landscape, vast, primal, quieting.

On that first trip, I saw eagles flying high above, and in the tall yellow grass, a placid herd of buffalo grazed. Drawn to the buffalos' enduring calm, I found myself returning to the Wichitas again and again: during my four years in Oklahoma, those mountains became *my* refuge, a place where I could dream, letting myself roam. Most often, my reveries took me to contemplation of native history, to aching empathy for the displaced and devastated tribes, the deliberately slaughtered buffalo— even as I felt, standing on that land, a power I had never before known. Walking the hills, I gathered sage to burn in ceremony; once, atop Elk Mountain, I encountered a lone buffalo who had climbed the mountain to die.

Of course, I also met in Oklahoma, as I expected, the conventional America I had both feared and desired. This was the world of suburban homes with well-kept yards and attached garages; the world of covered-dish church dinners and state fairs, Sunday football games and afternoon barbecues—the world of the state trooper. In my own way, and much to my surprise, I learned to live in this world—buying a small house and keeping my lawn mowed, discovering the pleasures of talking with neighbors over the back fence and preparing vegetables grown in my own garden. In this Oklahoma I encountered the ordinary decency of middle America. Quietly and easily, I made my peace with it.

But the real drama of my life lay elsewhere, in my unexpected awakening to the abiding beauty and power of the land and to the lives of its indigenous peoples. It was in Oklahoma, surrounded by the spirits and touched by the lives of contemporary Indians, that I discovered the kind of American I wanted to be: one with respect for ancestors, responsibility for future generations, and love for the land upon which I walk. And when I left Indian Territory to take a job in Louisiana, I retained my engagement with native life, seeking out the Houma tribe in southwestern Louisiana and finding my way to a Creek teacher in Folsom. From Medicine Hawk and his wife, Looks-Within-Woman, I imbibed my deepest lessons, privileged to receive their most sacred teachings. "All my relations," I heard as I entered the purification lodge and shared in the pipe ceremony. "All my relations," I repeated, as I undertook a vision quest and spent four days and four nights alone on the land. As ants crawled over me and brown Mississippi dirt caked my sweating skin, I let myself sink, unresisting, into earth.

All my relations. My initiation into native ways led me back, inevitably—to my own family and to our Egyptian origins. Working to repair the web, I talk regularly now with my mother, and I make steady efforts to reconnect with all the members of our extended (and internationally dispersed) family—even while continuing to live my "American" life with a lover, a job, a home of my own. A year ago, no longer able to tolerate the gap in my knowledge, I committed myself to studying Arabic. Twice a week these days, I race up the steps of my university's Education building, hungry to hear and repeat the sounds that return me to the rhythms and intonations of my native land. My English Ph.D. suddenly irrelevant, I find it is Arabic literature I want to study, Egyptian culture I need to know.

And just this year, summoning all my courage, I ventured at last to

Cairo, back to the land my parents had felt forced to abandon. To my surprise, I found myself warmly greeted by Muslims, Copts, and the few Jews I managed to find. In answer to their repeated questions, "Where are you from?", I would hesitatingly confess that I was Jewish, born in Cairo, living now in the U.S., and returning for the first time. "Welcome to your homeland," they all said, smiles blossoming in dark faces. "This is your homeland. Welcome." When I ordered tea with mint, *"be naanaa,"* the waiter in my hotel beamed. "Egyptian! Egyptian! Really Egyptian!" he exclaimed, bringing me a fragrant sprig of green mint in a clear glass cup.

It was Ramadan during my visit; during the day, I fasted with the sixteen million inhabitants of Cairo, and in the evenings, I shared *Ifftar* with Muslim friends. I prayed in the synagogue where my parents had been married and explored the elegant neighborhood—now a business district—where my mother had grown up. Enchanted, I wandered the ancient streets of Coptic Cairo, lighting candles in dim churches. Alone, I visited the Pyramids and walked into the vast openness of the desert. Wherever I went, I found myself surrounded by warm faces mirroring mine; looking deeply into dark eyes, something within me let go: I was home.

On the morning of my departure, I wept, not wanting to wrench myself away. Sitting alone in the barren airport, watching a gray cat wander beneath orange seats, I suddenly understood. "I am Egyptian," I thought for the first time, "I'm Egyptian. That's who I am." Not a Jew who happened to have been born in Cairo, not an American tourist on a sentimental journey, not even an Egyptian Jew, but an Egyptian, pure and simple, bound by skin and blood and bone and heart to an ancient land and people. I am Egyptian. In recognizing and affirming this identity, I become American in a new way. With the certainty of belonging to one land, I can now walk freely upon another—with care. "Al-din li'llah wa'l-watan li'l-jami," I want to say now with the nationalists of the 1919 uprising against the British. "Religion is for God and the homeland is for all," adding only that Earth Mother is our one true homeland, and we all belong to Her.

EDITOR & CONTRIBUTOR BIOS

MERI NANA-AMA DANQUAH was born in Ghana and raised in the Washington, D.C., area. She is the author of the memoir *Willow Weep for Me: A Black Woman's Journey Through Depression* (North/Ballantine). Danquah, who earned her MFA in Creative Writing and Literature from Bennington College, is presently writing a book, to be published by Riverhead, about her first return visit to Ghana after twenty-six years of living in America as an immigrant. She lives in Los Angeles with her daughter.

NINA BARRAGAN (the pen name of Rocío Lasansky Weinstein), was born in Cordoba, Argentina, and received a B.A. from the University of Iowa. Her prize-winning collection, *No Peace at Versailles*, appeared in 1991. A new novel on Argentina will be forthcoming from the University of New Mexico Press in 2001. She lives in Iowa City with her artist husband, Alan Weinstein, and their four children.

LILIANET BRINTRUP was born in the Province of Llanquihue in southern Chile. Since 1990, she has been a professor of Hispanic American Literature and teaches Spanish at Humboldt State University in Northern California. She is the author of the poetry collections *En Tierra Firme* (Santiago de Chile: Ed. El Azafran, 1993), *Amor y Caos* (Santiago de Chile: Ed. La Trastienda, 1994) and *El Libro Natural* (Santiago de Chile: Ed. La Trastienda, 1999). Presently she is at work on two other collections of poetry.

VERONICA CHAMBERS is a culture writer at *Newsweek* and is the author of *Mama's Girl* as well as several books for younger readers, including *Marisol and Magdalena: The Sound of Our Sisterhood*. She lives in Brooklyn, New York.

JUDITH ORTIZ COFER is the author of seven books, including the novel *The Line of the Sun*, *The Latin Deli: Prose and Poetry* and the memoir *Silent Dancing: A Partial Remembrance of a Puerto Rican Childhood*. A native of Puerto Rico, she now lives in Georgia and is a professor of English and Creative Writing at the University of Georgia.

EDWIDGE DANTICAT was born in Haiti and came to the United States when she was twelve years old. She is a graduate of Barnard College and Brown University and is the author of *Breath, Eyes, Memory; Krik? Krak!* and *The Farming of Bones*.

GABRIELLE DONNELLY was born in London and emigrated to Los Angeles in the 1980's. A journalist and novelist, she is the author of, most recently, the mystery *The Girl in the Photograph* (The Berkley Publishing Group). She lives in Venice, California, with her husband, Owen Bjornstad, and is at work on a new novel on the subject of American immigrants.

LYNN FREED'S novels include *The Mirror*, *The Bungalow*, *Home Ground*, and *Friends of the Family*. Her short fiction and essays have appeared in numerous publications, including *The New Yorker*, *Harper's*, *The Atlantic Monthly*, *Southwest Review* and *The New York Times*. She lives in Sonoma, California.

AKUYOE GRAHAM is a writer, actor and educator. She has appeared in numerous television shows and motion pictures, such as *Picket Fences*, *Chicago Hope*, and *American Pie*. Her critically acclaimed one-woman play, "Spirit Awakening" was hailed by the *Los Angeles Times* and is currently in development as a major motion picture. She lives in Los Angeles.

LUCY GREALY was born in Dublin, Ireland, and raised in Spring Valley, New York. She is the author of the memoir *Autobiography of a Face*, numerous essays and a novel to be published by Doubleday in 2000. She lives in New York.

SUHEIR HAMMAD is the author of the poetry collection *Born Palestinian, Born Black*, and the memoir *Drops of This Story*, both published by Harlem River Press. She has been the recipient of numerous awards, including the Audre Lorde Poetry Award, and her column, "Psalm 26:7," appears regularly in *Stress* magazine. She lives in New York.

GINU KAMANI, Bombay-born, is the author of *Junglee Girl*, a collection of fiction exploring sexual self-knowledge and issues of power. She speaks regularly on bi-cultural sexual issues and was Distinguished Visiting Writer at Mills College, Oakland, CA, from 1997 to 1999. She is currently finishing a novel.

NOLA KAMBANDA was born in Burundi to Rwandese parents. After moving to the States to pursue her university studies, she received a BS in Electrical Engineering from California State University, Los Angeles. She works as an engineer/scientist for a major aerospace company in Southern California, where she lives.

HELEN KIM'S first novel, *The Long Season of Rain*, published for both the adult and young adult markets, was nominated for the National Book Award in Juvenile Literature in 1996, and has been translated into seven languages. She is currently working on her second novel, *Between the Bodies of Water*. She teaches and lectures in Seattle.

HELIE LEE received her BA in Political Science from UCLA in 1986. She is the author of the memoir *Still Life With Rice* (Scribner). Her work has also appeared in *Mademoiselle, Essence, Korean Journal* and other notable publications. Lee's daring rescue of nine family members from North Korea was the feature subject of an episode of *Nightline*. She lives in Los Angeles and lectures frequently throughout the country.

KYOKO MORI is the author of *Shizuko's Daughter* and *One Bird* (novels); *Fallout* (poetry); and *The Dream of Water: a Memoir* and *Polite Lies: on Being a Woman Caught Between Cultures* (nonfiction). She is a Briggs-Copeland Lecturer in creative nonfiction at Harvard University.

IRINA REYN'S features and book reviews have appeared in numerous publications. Presently, she is a graduate student in Russian Literature at the University of Pittsburgh. She is also at work on her first novel.

NELLY ROSARIO was born in the Dominican Republic and raised in the United States. She received her MFA from Columbia University. She lives in Brooklyn, and is working on a novel.

UTE MARGARET SAINE was born in postwar West Germany, emigrating to the United States when she was twenty-one. Her first book of poetry,

Bodyscapes, was published in 1995 by the Pacific Writers Press. She is a founding member of PEN Orange County and is active in PEN West's Freedom-to-Write program.

ROSANNE KATON-WALDEN has, for thirty-five years, maintained a successful career as a stage, film and television actress and screenwriter. She and her husband, Richard, live in Los Angeles with their two children.

ANNETTE GALLAGHER WEISMAN is a freelance writer who was born and raised in Dublin, Ireland. She has won an Associated Writing Programs award for nonfiction, received an MFA from Bennington College and is a member of the National Book Critics Circle. She is currently working on a collection of memoir-linked essays called *Irish Times* and lives in Cincinnati, Ohio, with her husband and two children.

MITSUYE YAMADA, born in Kyushu, Japan, spent most of her formative years in Seattle, Washington, until a few months after the outbreak of World War II, when her family was removed to a concentration camp in Idaho. Her most recent work, *Camp Notes and Other Writings*, is a newly combined edition of her first two books and was published by the Rutgers University Press in 1998. She is presently Visiting Associate Professor in Asian American Studies at University of California, Irvine.

BELLE YANG, though born in Taiwan, spent part of her childhood in Japan. At age seven, she emigrated to the United States with her family. She graduated from the University of California, Santa Cruz, with honors in biology, but went on to pursue fine art at the Pasadena Art Center College of Design and the Academy of Traditional Chinese Painting in Beijing. She is the author of *Baba: A Return to China Upon My Father's Shoulders* and *The Odyssey of a Manchurian*, both published by Harcourt Brace and Company.

JOYCE ZONANA is Associate Professor of English and Director of Women's Studies at the University of New Orleans. She is a winner of the Florence Howe Award for Feminist Criticism. Currently, she is completing a memoir entitled *Aroosa*.